The Upstart Guide to Owning and Managing a Restaurant

Second Edition

by Roy S. Alonzo

PUBLISHING

New York

This book is dedicated with sincere thanks to Donald H. Strickland for his wisdom and many years of friendship.

Editorial Director: Jennifer Farthing
Acquisitions Editor: Victoria Smith
Associate Development Editor: Joshua Martino
Production Editor: Karen Goodfriend
Production Artist: International Typesetting and Composition
Cover Designer: Kathleen Lynch

© 2007 by Roy S. Alonzo

Published by Kaplan Publishing,
a division of Kaplan, Inc.

Printed in the United States of America

April 2007

07 08 09   10 9 8 7 6 5 4 3 2 1

ISBN 13: 978-1-4195-8332-2
ISBN 10: 1-4195-8332-8

Kaplan Publishing books are available at special quantity discounts to use for sales promotions, employee premiums, or educational purposes. Please email our Special Sales Department to order or for more information at kaplanpublishing@kaplan.com, or write to Kaplan Publishing, 888 7th Avenue, 22nd Floor, NY, NY 10106

C o n t e n t s

Has the thought of becoming a restaurateur ever crossed your mind? If you enjoy dining out, entertaining guests, or cooking, that would not be an unusual thought. Most people would like to earn their livelihood by doing something they enjoy.

America's love affair with restaurants has never been greater. With annual sales of approximately a half trillion dollars and its growth showing no signs of leveling off, estimates show that within the next ten years, over 50 percent of Americans's budgeted food dollars will be spent in restaurants. This growth promises many opportunities for people interested in entering the business.

The purpose of this book is to give you a sense of what the restaurant business is like, make you aware of what is required to enter it, and help you evaluate whether it is the right business for you. It is also intended to acquaint you with a logical course of action for starting up a restaurant, should you decide to enter the business, and to give you insights and techniques for operating a restaurant successfully. It covers the spectrum from the initial idea to the grand opening and beyond.

The very favorable response to the first edition of this book showed that an ongoing need exists for guidance on the process of starting up, owning, and managing a restaurant. The contents of this book are presented as a source of ideas, methods, and strategies for improving your chances for success.

The National Restaurant Association, institutions of higher education, and restaurant and hotel chains have been very active in developing management systems and control procedures for the industry. However, even with such well-developed resources available, many independent restaurants still function with inadequate controls, a shortcoming this book will address.

It should be noted that laws vary from state to state and among the various levels of government. This book discusses laws only to make the reader aware of their existence. Consequently, nothing in this book is offered as legal advice or an interpretation of a law, and it should not be construed as such. Information of that kind should be obtained from attorneys and the appropriate government officials, just as advice on accounting and technical matters should be sought from specialized professionals in those fields.

The mention of any product names in this book is done merely for illustrative purposes and should not be deemed an endorsement. Likewise, where products are mentioned, the omission of any products is not in any way a reflection on such products.

Finally, this book is intended to stimulate thinking about the restaurant business, answer a variety of questions, and present an assortment of management tools that may be used to operate a restaurant. To those of you who may become restaurant owners, we wish you a full plate of success and an overflowing cup of happiness as you pursue your goals.

Many people and companies contributed to make this book possible. I would like to thank Matthew Wheeler and the Hobart Corporation of Troy, Ohio; Scott Schloerke and the Perlick Corporation of Milwaukee, Wisconsin; the Starlite Diner of Daytona Beach, Florida; Chad Hale and Perkins Equipment Corporation of Manchester, New Hampshire; Acorns Restaurant and Lounge at the New England Center, Durham, New Hampshire; and Jaime Brannan of Benghiat Marketing & Communications and RATIONAL USA for information and photos.

I would also like to thank Kevin Tacy and Paul Murphy, proprietors of Fosters Downeast Clambake of York Harbor, Maine for photos and sharing their entrepreneurial experiences; Datamonitor for information on megatrends; The American Amusement Machine Association for demographic information on the Y generation; Barbara Balboni, editor at R.S. Means Publishing Company; Joseph Danehy of the University of New Hampshire for his computer assistance and the reference librarians at the university for their research assistance; as well as Karin Witmer of the National Restaurant Association—Educational Foundation in Chicago, Illinois.

Finally, I would like to thank The Portsmouth Athenaeum for use of the historical photo of Gilley's Diner, Mark Roy and Ken Roberts for photographic assistance, and the editorial staff at Kaplan Publishing, Inc. for their support.

1

THE RESTAURANT BUSINESS

Dining out is an integral part of the American lifestyle. We eat out not just because we're hungry but also for entertainment, relaxation, to socialize, to avoid cooking at home, and sometimes to conduct business. It is convenient and fits well into our faster paced 21st century lifestyles. But it wasn't always this way.

Historically, the concept of a *restaurant*, as we know it, is a relatively recent one. It is asserted by some that the first restaurant in Europe was the Champ d'Oiseau, started by a chef named Boulanger in Paris in 1765. Others claim that the honor goes to another Parisian public eating house, La Tour d'Argent, opened in 1533. Whatever the case, it was not until after the French Revolution, in 1789, that the concept of a restaurant began to spread. Prominent chefs, once employed by the deposed wealthy, found themselves out of work, and the more enterprising ones opened establishments to feed the public.

Prior to the 1700s, the only places where ordinary people could obtain a prepared meal for a fixed price in England were inns and taverns, also called *ordinaries*. The meals were not of the customer's choice, and their price included a fee for lodging, which had to be paid whether or not the diner slept there.

THE AMERICAN RESTAURANT SCENE

In colonial America, the establishment of taverns and roadhouses was decreed by law, as an aid to expanding the frontiers. The crude hostelries provided a simple meal and a sleeping accommodation, commonly shared with a fellow traveler.

As time progressed, a genteel class emerged in the colonies, and inns fashioned after those in England were built to serve them. The inns would accommodate guests who wished to dine only but required them to pay for both food and lodging, as was the custom in England.

Few changes occurred in the public hospitality field after the colonies received their independence. Not until the economy of the United States began to shift from agriculture to mining and manufacturing in the 1800s did significant innovations take hold.

By the 1820s, eating establishments were being opened for the sole purpose of serving food and drink to the public. Such leaders as the Union Oyster House, founded in 1826 in Boston, Massachusetts, and Delmonico's, founded in New York City in 1827, were soon followed by others. The expansion of railroads throughout the rest of the century created a great demand for eating establishments to accommodate travelers. This demand was met by the gradual emergence of cafes, lunchrooms, lunch wagons, tearooms, cafeterias, coffee shops, diners, and full-service restaurants.

Major changes occurred in the restaurant industry after World War II as a result of America's changing lifestyles. The spectacular growth of the automobile industry and the building of the national highway system gave people greater mobility. Families that formerly could not afford one car now had two or three. Americans took to the road in record numbers, and restaurants popped up at every destination to serve their needs.

Some of the more important changes that impacted the restaurant industry in the second half of the 20th century were the following:

- The franchising of fast-food establishments made eating out convenient and more affordable.
- The growth of airlines made business and vacation travel commonplace.
- A large number of women entered the workforce.

FIGURE 1.1 *Gilley's Diner, drawn first by a horse was, as shown, pulled by a tractor in the early 1900s. Later, it was drawn by truck, and now, after several remodelings, it sits on a foundation on a side street in downtown Portsmouth, New Hampshire. (Photo courtesy of the Portsmouth Athenaeum)*

- The women's movement of the 1970s and 1980s helped to bring about more equitable compensation and gave women greater buying power.
- Eating out became routine for families with two working parents and for single working parents.

By the 1980s, there were restaurants for every pocketbook, palate, and work schedule. The restaurant industry had reached its age of majority.

WHAT ATTRACTS YOU TO THE BUSINESS?

Many people who like to cook or eat out are fascinated by the restaurant business, and some would like to own an eating establishment of their own. They enjoy meeting people and satisfying the palates of others with their culinary skills. Consequently, they view the business first as a creative venture that also brings social and financial rewards.

It is true that there are many enjoyable aspects to the business—it can be creative, it presents opportunities to meet interesting people, and it allows many people to work at something they enjoy. Beyond that, restaurateurs are usually well regarded by their customers and are often acquainted with the leaders of their community. These are attractive lures, but they should not be the principal reasons for entering the business.

SOME CONSIDERATIONS

Not everyone who cooks well or likes to eat out should be in the restaurant business. As a matter of fact, you will probably have much less time available to eat out if you enter the business.

Restaurants can have excellent profit-making potential if they are run well; however, they are anything but your typical nine-to-five job. They require infinite attention to details, long hours, working on weekends and holidays, and occasionally dealing with nuisance customers. Does that make it bad? No, it depends on you—your lifestyle and your personal needs and goals.

It is not unusual today for professional and commercial people to experience the same demands from their work. Doctors, nurses, airline pilots, police officers, fire fighters, entertainers, and increasingly people in the retail field all work odd hours and days as well as weekends and holidays. When you own your own business, the redeeming feature for enduring such hardships is that you harvest the fruits of your labor—the profits are yours.

CAN YOU START A RESTAURANT WITH LIMITED CAPITAL?

Is it possible for an entrepreneur with limited means to succeed in the restaurant business in this age of highly capitalized chain restaurants and stamped-out franchises? Yes, if the owners operate within their means and take full advantage of what small businesses can do best. They must get to know their customers' wants and needs and serve them well. Following is a profile of a highly successful food service venture that exemplifies the wide-ranging opportunities for small investors in the industry today.

Profile: An Entrepreneurial Success

Going from college to the White House is a ride that few restaurateurs/caterers can imagine, but Kevin Tacy and Paul Murphy actually experienced it. In their resumes are such eye-widening items as: catered Down East clambake for the entire Congress on the White House lawn; catered clambakes at the elder President Bush's Kennebunkport home; and catered a clambake for a contingent of soldiers returning from the Gulf War and their welcoming families, friends and dignitaries—4,600 people—at Westover Air Force Base.

It all started when Tacy was a graduate student studying marine biology. He became involved in a sea grant program where his work focused on cultivating the European Belon oyster. When he graduated, he realized that his main interest was in raising oysters commercially, and he and his similarly inclined college friend, Murphy, started a fledgling business. Before long, they were also shipping snails and lobsters overseas.

One of their lobster customers, a salty Mainer named Bill Foster, wanted to retire from his clambake business in York Harbor, Maine. Though rudimentary, the business had built a reputation for serving a remarkable, old-fashioned New England clambake and had a good local following. He asked Tacy and Murphy if they might be interested in buying it.

The prospects of the business intrigued them, but they lacked the finances to buy it. With the help of a balloon payment loan, however, they were able to buy the business in 1985. With long hours and hard work, they managed to make their monthly payments on time and never missed a payment.

The years passed swiftly as they struggled to get on their feet, and soon the large balloon payment that made the purchase possible was due. This led to a major crisis. They could not renegotiate the large balloon payment. At the same time, the economy and the real estate market were mired in a severe slump, and banks were not extending risky loans, particularly to restaurants. Weeks of gut-wrenching anxiety followed. The bank was threatening to foreclose, and they stood to lose everything. Finally, Tacy asked for a meeting with the bank president and tossed the keys to the restaurant on his

(continued on next page)

desk, saying, "We've always made our payments on time, and now the bank won't even try to help us work through this. Take them, the keys fit every door in the place. It's all yours now."

When he turned to leave, the surprised bank president called him back, settled him down, and offered assistance. Soon after, Tacy and Murphy were able to acquire a small business development loan that resolved their crisis. From that point on, the business grew steadily each year.

Foster's Downeast Clambake is located on five acres on Route 1A, not far from the cold Atlantic water from which the celebrated Maine lobsters are trapped. The main restaurant building, called the Pavilion, is a large, single-story structure that is unified by an attractive nautical motif. It can seat up to 400 diners, houses the company offices and the holding tanks for live lobsters, and includes a gift shop. In a rear courtyard are the clambake ovens and their peripheral equipment. On the grounds behind the Pavilion are facilities for wedding receptions and outdoor functions with diversions such as a volleyball court, shuffleboard courts, and a horseshoe pit.

Walk-in business is welcomed at the full service restaurant in the Pavilion, but it actually accounts for only 10 percent of the company's

FIGURE 1.2 *The Fosters Downeast Clambake facility in York Harbor, Maine. (Photo courtesy of Kevin Tacy)*

revenue; the   principal source of revenue is from its group functions. It caters corporate functions, tourist bus groups, senior citizens
groups, weddings, governmental and civic functions, and virtually any
group of 35 or more people who want to experience an authentic
New England clambake (sometimes called a "lobsterbake"). The clambakes are done by reservation only. If an entire room is not booked for
a function, several smaller groups may be clustered together to fill the
room. A local piano player and singer entertains the diners.

The menu is tried and proven and does not change, except that
upon request, a barbequed half-chicken with sweet-and-sour hickory
sauce may be substituted for a lobster. The standard menu includes
their prize-winning clam chowder, cultivated mussels, steamed
clams, a $1\frac{1}{8}$ pound Maine lobster, sweet corn on the cob, roasted
red bliss potatoes, roasted onions, rolls, hot drawn butter, and Maine
blueberry crumb cake.

In 1991, when the Bushes decided the annual congressional
picnic would be a New England clambake, Barbara Bush called the
Department of Fisheries to ask who could do it. They, in turn, called
their counterpart agency in the state of Maine, which called around
and heard that Foster's puts on a really good bake and caters. That's
how they got the job. It took Tacy one whole week just to plan for
the function, but it has paid off ever since.

Foster's Downeast Clambake now sells over 35 tons of lobsters a
year. On average, it does at least six clambakes for groups of over a
thousand guests each year, and it will put on a clambake anywhere in
the country, indoors or outdoors. Some equipment is transported by
employees in rented trucks, and other equipment is rented from a
supplier at the destination; on occasion Foster's partners with a reliable caterer near the site. The lobsters, shellfish, and clam chowder
are shipped by air freight.

All of Foster's clams are retained in special holding tanks before
being steamed, so that they will be completely purged of sand. The
water in the holding tanks is constantly circulated out of and back into
the tanks, in the process being purified of bacteria by ultra violet rays.

Asked what was the most hair-raising experience they have
encountered over the years, Tacy replied, "When we did the clambake

(continued on next page)

at the White House. Everything went well; we had just finished loading up the rental truck and were ready to head home. I got into the truck, which was parked just feet away from the building, to start the engine, and the key broke in the ignition keyhole. I immediately thought, 'Oh-oh, this doesn't look good. We could be stuck here for days.' The sweat poured from my brow as I struggled to turn the key stub with a pair of needle-nose pliers. It worked, the truck started, and we drove all the way back to Maine without turning off the engine."

On the subject of labor, Tacy explained that because of the seasonal nature of the business, only a small percentage of their 110 employees are year-round full-timers. Many are teachers and students; some start while in high school and come back every year until they finish college. They like the atmosphere, the flexibility of the schedule, and the exciting places the work sometimes takes them to. Employees are given thorough training and treated well and, as a result, are dependable and conscientious.

As for the outlook of the lobster industry, Tacy is optimistic. He says, "It's one of the best-managed fisheries, and consequently the number of lobsters caught each year is stable. But the cost of catching them is up, and that puts pressure on the lobstermen and eventually impacts the retail price of lobsters."

Foster's Downeast Clambake is an example of a well-run food business. It knows each segment of its customer base and strives to give its customers what they want. It's still a hands-on business for Tacy and Murphy; walk into their offices any day and you're apt to find them wearing rubber boots and shorts. The business is never boring, and both of them, industrious problem solvers, find it challenging. Over the years, Foster's Downeast Clambake has achieved brand recognition and a reputation for high quality, and it continues to grow.

TYPES OF RESTAURANTS

The restaurant industry offers a wide variety of opportunities for entrepreneurship. There is a type of restaurant for just about everyone who is attracted to the business. Early risers can operate breakfast and lunch establishments, and night people can run dinner restaurants. Below is a partial list of the kinds of eating establishments. Each type of establishment has its own characteristics and clientele.

Breakfast and lunch	Seafood restaurant
Dinner restaurant	Ethnic restaurant
BBQ restaurant	Coffee and donut shop
Diner	Buffet restaurant
Truck stop	Tearoom
Ice cream restaurant	Fast food
Pizza restaurant	Sub shop
Steak house	Fish or clam shack
Chicken restaurant	Natural foods restaurant

The principal differences among eating establishments are the kind of food served, the style of presentation (table or counter service, or take-out), the atmosphere (formal or casual), the hours of service, and the price range.

A TYPICAL DAY IN A RESTAURANT MANAGER'S LIFE

The size of an establishment determines the roles that a manager may assume during the course of a day, as will the skills and interests of the manager. In a small, start-up operation, a manager will do many things that in a large establishment would be delegated to other people.

A manager's duties in a small, start-up restaurant could include: checking the previous day's receipts and preparing the bank deposit, inventorying supplies on hand, calling purveyors for competitive prices, placing orders, preparing work schedules, working on payroll, talking to salespeople, interviewing job applicants, placing advertisements with media, repairing a piece of equipment, conducting meetings with employees, planning new menus, pricing menu items, calculating food and beverage costs, working up new sales promotional ideas, checking on quality and customer service, and working the dining room floor to greet the clientele.

Such a wide variety of duties can draw on the finest skills a person has to offer. Few other fields of employment offer such a diversity of activities. One thing is certain in the restaurant business—it is never boring.

CAN SOMEONE ELSE MANAGE YOUR RESTAURANT?

Yes, this has been amply demonstrated by the many successful restaurant chains one sees represented on the main business strip in most communities. Those organizations conduct in-depth training and have well-tested policies that merely require execution by a competent manager.

In the case of smaller, independent restaurants, much depends on the knowledge and dedication of the hired manager. If that person is willing to make the same kind of personal sacrifices as the owner, very possibly someone else can manage your restaurant successfully. However, the degree to which such people succeed will depend a great deal upon their motivation and how you structure their rewards.

IS RESTAURANT OWNERSHIP FOR YOU?

The restaurant business is an entrepreneurial experience and as such has risks, disappointments, seemingly endless demands for time and money, and no guarantee of success. External factors, such as bad weather, a natural disaster, a lengthy highway project in front of your location, or a downturn in the economy can impact your chances of success. Some people thrive on such challenges, which bring out their best qualities, but others feel insecure when faced with uncertainty.

The main question you must answer is: Are you cut out to be an entrepreneur? In other words, are you willing to risk your savings for a business? Would you be willing to take out a second mortgage on your house? Are you willing to borrow from friends and relatives? Is your family willing to undergo the lifestyle changes that might be required during the business's infancy? Are you willing and able to work 12 hours a day, 7 days a week, if necessary? Can you stand the uncertainty and pressure of the start-up period, which might be longer than expected?

Your answers to these questions will reveal your passion for entering the restaurant business. Most people prefer the stability of a nine-to-five job with a steady paycheck, and there is a great deal to be said for that. But if you enjoy seeing your creation grow and thrive on challenges, in spite of unusual demands, the restaurant business may be an exhilarating and profitable experience for you. Only you can answer the question: Is it for you? The goal of this book is to help you operate successfully, should you decide to enter the business.

Action Guidelines

☐ Determine your tolerance for business risks by giving yourself an entrepreneurial test.

☐ Inventory your goals and priorities, then match them with a list of the benefits and rewards the restaurant business might provide, to determine if you will receive the satisfaction you seek.

☐ List your interests, skills, and experience and assess how closely they match up with those that are required or useful in the restaurant business.

☐ Research the industry in your locale and talk to restaurant people in noncompeting markets to get the benefit of their knowledge and advice.

☐ Read books and trade publications, and take courses pertinent to the restaurant business, to become acquainted with the field.

2

CHANGE AND INNOVATION

Chapters 3 through 16 of this book will guide you through the process of starting your own restaurant, but first let's take a look at some of the trends and changes that are shaping the way the restaurant business is conducted and some of the innovations that have been developed in response to those challenges.

We live in an era when change—social changes, lifestyle changes, and changes in the way businesses operate—is coming at us so fast we can barely keep up with it. Some people's first reaction is to hunker down and resist change. But history shows us that when businesses embrace changes, they manage them better, while those that resist change are often swept aside. Restaurateurs must be aware of changes and emerging trends if they are to prosper.

TRENDS THAT AFFECT THE RESTAURANT BUSINESS

A number of megatrends have been identified by Datamonitor, a global market analysis firm. These trends concern behavioral changes and shifting spending patterns in such areas as convenience, health issues, age complexity, gender complexity, life-stage complexity, income complexity, individualism, sensory needs, comfort needs, and connectivity. It is important for restaurant owners to be aware of such trends and to consider their potential impact on operations. Listed below are some current trends, followed by challenges that one may extrapolate from them.

- Lifestyles have become faster paced, and multitasking among work, home, and family responsibilities is common. This has driven people to seek easier ways of coping with the many demands on their time. Consequently, *convenience* has become a major factor when making consumption decisions. The challenge: How can you make your restaurant more accessible and time-efficient for your target clientele?
- A growing awareness of the importance of *health maintenance* has raised the demand for healthier choices in restaurants as well as in take-out foods. Health issues and diet consciousness increasingly influence what and where people choose to eat. The challenge: How can your restaurant attract and better serve this growing segment of the market by offering healthier choices?
- Many people are defying the stereotypical patterns linked with their age group. These *behavioral changes* express themselves as older adults become more accepting of casual dress wear and activities usually associated with younger adults, teens walk around with wallets full of allowance money, and young people with first-time credit cards are eager to exercise their spending power. The marketing strategies and advertising pitches that have been used to attract these groups must be reassessed. The challenge: How can your restaurant keep up with the products and services that these groups now seek and expect?
- *Modern lifestyles*, such as younger people not marrying until later in life, single-parent households, and gender complexities are also affecting spending patterns, requiring businesses to evaluate how well they meet the needs of these groups. The challenge: How can your restaurant broaden its appeal to give these groups more reasons to favor you with their patronage?
- Many people seek *relief from daily stress* through small indulgences, such as comfort foods that help them escape the day's

pressures. The challenge: How can your restaurant satisfy those needs through in-house or take-out offerings?

- Consumers are bombarded with commercials touting the good life and increasingly *want to participate* in it. Lower- and middle-income earners are searching for experiences that give them a taste of luxury on a low budget. The challenge: How can you upgrade your menu, service, or ambiance to satisfy those desires while keeping your prices affordable?

- Diners appear to be seeking *greater sensory fulfillment* and are more willing to experiment with new foods. Your guests' experience includes what they see, hear, touch, taste and smell at every point in your restaurant. The challenge: How can your restaurant match their expectations?

- The growth of *ethnic populations* in America presents opportunities to restaurants that are welcoming and address their wants and needs. These market segments represent a huge volume of buying power. The challenge: How can your restaurant extend its marketing outreach to these groups and capitalize on the opportunities they present?

Reports on these and other trends are available from Datamonitor. The National Restaurant Association also informs its members on industry trends through its newsletter, *SmartBriefs*; its annual Restaurant Industry Operations Report; and its Educational Foundation publications.

BALANCING TECHNOLOGY WITH YOUR BUDGET

Many of the procedures discussed in this book can be performed better and faster by computerized systems and technological devices, but such technology can be costly. In case you can't afford all of it when you start out, the topics in this book are presented with both the person of abundant resources and the person of limited resources in mind.

Since the era of franchising and rapid market saturation has come upon us, the old fashioned pay-as-you-go model for growth has become rare. In that era, a hot dog stand might pop up on a roadside one year, the next year an ice cream stand might be tacked on to one end of it, and a few years later a dining room and kitchen would be added at the other end of the building, largely financed by previous years' earnings. Today that is highly unusual, but periodically, an example reminds us that it is not impossible.

No doubt, one would prefer to have ample finances to do what is needed in the most up-to-date way. However, a well-run, small restaurant with limited finances, which operates within its means and serves great food or has a unique concept, can build a loyal clientele and upgrade gradually. Remember, however, that at any level of operations, a certain amount of financing is necessary, an amount below which a restaurant runs a serious chance of failure. If that amount cannot be raised, it is better to postpone the project until adequate financing is available.

INNOVATIONS THAT ARE CHANGING THE RESTAURANT INDUSTRY

A hallmark of 21st-century marketing is proving to be quickness to identify changes. Changes often create problems, but problems can present opportunities for those who respond with creative solutions. Following are some of the many technological advances that are being adopted in response to societal changes, labor shortages, and shifting consumption patterns:

- *Handheld devices and digital ordering stations,* capable of transmitting guests' food orders from the dining room to the kitchen or bar, have reduced footsteps for servers, speeded up service, and increased table turnover. Likewise, *silent pagers,* which notify guests when their table is ready, have eliminated the intrusive sound of a cook on a speaker system notifying wait staff that an order is ready.
- *Wi-Fi networks,* which allow guests to access the Internet with their personal digital devices, are becoming increasingly popular in places where people dine or drink casually. They appeal to those who want to be productive or be entertained online while they

relax with a drink or wait for their food to arrive. Such networks are particularly suited to sidewalk cafes and courtyard seating.

- *Self-service kiosks with built-in technologies,* a lower-cost way to extend your brand to consumers, continue to grow in popularity at venues with a high volume of foot traffic, such as malls and the lobbies of high-rise buildings. Busy people often want grab-and-go food in the most convenient way possible. Therefore, the kiosks that use new technologies for holding foods in oven-fresh condition and accept multiple payment methods are likely to become the most popular. They may be independent businesses or satellites of traditional restaurants.

- *GPS devices* grow in popularity as the meal delivery concept grows among traditional restaurants. They assist delivery drivers in finding a customer's location faster. They also allow employers to track delivery vehicles.

- Still in its infancy, *RFID (radio frequency identification)* technology is on the cusp of changing the future of the hospitality industry. RFIDs are chip-based tags that can be mounted onto products or containers (wood, metal, plastic, or cardboard) to help processors monitor storage conditions, record usage of products, locate goods, and issue warnings, among an ever-growing list of applications. They can even (with the help of a tilt switch) monitor how much liquor is being poured from a bottle and if the bartender is sticking to the recipe.

- *Video cameras* are being used more and more to monitor operations for theft deterrent and security reasons.

- *Scannable gift cards* are finding widespread acceptance. They not only replace paper gift certificates, which are often lost or torn, but they can provide an alternative method of payment for guests who on occasion want the pleasure of a cashless, prepaid dining experience.

- *Infrared scanning thermometers* have made checking on food freshness and spoilage, always a concern in the restaurant business, easier and more accurate. Handheld digital devices, which are faster to use and more sanitary than traditional thermometers, can check both the surface and subsurface temperatures of foods with infrared scans and probes. They can also issue alarms.

- *Point-of-sale (POS)* systems are constantly being expanded to interface with peripherals to perform more time-saving and information-gathering functions. Essentially, POS systems integrate all functional activities and accounting procedures of a restaurant that are affected by a transaction. Comprised of hardware and software, the systems are applied to such tasks as order taking, cashiering, inventorying, record keeping, and accounting, and the systems can wirelessly share information among departments to avoid duplication of effort and generate valuable reports for management.
- *Waterless urinals*, odorless and sanitary, are just starting to replace traditional ones in men's rooms. They resemble traditional urinals without flush valves. Because the bowl surface is urine repellant, drainage occurs by gravity without flush water. They reduce costly maintenance and save on water and sewer bills. Sewer gases and odors are trapped by a biodegradable liquid solution that floats on the discharge. Daily cleaning procedures are the same

FIGURE 2.1 *The various models of the SelfCooking Center manufactured by RATIONAL. The SelfCooking Center detects product-specific requirements, the size of the food product to be cooked, and the load size. Then the SelfCooking Center automatically calculates cooking time and temperature and maintains the ideal climate for the product. (Photo courtesy of RATIONAL)*

as for traditional urinals. Their return on investment is claimed to be less than one year.

- *Robotic machines* are now available to mix drinks and perform numerous other functions. Automatic floor washers and pot-and-pan-washing systems that eliminate soaking and scrubbing are gaining popularity. They are seen as partial solutions to the tight labor market.

- Back to the future? Cell phone usage is discouraged or prohibited in some dining rooms because of complaints from other guests. But to avoid making cell phone users feel unappreciated, some restaurants provide an alternative—*telephone booths*. Unlike the familiar, old-fashioned ones, the new booths have no phone. Instead, they have a comfortable seat and a pleasant ambiance for cell phone users.

- *New cooking equipment* that automatically adjusts dry heat and moisture for optimal finishing allows for holding food without losing its fresh-cooked taste and appearance. Such systems give chefs greater flexibility in scheduling cooking times and equipment usage.

- *Attention getters* are characters that appear lifelike in appearance, size and dress. They can move their heads and speak (electronically with convincing voices and lips that move) to deliver any message desired when people come within their sensory range. They may be seated on benches or propped up in any realistic position to invite people to enter an establishment.

CREATIVE SOLUTIONS FOR CHANGING CONDITIONS

Following are examples of creative solutions that are being adopted by restaurants throughout the industry to meet changing consumer tastes and to cope with shifting trends in the business environment:

- *Fusion cooking.* With its spicy embellishments and introduction of overlooked ingredients from other cultures, fusion cuisine is adding excitement to many menus. It is a welcome addition for customers who seek a bolder flavor in their dining experience.

- *Gourmet dining at a counter seat.* In locations where the cost of leasing square-footage has become too expensive, some restaurateurs are leasing previously unthought-of storefronts that are narrow but deep and capable of accommodating a long serving counter. The pioneer restaurants of this concept are luxuriously furnished and appointed with the niceties of an upscale restaurant, the high-end décor and ambiance reflecting gourmet menus.

- *Special requests.* In a departure from traditional policies, some restaurants are experimenting with accommodating special requests from regular customers, if they can be easily prepared within the scope of the kitchen's normal operations.

- *Using the Internet.* Some chefs are searching the Web for exciting new recipes and to get in front of new trends. Internet sites are also being used to show pictures of dining rooms and menus to prospective diners and to give them directions to the restaurant.

- *Cost-cutting programs.* Reeling from escalating energy costs, restaurants are training employees to turn off lights and adjust thermostats in empty rooms, and they are replacing inefficient equipment with energy-saving models.

- *Portion sizes.* Similarly, the rising cost of food products is putting pressure on menu planners, and some restaurants are re-evaluating portion sizes. If plate-waste studies show that a lot of certain items are not being eaten, their portion sizes are being reduced.

KEEPING IT ALL IN PERSPECTIVE

Adopting new technologies is not a cookie-cutter situation; what works for one market segment may not work for another. More than ever, restaurants must stay in close touch with the wants and needs of their particular clientele. For example, tabletop televisions may work for one demographic but not for all. Also, restaurants should stay informed about emerging technologies to benefit from those that are appropriate to their needs. When changes come along, be open-minded and flexible—pan them to discover the nugget of opportunity that may be hidden under the surface.

Action Guidelines

☐ Keep abreast of news developments and emerging trends in your locale. Consider their impact on the food and beverage industry and try to identify their challenges or opportunities.

☐ Join industry associations and network with other people in the industry.

☐ Read industry publications and newsletters.

☐ Attend hospitality industry trade shows.

3

START-UP REQUIREMENTS

If after considering the opportunities and challenges of the restaurant field, you decide that your goals and personality attributes are a good fit for the business, the next step is to determine what is required to open a restaurant. In general, the requirements fall into four main categories:

1. Financial requirements
2. Personal requirements
3. Location requirements
4. Legal requirements

FINANCIAL REQUIREMENTS

The amount of money needed to start a restaurant will depend on the size and type of establishment you have in mind, the geographic area in which it will be located, and the condition of the local economy at the time. Obviously, leases and building costs are relatively expensive in prestigious areas and, similarly, in locations near attractions that draw large numbers of people, such as beaches, civic centers, and athletic stadiums. Construction costs are more expensive during economic booms than in slack times.

The various expenses of starting a restaurant can be divided into three general categories:

1. *Initial planning.* Accounting and legal resources, market research, and general and administrative expenses, such as telephone, photocopying, transportation, and the services of consultants as well as designing and cost estimating
2. *Construction and acquisition of equipment and supplies.* Building or renovating a facility, purchasing and installing the necessary equipment, obtaining initial inventories, and appropriate operating supplies
3. *Preopening expenses and working capital.* Advertising, hiring and training a staff, cleaning up the premises after construction, and having adequate funds to meet payroll and pay other bills until your cash flow can sustain current operating costs

One of the biggest mistakes some prospective entrepreneurs make is wanting to start out with their ultimate dream, the perfect restaurant, the one they have been planning for months if not years. But even in our land of great opportunity, you cannot start out that way, unless you have unlimited financial resources. It is true that people have gone from pushcarts to plush restaurants, but they started with pushcarts. They began with what they could afford, built a good reputation and a loyal customer base, and moved up to their dream restaurant in stages.

Sources of Financing

Traditional lending institutions are wary of granting a loan for a new restaurant if the applicant does not have a proven track record in the business. Their caution is due to the historically high failure rate in the industry by inexperienced people. Unless a borrower has adequate collateral to make a loan virtually risk-free, banks will usually apply rigid lending practices. You will have to depend upon your own resources and those of partners or investors to a great extent.

Be prepared for the fact that a major investor will want to be the majority owner until their investment has been recouped, after which you may become the majority owner.

Following is a list of sources of funds, including some that are often overlooked:

- Soliciting partners
- Incorporating (selling stock)
- Personal savings
- Loans from relatives
- Collateralized bank loans (secured by home equity or tangible assets)
- Credit terms from equipment suppliers
- Credit terms from food suppliers
- Cash value of life insurance policies
- Loans from finance companies
- Small Business Administration loans
- Venture capitalist's loans

Understand that when you seek capital from others, no one will invest in a vague idea. You will be asked many questions and must be able to answer them convincingly. To do that, you must have a persuasive business plan that shows a clear path to profits and is supported by detailed financial data. Due diligence in developing your business plan will demonstrate your ability to think through the complexities of starting up and running a profitable business.

PERSONAL REQUIREMENTS

Beyond the personal requirements discussed in Chapter 1, certain skills can enhance an entrepreneur's chances for success in the restaurant business. The skills required of an owner are largely determined by the extent to which that person wishes to become involved in the daily operations of the business.

Some skills, such as cooking or bartending, are particularly useful when an employee does not show up on time or during an unexpected rush period. Likewise, some accounting knowledge is essential for understanding the books and for budgeting and filling in when the bookkeeper is on vacation. Public relations skills are vital when dealing with a disgruntled guest, and personnel management skills are necessary to motivate employees.

Must you have all of these skills yourself? Not necessarily. In large operations, many duties and responsibilities must be delegated to others, because an owner or manager cannot be in all places at once. In smaller establishments, where monetary constraints are a problem, the owner or manager commonly fills in wherever needed. The financial condition of a business will usually dictate how many hats an owner or manager will wear until the business gets established.

Some skills can be acquired by taking a job to acquire experience or by taking courses at high schools or colleges. Other skills can be acquired from a paid consultant. Beyond that, free advice and training may sometimes be obtained from retired professionals who volunteer their expertise to fledgling businesses through the nonprofit Service Corps of Retired Executives (SCORE) organization. Their availability can be determined by calling your local Small Business Administration.

LOCATION REQUIREMENTS

A good location is critical to the success of a restaurant—extreme care must be taken when selecting a site. Many locations will not have the right demographic makeup or the right zoning for your business. Others may appear ideal but may have environmental problems or historical restrictions.

Accessibility to your target market is important. If customers will be arriving by car, the location must provide adequate space for convenient and safe parking. If you wish to attract tourists, the restaurant should be located near tourist attractions. If you intend to cater to businesspeople, it should be within a few minutes of their workplace. Choosing a good location is perhaps the most important task in the entire process of starting a restaurant. Site selection is discussed in detail in Chapter 4.

LEGAL REQUIREMENTS

The food service business is entrusted with the health and safety of the public. People dine in restaurants with the expectation that the food they eat will be wholesome, that it will be properly served, and that they will not become ill from the experience. Consequently, the restaurant industry is tightly regulated by governmental agencies, and without all of the necessary licenses, permits, and approvals, you cannot open your doors for business.

There are three levels of control for restaurants—federal, state, and local (city, town, and county). The federal laws apply uniformly in all 50 states and the District of Columbia, but the state and local laws vary considerably from state to state and from one jurisdiction to another.

Early in the planning stage of your project, you should consult with the appropriate officials at all three levels of government to determine the specific requirements that apply to your situation. Moreover, you should remain in contact with those officials throughout your start-up process to ensure that you are progressing properly toward the satisfaction of all requirements. For the current addresses of licensing commissions and other agencies, see the appendixes at the back of this book.

State and Local Requirements and Controls

On a day-to-day basis most of a restaurant's dealings are with local and state agencies. These agencies typically deal with adherence to health codes, liquor laws, and public safety.

Food service licenses. All states have food service sanitation codes that require restaurants to obtain food service licenses before they can open for business. The name of this license may vary from state to state. Some call it a health permit (Massachusetts calls it an "Innholder/ Common Victualler license"), but no matter its name, the intent is the same—to ensure that food service establishments are operated in a sanitary and safe manner that complies with food sanitation codes.

Without such a license, restaurants cannot sell food to the public. Furthermore, if at any time after opening, a restaurant fails to comply with the requirements of the food service sanitation code, its license may be revoked. Licenses are issued for one year at a time.

State and local public health authorities cooperate closely with each other on public health matters. In some jurisdictions, local health departments administer inspections of restaurants and issue food service licenses subject to approval by the state public health department. In others, state public health officials administer all aspects of the food sanitation code.

The typical process for obtaining a food service license is as follows:

1. Advise local officials of your proposed restaurant:
   • Building inspector
   • Planning board
   • Zoning board
2. Submit floor plans of your restaurant to the local health department, which will advise you if it is necessary to submit them to the state health department. Call to make an appointment to bring in the plans for review.
   • The placement of all major equipment must be shown as well as the locations of sinks and restrooms. A list of materials to be used for floors, walls, ceilings, and food contact surfaces should be included.
   • A copy of your food and beverage menus must be included.
3. Complete and submit a license application with the appropriate fee to the local or state health department, as directed.
4. Call the health department for a preopening inspection at least seven days prior to your planned opening date.
5. If all goes well with the preopening inspection, a food service license will be issued, and periodic inspections will follow.

When planning a restaurant, particular attention should be paid to toilets and hand-washing facilities, sewage disposal, plumbing, lighting, ventilation, dish-washing and glass-washing facilities, and all work surfaces. These are areas of vital concern to public health authorities.

Fire permits. Fire safety is just as important as food safety—a restaurant cannot open for business until it has been issued a fire permit. The state fire marshal's office and local fire departments work hand in hand, but as a rule, the local fire departments do the on-site inspections.

The local fire department places a limit on the number of patrons allowed into a restaurant. That capacity is determined by square footage and other factors contained in the state and local fire codes, modeled after the National Fire Protection Code.

Local fire departments issue permits upon passage of an inspection that includes, but is not limited to, the following items:

- *Clearances.* Gas-fired and other fuel-burning equipment must be installed with specified clearances from walls, ceilings, and floors.
- *Exits.* The correct number of exits must be in the right locations. They must be unobstructed and have illuminated exit signs. External exit doors must swing outward and be mounted with crash bars.
- *Fire detection.* Smoke detectors and appropriate fire suppression systems (such as sprinklers, CO_2, and dry chemical) must be in place as well as an emergency lighting system.
- *Sprinklers.* These must not be covered, blocked, or otherwise impaired from performing as intended.
- *Fire extinguishers.* An adequate quantity and type must be correctly placed throughout the premises. Usually, they must be located within 75 feet from any point, have a particular rating, and be visible.
- *Electrical.* All electrical work must conform to applicable building codes and be done by licensed electricians, using approved materials. An adequate electrical supply must be in place to meet the load required by the equipment and other electrically powered systems safely.
- *Flammable liquids.* The storage, use, and disposal of any flammable liquids (such as cooking oils) must be by approved means. Cooking equipment that uses combustible liquids must be protected by fire hoods with built-in suppression systems.
- *Storage.* Aisles of at least 36 inches should be provided between shelves. Approved metal containers must be provided for debris or other combustible materials.
- *Miscellaneous.* Chimneys, heating equipment, and vent systems must meet code requirements.

Building permits. In most communities, it is necessary to check with several other agencies before applying for a building permit. Following is a typical sequence of events for obtaining a building permit and a certificate of occupancy:

1. Check with the zoning board to determine whether the zoning at your proposed location allows a restaurant.

2. Obtain a site approval from the planning board. This is an important step if your restaurant will serve alcoholic beverages, because this is when public hearings will be held and neighbors may voice objections to your plans. It is best to know of any objections early on. The board will consider such factors as your business's potential impact on traffic conditions and the environment.

3. Next, a plan review meeting is held with an official from both the building and the fire department present. They will review the plans in detail, paying particular attention to the structural integrity of the building, the occupancy capacity for which it is rated, fire detection systems, and conformance to all applicable codes.

4. Finally, you make formal application for a building permit.

If everything checks out well in the above stages, a building permit is issued, and construction may be started. From this point on, the building inspector will make periodic inspections of the construction or renovation to determine compliance with codes. You must use licensed electricians and plumbers.

When the construction is completed, the building inspector and the health inspector will make a final inspection, and upon passage of that inspection, a certificate of occupancy is issued to the owner of the business.

Other state and local departments. A restaurant must register its name and comply with the state's labor laws, handicap access regulations, and environmental regulations. It must also collect sales or meals taxes as required. For specific details on these requirements, you should check with the appropriate agencies in your state:

- *Secretary of state.* To register the name of the business and to incorporate if that is the legal form of business chosen
- *Commission on the handicapped.* To inquire about accessibility requirements for new construction and renovations
- *Bureau of weights and measures.* For inspection of any scales to be used in commercial trade
- *Department of revenue.* For information on sales taxes or meals taxes that may have to be collected
- *Signage commission.* Many communities now have an agency that controls signage and requires that a permit be obtained before a

sign may be installed. They are primarily concerned with the size (square footage) of the sign, its height from ground level, and the type of illumination planned for it.

- *Historical commission.* Should you have plans to use a designated historical building for your restaurant, you may not be able to do what you want with it.
- *Wetlands commission.* Swamps and marshes are protected lands. If you are looking at a property for your restaurant site that contains wetland, you may not be able to drain it or fill it in for your parking lot. Inquire first.

In recent years, water supply and septic systems have come under much tighter control, as has the disposal of hazardous materials. These are important matters to investigate when buying a property, particularly in suburban areas where wells and septic systems are common. Also, beware of underground fuel tanks; they may have to be removed at considerable expense.

Liquor licenses. If you plan to sell alcoholic beverages in your restaurant, you will want to investigate the availability of a liquor license early on. Many restaurant plans have been aborted because a liquor license was not available at the intended site.

All states require a liquor license to sell alcoholic beverages. Liquor laws vary from state to state, but they all have regulations governing what you can sell, where you can sell it, when and to whom you may sell it, and how you may advertise and promote it.

The availability of licenses also differs from state to state. They are more difficult to obtain in some states due to the number of licenses already in existence in relation to the size of the population. In other states, they are readily issued as long as the applicant and the premises meet the requirements. Applicants for liquor licenses are checked thoroughly. Of greatest concern to state liquor control boards is an applicant's ability to obey laws and be financially responsible. The general requirements for a liquor license are that the applicant must

- be 21 years of age or older;
- be financially responsible; and
- have good moral character.

Other requirements concerning American citizenship, registered alien status, and criminal background vary from state to state.

The license for a restaurant that sells alcoholic beverages for consumption within the licensed premises only is called an *on-premise* license (as opposed to an *off-premise* license for a business such as a liquor store). There are different types of on-premise licenses—beer only, beer and wine, and all alcoholic beverages. The effective term of a license is one year, and it applies only to one specific location.

Allowing for variations from one jurisdiction to another, liquor laws typically cover the following items:

- Types of licenses available, fees, and the application process
- Requirements for acquiring a license
- Hours and days of operation
- Proximity to churches, schools, and hospitals
- Who may be employed in a licensed establishment
- Who may not be served alcoholic beverages
- Change of ownership or managers
- Changes or alterations to the licensed premises

All states have an alcoholic beverage control agency. In some states, only the state agency can issue a liquor license. In others, cities are allowed to issue a liquor license, provided the state agency approves the issuance of the license.

States fall into two categories as regards to governmental control of the liquor business: *license states* and *control states.* In a license state, liquor products are distributed by private wholesalers, which have salespeople that call on restaurants and bars. In a control state, restaurants must buy their liquor products from state liquor stores or warehouses. There are 18 control states (and Montgomery County in Maryland), and each has its own regulations and ways of doing business.

Federal Requirements and Controls

The federal control agencies are the Department of Labor, the Internal Revenue Service (IRS), and the Bureau of Alcohol, Tobacco, and Firearms (BATF).

The Department of Labor administers the provisions of the Fair Labor Standards Act. Its principal concerns are compliance with the federal minimum wage laws and discriminatory practices. Where state and federal minimum wage levels are not the same, the higher of the two minimum wage rates prevails. Most of a restaurant's dealings on labor issues are conducted with state labor departments.

The Internal Revenue Service requires businesses to obtain an Employer Identification Number (EIN). This is done by filing IRS form number SS-4. It also requires restaurants to pay estimated federal income taxes on a quarterly basis. Employers are also required by the IRS to withhold federal income taxes, Social Security (FICA) taxes, and Medicare taxes from their employees' pay. All such withholdings must be forwarded to the IRS by certain dates, depending on the size of the payroll. It is advisable to have a competent accountant set up routines that conform to IRS requirements for these matters, when you start your business. To calculate payroll withholdings, an employer should refer to IRS Circular E, "Employer's Tax Guide."

Special occupational tax stamp. If you plan to sell alcoholic beverages in your restaurant, you will need to obtain a Special Occupational Tax Stamp from the BATF, a division of the Treasury Department. Without that stamp, a restaurant cannot legally sell alcoholic beverages. The Special Tax Stamp is a receipt for payment of the Special Occupational Tax. It is not a federal license, and it does not confer any privileges on the retail dealer.

The law defines a *retail dealer* as "a person who sells alcoholic beverages to any other person other than a dealer." This includes all restaurants that sell alcoholic beverages for on-premise consumption. The Special Occupational Tax must be paid each year, on or before July 1.

For complete details on the federal liquor laws and regulations, call your nearest BATF office and ask for the free booklet TTB P 5170.2.

Action Guidelines

☐ Consult an accountant familiar with the restaurant business and an attorney familiar with the requirements for obtaining licenses, opening restaurants and payment schedules of applicable taxes.

☐ Obtain specific information on the requirements for opening a restaurant in your location by doing the following:
- Contact your local regulatory agencies:
  - Public health department
  - Liquor commission (if you plan to serve alcoholic beverages)
  - Building department
  - Fire department
- Contact your state regulatory agencies:
  - State public health department
  - Alcoholic beverage control board (only if you plan to serve alcoholic beverages)
  - Secretary of state
  - State finance and taxation department
- Contact the Bureau of Alcohol, Tobacco, and Firearms
- Contact the Internal Revenue Service

☐ Estimate the approximate costs of starting the type of restaurant you have in mind and match this with your possible sources of funds, using the resources described in this chapter.

C *h a p t e r*

4

STRATEGY FOR SUCCESS

Business scholars have studied the ingredients of success for many years, but to date no one has come up with a formula that works in every case. The best one can hope for is that with training, experience, good planning, and a lot of hard work, you stand a chance of succeeding. That is why 80 percent of all new businesses fail within the first five years of their existence. However, you can increase your chances of success by learning from the experience of others.

Some people believe that restaurants can endure the harshest of economic times and survive poor management better than most businesses, because people have to eat. That is a misconception; the facts show that many restaurants fail every year. But at the same time, some restaurants do extremely well and reward their owners handsomely. Why the difference?

REASONS SOME RESTAURANTS FAIL

The two main causes of failure are undercapitalization and lack of knowledge about the restaurant business.

Simply put, *undercapitalization* means "not having enough money to do the job." It usually results from not having a financial plan when entering a business. Some entrepreneurs spend too much of their funds to construct their restaurant and consequently do not have enough money left to meet their bills during the start-up period. A common mistake is overspending on new equipment or renovations, rather than phasing in changes gradually as cash flow increases. If a prospective restaurateur does not have enough capital to enter the business safely, it is best to hold off until the capital position is improved.

Lack of knowledge of the business covers a broad spectrum, from not possessing the required skills to not knowing the customers' wants and needs. Some training or experience must be acquired before attempting to enter the field. Money alone cannot buy profitability. Some investors with adequate funds attempt to enter the restaurant business but lack the interest or ability to manage it properly. These investors wind up with losses instead of profits.

Close supervision and sound policies are required, because a restaurant business is made up of so many details that, if not properly tended to, can ruin it. Owners must constantly monitor their operations and look for weak spots that need improvement.

The following recommendations will help you stay in business:

- Broaden your knowledge of the restaurant business as much as possible through
  - personal research;
  - reading trade journals and books on the hospitality field;
  - obtaining information from food and beverage salespeople; and
  - attending professional seminars and taking useful courses.
- Conduct a feasibility study before buying an existing restaurant or starting a new one.
- Seek guidance from a reputable accountant and lawyer, preferably ones who are well acquainted with the restaurant field.
- Join local professional associations and network with other, non-competing restaurant owners.
- Stay current by obtaining information on new products, trends, and promotional ideas from your suppliers and other educational resources.
- Develop a financial plan (cash-flow budget) for your first year in business.

- Compare your actual performance against your business plan at frequent intervals during the year and make adjustments where necessary.

- Control the following profit centers carefully from the outset of the business:

  - *Purchasing.* Establish specifications for each product (purveyor, brand, size, and maximum and minimum stock levels).

  - *Receiving.* Count and inspect all incoming shipments for proper quantity, quality, and pricing before signing invoices.

  - *Storing.* Put away all incoming shipments of foods, beverages, and supplies in secured storage locations. As few keys as possible should be issued and those only to staff who require them.

  - *Issuing.* All shipments received and all issues of products from the storeroom should be recorded in an inventory book or the computer system.

  - *Inventory.* A physical inventory (actually counted) should be taken at least once a month to verify the accuracy of the balances on hand shown in the inventory book or computer system.

  - *Standard recipes.* Use standard recipes to ensure consistency of product quality.

  - *Portion control.* Establish standard portion sizes and use measuring tools, such as scales and numbered scoops and ladles, to ensure consistency of production cost and customer satisfaction.

  - *Cashiering.* Make sure every product served is accounted for according to your policies. If you want to give away a complimentary meal—fine. It is your business, after all. But no one else should have the right to give away your profits.

- Know your customers. The better you know them individually and as a class, the better you can serve them. Here are some ways of viewing your customers:

Age	Type of jobs
Sex	Education levels
Income	Type of transportation
Interests	Food and beverage preferences

- Observe your customers' spending habits:
  - Where are they spending their money?
  - What are they buying?
  - How much do they tend to spend?
  - What time do they arrive? How long do they stay?
  - Do they come alone or with friends?
- Make your customers feel welcome. Talk to them and get feedback.
- Establish and adhere to responsible business practices. This will affect your relations with your community.
- Keep up-to-date on laws and regulations that pertain to the restaurant business.
- Advertise effectively to attract the type of clientele you desire.
- Give your customers reasons to come back again soon. Develop a steady flow of menu specials and promotional events and announce them on table tents and wall posters.
- Price your menu competitively according to your particular style of service and serve high-quality food consistent with your prices.
- Keep your premises clean and up-to-date.

DON'T ASSUME SUCCESS WILL HAPPEN

Management should conduct periodic surveys of the restaurant to identify problems and anticipate possible causes of failure. Corrective actions should be taken as soon as possible, and they should be assessed shortly after their implementation to determine their effectiveness.

For example, suppose Restaurant A is losing customers to Restaurant B, a new competitor that features a piano player in its dining room. So in response, A begins to offer musical entertainment. After two weeks, A reviews the situation and finds that sales are still declining, and on top of that, profits have shrunk because they are now paying for entertainment. The corrective action must be reassessed. Possibly, they have engaged the wrong type of entertainment for their particular clientele. Or maybe the competitor's entertainment is not drawing customers away after all. Perhaps the quality of A's food has slipped, or any number of other factors are causing the decline. Restaurant A must recognize that the corrective action has not achieved the desired result and, therefore, must be modified.

You should be your severest critic, because no one else cares as much as you do about the success of your restaurant. To stand a chance of succeeding, its management must be honest and objective in its appraisal of how well the restaurant is performing.

START FROM SCRATCH OR BUY?

There are two ways to enter the business: one is to start a new restaurant from scratch; the other is to buy an existing one. Neither way is a surefire guarantee of success. However, having a knowledge of the factors involved in each approach can significantly improve your chances of succeeding.

Should You Start a New Restaurant?

People who have a truly unique concept and the necessary money to finance their idea will probably want to start a new restaurant. Extensively renovating a going restaurant eradicates most of the savings associated with buying an existing business and oftentimes compromises the initial plan.

With a new restaurant, you will have to do everything that would have already been done in an established restaurant—but you will be able to do it your way.

You will have to address all of the responsibilities associated with a business start-up. For example, you will have to establish an organization, find a suitable location, develop your menus, determine prices, project sales, purchase equipment, develop a floor plan, select your decor, develop a service system, hire and train a new staff, and, when applicable, plan your entertainment. If you have a brand-new concept, you will also have to advertise it aggressively until you achieve name recognition.

When all of these things are done, you will open your doors to the public and hope your new restaurant becomes a success.

The typical progression of start-up activities as depicted in Figure 4.1 is for a project with adequate internal funding in place. If external financing is required, the project would be planned up to the point of estimating its cost and potential return before approaching investors or lenders.

FIGURE 4.1 *A typical flowchart of activities for a start-up restaurant business. Legal, accounting, and food service professionals as well as licensing agencies should be consulted early in the process*

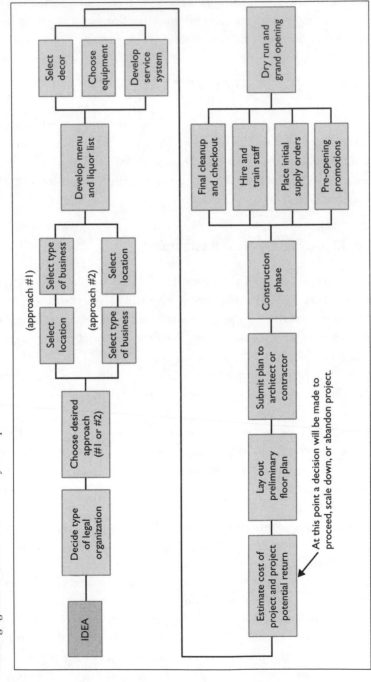

The cost of the project must be reasonable in terms of its potential return; otherwise, it will not attract investors. If the estimated cost is too high, you will have to loop back in the process and make the necessary changes.

The talents, financial resources, and experience of the principals make every start-up situation unique; however, the basic process tends to be the same. The actual steps will be determined by the restaurant's size and scope. If new construction for a large restaurant were required, you would want to bring in an architect at the beginning of the process. On the other hand, if you were planning a small luncheonette to go into a rented space, you would not need an architect at all. With the proper approvals and help from some equipment salespeople, you could plan your own layout and, given the necessary skills, do some of the general work yourself. Electrical, gas, and plumbing work must be done according to building codes and should be subcontracted to licensed tradespeople. Heating, ventilation, and air-conditioning as well as the fire suppressant system should be done by professionals. Frequent consultation with building, fire, and health inspectors is prudent.

Should You Buy an Existing Restaurant?

The biggest advantages to buying an existing restaurant are that it comes with (a) an immediate cash flow, (b) an experienced staff and (c) production and service systems that are in place. In effect, you save the start-up costs of a new business—but care must be taken to assure you do not inherit unwanted problems, such as an irreparable bad reputation, an incompetent staff, outdated equipment or a short lease. Be aware also that if the success of an existing restaurant is intricately tied to the image of the present owner or chef, there is no guarantee its success will continue after the business changes hands.

Arrange to have an equipment specialist accompany you when you inspect a restaurant that you are seriously considering buying. The small cost for this service is well worth it. Check the age and condition of the equipment to determine if a great deal of it is obsolete or about to fail and consider how appropriate the equipment would be for producing the menu that you may have in mind.

HOW MUCH SHOULD YOU PAY FOR AN EXISTING RESTAURANT?

There is no one rule of thumb. The answer to this question will vary with the facts of each situation. For instance, if you were considering buying a restaurant in its entirety—that is, a going operation with a successful track record and an attractive cash flow—it would be valued one way, whereas if you intended to buy just the assets of a business, they would be valued quite differently. In the first case, the price would be based on the value of the assets plus the value of a proven income stream. In the second case, the price would be based solely on the value of the assets, which, unless used properly, may or may not ever produce profits.

Likewise, a restaurant in an extraordinarily good location will command a substantial premium over one in a mediocre location.

Potential buyers can use several techniques to assess an existing restaurant, determining the high and low end of an acceptable price range within which you can dicker. In this process, you should work closely with your accountant. Four of the more common methods are listed below:

1. *Comparable values of similar going concerns.* This method arrives at a value based on what similar restaurants have sold for.
2. *Reproduction or replacement value.* This method is based on the open market cost of reproducing the assets of the business. It is most useful when only the assets are being purchased.
3. *Earnings approach.* Here the focus is on the annual earnings of the business. Earnings can be used to calculate your potential return on investment; however, some cautions are important.

   Earnings can vary with methods of accounting. For example, in the case of a sole proprietorship, where an owner may work but is not an employee and is not paid a salary, the business's earnings would appear much higher than they should, as the cost of the owner's labor is not accounted for. Also, if economic conditions have shifted and are now declining, past performance may not be a good indicator of future earnings.

   Some people will use a multiple of five or six times annual earnings to establish a theoretical value that fits their amortization timetable, while others who may be considering a business with potential uncertainties would likely want a faster payback period. However, in the end you should regard earnings as just one measure that must be looked at alongside others.

4. *Book value*. Essentially, this is the "adjusted book value" of a restaurant, arrived at by subtracting total liabilities from total assets and adjusting for any intangibles such as goodwill. Although the data is based on a firm's most recent balance sheet, the value of the assets should be tested for fair market value and, if necessary, so restated.

HOW MUCH SHOULD YOU PAY FOR RENT?

The concepts of time and place are all important. *Time* refers to what is happening at a location within a given period. For instance, a storefront one block away from the site of a major event like a World's Fair or an Olympic stadium during a given year will fetch a far greater rent than it would at another time. *Place* refers to location. A site between two high-volume anchor stores in a prestigious mall would fetch a higher rent than a store in a less desirable area.

Rent is also influenced by factors other than the traffic count. The age of a building and the desirability of its address as well as the provision of amenities, such as heat, light, water, parking, and snow removal, affect rents. When expenses such as property taxes, insurance, and maintenance are paid by the lessee, the lease is referred to as a triple net lease. A National Restaurant Association annual publication titled *Restaurant Industry Operations Report* shows occupancy costs—which include rent, property taxes, and insurance. For example, in 2004 occupancy cost for full-menu, table service restaurants that sell both food and beverages averaged 3.5 percent to 9.5 percent of total sales that year.

When budgeting for expenses, it is important to be conservative in estimating total sales so as to not overstate expenses that are forecast as a percentage of sales.

EVALUATE BEFORE YOU INVEST

It is critical that you research an existing restaurant thoroughly before buying it. Figure 4.2, a checklist for surveying an establishment, may draw your attention to areas that might be overlooked.

FIGURE 4.2 *Checklist for Surveying an Existing Restaurant*

Areas to Evaluate	Comments
• Purchasing and receiving procedures	
• Storing and issuing methods	
• Equipment and layout	
• Location of equipment	
• Maintenance of equipment	
• Suitability of equipment for menu	
• Functional aspects of equipment	
• Ability to be cleaned	
• Attractive design	
• Ease of operation	
• Food preparation methods	
• Quality control of recipes	
• Use of premixes	
• Portion control	
• Presentation	
• Inventory	
• Item popularity	
• Product availability	
• Price range	
• Turnover rate	
• Personnel	
• Staffing	
• Duties and responsibilities	
• Grooming	
• Uniforms	
• Productivity	
• Morale	
• Labor	
• Turnover of employees	
• Training on the job	
• Overtime policies	

(continued on next page)

FIGURE 4.2 *(Continued)*

Areas to Evaluate	Comments
• Food and beverage costs	
• Standard recipes	
• Inventory control records	
• Pilferage control	
• Cost percentages	
• Food presentation methods	
• Size of portions	
• Garnishes	
• Variety of colors and textures	
• Service system	
• Order taking	
• Pickup system	
• Guest check controls	
• Delivery system	
• Dining room and lounge	
• Number of servers	
• Tables per station	
• Style of service	
• Decor	
• Type of clientele	
• Average guest check size	
• China, glassware, utensils, and paper supplies	
• Backup inventory supply	
• Inventory-taking procedures	
• Reorder policies	
• Advertising and sales promotion	
• Types and frequency of ads	
• Media used	
• Effectiveness of ads	

(continued on next page)

FIGURE 4.2 *(Continued)*

Areas to Evaluate	Comments
• Sanitation	
• Inspection policies	
• Training	
• Equipment	
• Method of supervision	
• Safety	
• Fire-extinguishing equipment	
• Fire exits	
• Fire-retardant materials	
• Emergency lighting	
• Fire detection and suppressant systems	
• Communications	
• Lines of authority	
• Supervision	
• Policy manual	
• Accounting controls	
• Food cost controls	
• Beverage cost controls	
• Labor cost controls	
• Controllable general expenses	
• Physical appearance of property	
• Building, exterior and interior	
• Furniture, fixtures, and equipment	
• Obsolescence factor	

OBTAIN PROFESSIONAL ASSISTANCE

Engage experts to help you evaluate a restaurant—talk to bankers, suppliers, and repair technicians. They can give you information about less obvious parts of the business. Also, talk to patrons, neighbors, and anyone else who may have information about the business. Try to find out how the restaurant has been doing in regard to sales, public image, and customer satisfaction. But most of all, be sure to get your accountant involved at this stage of your evaluation.

Insist that your accountant be permitted to examine the official books of the business. Check for outstanding bills or liens if you buy the restaurant in its entirety. If deposits for future functions (banquets booked in advance) have been accepted by the current owner, adjustments should be made during the closing process. In addition, determine whether all taxes have been paid or whether tax issues are outstanding with the IRS or state revenue agency.

Closing the Deal

It is wise to hire an attorney who is familiar with the restaurant industry. If you do not know such a lawyer, contact your local bar association. Their referral service will give you several names to choose from. Have your attorney review all documents before you sign them. You will be encountering contractual matters that are beyond the ability of the average layperson to cope with. Be sure to make any agreements you enter into contingent upon your acquiring the necessary licenses and permits, because without the required licenses and permits, you will not be able to open for business. To ensure that everything is done properly and in your best interest, have your lawyer present at the signing.

Choosing a Legal Form of Business Entity

In general, the three most common legal forms from which you may choose are: the sole proprietorship, the partnership, and the corporation. Each has its advantages and disadvantages. Which legal form of business entity is best for you should be worked out with your lawyer and your accountant. At issue will be how much money you have to invest, how much personal involvement in the business you wish to undertake, and the tax implications and liability and disclosure requirements of each form.

Sole proprietorship. The idea of not having a boss or committee meetings is very appealing to many people. Sole proprietorship is very popular, because it gives the owner complete control over a business. The owner can make the rules and set the policies, take time off at will or work long hours. Best of all, the owner doesn't have to split the profits with partners or stockholders, and the profits are taxed as if they were personal income. In addition, the owner enjoys prestige, hires and fires people, and has final authority for everything.

Counterbalancing the above, the owner must carry the entire financial burden and be competent at all of the roles in the business. Beyond that, the owner must deal with all of the business's problems alone. The greatest disadvantage of a sole proprietorship, however, is that it has unlimited liability. Everything of value that the proprietor owns is at risk if the business fails. In other words, if you end up owing money, creditors can come after your personal assets.

Partnership. Partnerships function best when the partners have complementary talents and each brings financial resources to the business. Small partnerships may enjoy some of the advantages of a sole proprietorship, except that everything you own, do, or earn is shared with one or more partners.

The two most common types of partnerships among small businesses are the *general partnership* and the *limited partnership*. In a general partnership, all partners bear the burden of unlimited liability. In a limited partnership, there must be at least one general partner who runs the business and has unlimited liability, but an unrestricted number of others may be limited partners who have limited liability and are not required to take an active role in the operations of the business.

It is important to have a partnership agreement drawn up by an attorney and signed by all partners. The agreement should include, at the very least, the names of all partners, the amount of each partner's investment, the share of the firm's profits to which each partner will be entitled, the role and responsibilities of each partner in the operations of the business, and what will happen in the event a partner dies or wants to sell their ownership share.

One partner's actions may jeopardize a business and create a liability that must be shared by all partners; therefore, it is essential to know and trust implicitly the individuals with whom you become a partner. As a general rule, you have no reason to consider the partnership form of business, unless you need the skills or the funds of other people to launch your business.

Corporation. A corporation is defined as "a fictitious person" by the U.S. Supreme Court. Therefore, because you are a real person, you cannot be a corporation. A corporation is held to be a separate entity from yourself. You may, however, be a stockholder, a director, an officer, or an employee of a corporation. Three or more persons are usually required to obtain a corporate charter, elect a board of directors who guide the corporation, and appoint officers to run it. Following is a list of advantages of incorporating:

- Raising additional capital for growth or expansion is easier than with a proprietorship or partnership.
- Your personal assets are protected from seizure or attachment by corporate creditors.
- Your liability is limited to your investment in the corporation, unless you misuse corporate funds or facilities.
- Stock can be used as collateral for loans, whereas owners in sole proprietorships and partnerships may have to use their personal assets.
- Filing a Subchapter S election allows gains and losses to flow directly through to stockholders, so that they can be treated as personal income. In this respect the Subchapter S corporation is like a partnership.

ACQUIRING ADDITIONAL CAPITAL

A corporation may issue additional shares of stock without affecting the workings of the company, because its owners are legally separate from the operations of the company. This is where the corporate form of business has a distinct advantage over other forms. A corporation can also obtain debt capital from professional lending institutions.

If a sole proprietor is an established member of the business community, is well networked in local financial circles, and has an upstanding reputation, borrowing as a private individual may not present a problem. However, if you are new to a community, you will find it very difficult to borrow money for a restaurant. A sole proprietor cannot sell stock and must, therefore, borrow additional capital on the strength of their personal and business reputation.

A partnership may bring new partners with investment capital into the firm. However, finding the right persons to associate with is not always easy. Extreme caution must be exercised because of the unlimited liability feature of a general partnership.

SELECTING A LOCATION AND A PROPERTY

The words *location, location, location* are sometimes referred to as the three keys to success. Without a good location, most fledgling businesses are doomed from their start, because the effort and funds required to offset the shortcomings of a poor site drain resources from more important aspects of the business.

The site analysis checklist in Figure 4.3 can be useful when evaluating restaurant sites, though not all items in the checklist are applicable in every situation. It can be very helpful to use a recording device for storing detailed information as you investigate potential sites.

Data may be obtained from tax offices, registry of deeds books, town or city clerks, Realtors and brokers, highway departments, chambers of commerce, and on-site inspections.

NAMING YOUR RESTAURANT

As with all businesses, names must be approved by and registered with the secretary of state of the state in which the business is domiciled. It is wise to submit three desired names in their order of preference, because your first choice may already be taken. The names will be screened through a computer, and if no one else has already registered the name you want, you will get it.

The actual process of registering a business name is an easy matter. Simply obtain the appropriate forms from the secretary of state's office (in your state capital), fill them out with your desired names, and return them to the secretary of state with a check for the stipulated fee. That is the legal side of selecting a name.

FIGURE 4.3 *Restaurant Site Analysis*

Address of site _____   Present owner or agent _____

City/state/zip _____   Address _____

Lot no. _____   City/state/zip _____

Map ref. _____ _____   Tel. _____

Date of inspection _____   Asking price _____

Physical Features of the Land

Size: Approach—visibility:

Shape: Accessibility to target market:

Slope: Clearance:

Expansion possibilities: Zoning:

Utilities: Nearby hazard or blights:

   Water, gas, electricity: Parking possibilities:

   Sewers: Snow removal or storage space:

Soil conditions: perc, tests,
drainage

Economic and Community Features

Economic trend: Wage trends:

Public transportation: Competition:

Local attraction: Income levels:

Civic promotional   Seasonal features:
agencies:
                                    Major highways nearby:
Labor supply:
                                    Population—number and makeup:
Traffic—passing daily:
                                    Fire and police protection:
Auto count:
                                    Food and beverage suppliers:
Pedestrian count:

Physical Features of the Structure

This is a partial list. Your Realtor can supply you with additional information.

Perimeter dimensions: Gas service—LP or natural,
                                    size of LP tank:
No. of rooms and sizes:

Traffic flow lines: Sewer—municipal or septic tank:

(continued on next page)

FIGURE 4.3 *(Continued)*

No. of restrooms:	Water—municipal or well, volume:
Flooring materials:	
Storage possibilities:	Handicap accessibility:
Insulation:	Heating/ventilation/air-conditioning:
Type of siding and roofing:	
Electrical service—amps, phase:	

Laws and Restrictions

Zoning of property:	Building height and setback requirement:
Land-use laws:	
Permits and licenses needed:	Lighting and signage requirement:
Building restrictions:	Parking regulations:
Wetland restrictions:	

Taxes

Property tax:	Meals and lodging tax:
Income or business tax:	State sales tax:
Assessment percentage:	Water and sewer tax:
City sales tax:	

Cost of Property

Land:	Necessary improvements:
Building:	Total investment:

The other aspect of selecting a name, the public relations aspect, is equally as important. Thoughtful consideration should be given to your name because it can serve many purposes, the most prominent of which is to convey specific information to the public. Some examples are:

- La Casa Napoli. Indicates an Italian restaurant.
- Fisherman's Landing. Suggests seafood and a nautical decor.
- The State Street Grill. Tells you where the restaurant is.
- The AM/PM Diner. Declares the establishment is open day and night.

Consider the most important message you want your name to convey in terms of who your target market is and what they want, then match their expectations.

RISK MANAGEMENT

A sound risk management plan must account for all kinds of disasters that could interrupt or destroy a business. Common considerations are floods, hurricanes, tornadoes, fires, collapsing roofs, lawsuits, medical emergencies, and other calamities.

A successful risk management program should include planning for the safety of both guests and employees and for the continuation of the business after the incident. This would include an evacuation plan for instances when exiting the premises is prudent and a shelter-in-place plan when evacuating would be too dangerous. It would also include setting sound company policies and training employees on their roles in event of a disaster and acquiring adequate insurance. It is advisable to have an insurance agent or broker design a complete insurance program for your business and discuss techniques for cost containment. Figure 4.4 shows the types of insurance available.

Action Guidelines

- ☐ List the relative merits of buying an existing restaurant as opposed to starting one.
- ☐ Acquaint yourself with accountants and lawyers who have experience in the restaurant industry.
- ☐ Select the legal form of business entity that is most appropriate for your restaurant.
- ☐ Choose three names for your restaurant and check the availability of those names with the secretary of state's office in your state.
- ☐ Evaluate several potential sites using the restaurant site analysis chart shown in Figure 4.3.
- ☐ Work with an insurance broker to develop a risk management program to meet the needs of your restaurant.

FIGURE 4.4 *Many types of insurance are available.*

Type of Insurance	Hazard Covered
Named peril	Covers property but is limited to specifically named losses.
General comprehensive liability	Covers claims for bodily injury and property damage due to an accident.
Personal injury liability	Covers law suits due to false arrest, libel, slander, defamation of character, and personal injuries.
Automobile liability	Covers damages or injuries that employees incur while driving their car or a company car in the performance of company business.
Liquor liability	Protects against suits resulting from damages or injuries to others by a person who becomes intoxicated in your establishment.
Property damage	Covers buildings, inventory, equipment, and fixtures against loss due to fire, smoke, explosion, or vandalism.
Product liability	Covers against suits based on damage or injuries resulting from a product that you served.
Fire	Covers damage to other buildings from a fire that originated on your property.
Workers' compensation	Covers employees' medical and rehabilitation costs for work-related injuries.
Business interruption	Reimburses you for expenses incurred and for revenues and profits lost as a result of unintended interruption of your business due to fire, major theft, or the illness of a key employee.
Bonds	Covers against law suits for financial loss incurred by others due to an act or default of an employee or to some contingency over which the principal may have no control.

Some carriers specialize in insuring food and beverage establishments. Their rates will vary according to the type of business, condition of the premises, degree of exposure to risks, and your risk management program.

5

PLANNING TO BE PROFITABLE

A common misconception among people who wish to go into the restaurant business for the first time is that they can't miss—their idea is so unique that it will be profitable from the start. These notions exude confidence and enthusiasm, which are fine qualities, but until an idea is tested in the marketplace, no one can be certain it will succeed. Yet plunging into the marketplace to find out if your idea will actually succeed is too risky. For that reason, it is imperative to conduct a feasibility study and prepare a business plan well before making any binding commitments.

THE FEASIBILITY STUDY

Simply put, the term *feasibility study* refers to doing research to determine if your idea is viable. It determines if the idea is wanted or needed by the people you envision as your clientele and if there are enough of them to sustain your restaurant profitably. It will answer questions such as the following:

- Is your concept truly unique?
- Is the economic climate in that location favorable for your idea?
- What competition will you encounter?
- What is the local labor market like? Skills? Wage levels? Availability?

The feasibility study minimizes your chances of entering an impractical venture.

WHY DO YOU NEED A BUSINESS PLAN?

Assuming that the feasibility study convinces you that your idea is viable, the next step is to prepare a business plan. A *business plan* gives you an advance opportunity to test your proposal on paper, to see if the numbers make sense and to assure investors, lenders, and yourself that you have not overlooked anything that might be critical to your chances of success. In essence, the business plan describes in detail how you intend to do what you are proposing to do.

It is a lengthy document that, if done well, compels you to confront all aspects of the business and to develop operational plans to capitalize on opportunities and cope with adversities.

In the course of its preparation, you challenge every assumption and defend every assertion that you make. You are forced to focus on what you wish to accomplish and how you intend to do it. Any weaknesses in your plans become evident when formulating the business plan.

Although the most common use of a business plan is to persuade potential investors or lenders to finance your project, its primary value should be to assure you, the entrepreneur—who has much to lose—that the enterprise is both feasible and potentially financially rewarding.

The business plan can also serve as a road map that can guide you through your start-up period, and it can be a reference point against which you can compare your actual performance.

Finally, a well-written business plan will convey to its readers the assurance that you can think clearly and have the ability to run a restaurant successfully.

ACCURACY IS IMPORTANT

Your business plan must be believable—be prepared to defend your statements. It is perfectly acceptable to present information in its best light, but inaccurate or incomplete information will be construed as undependable or deceptive by investors and lenders, very likely deterring them from participating in your project.

The main reason for being accurate and complete is that you will need the most reliable information available to make sound decisions. Inaccurate information will mislead you, perhaps causing decisions that lead to failure of the business.

ESTIMATING YOUR START-UP COSTS

As with any business investment, the cost of the project is a primary concern in everyone's mind, because the best of ideas are of little value if they cannot be funded. Knowing the cost, early on, can save a lot of wasted time and effort.

Information on costs can be obtained from a number of sources. On small jobs, certain information can be obtained for free from vendors, but on larger projects that involve time and research, you should expect to pay a consulting fee.

Equipment suppliers can provide you with working figures on dining room, kitchen, and bar equipment. Commercial Realtors can supply cost data and advice on suitable rental properties for your venture. Architects and contractors, interested in getting your business, can give you ballpark figures as you consider the feasibility of your project.

Distributors of food, liquor, beer, and wine products can assist you in estimating inventory costs. Because you may be one of their customers in the future, their best interest lies in helping you with your early planning. Wherever possible, cross-check information with more than one source.

If your business is a sole proprietorship or partnership, you may have limited capital to work with; consequently, the matter of estimating start-up costs will happen in stages, starting with ballpark figures. As your ideas become better defined, your estimates will become more dependable. At each stage of the process, you must answer the question: Can I afford it? If you believe you can, you will want to obtain final figures, perhaps hiring a consultant to develop a reliable estimate.

If you do not feel you can afford the project, as the ballpark figures show it, you must go back to square one and scale down your ideas to a level that you can afford—or simply abandon the project.

In the case of a corporation, the opportunity exists to raise additional funds through the sale of more stock. However, potential investors will scrutinize your business plan carefully and will want to be convinced of both the business's chances of success and the anticipated rate of return on investment.

BUSINESS PLAN FORMAT

Business plans may vary in format, but certain kinds of information are expected to appear in all business plans. An outline of a typical business plan for a restaurant is shown in Figure 5.1. Each section of the outline contains an example of the type of information that might appear in that section. A complete sample business plan for a restaurant appears in Appendix A at the back of this book.

HOW TO CONSTRUCT A BUSINESS PLAN

Cover Page

The cover page tells the reader with whom they are dealing. It should include:

- The legal name of your business and, if your restaurant will be doing business under another name (DBA, or "doing business as"), that name as well
- The date the business plan is issued
- The name and title of the principal person submitting the plan
- The address and telephone number of the business

If you are submitting copies of the plan to several people or firms, you may wish to number each copy. The number should appear on the cover page.

The Table of Contents

The table of contents tells what is contained in the plan and where it appears. Page numbers should be inserted after the plan is complete in every other respect.

FIGURE 5.1 *Using a business plan outline can ensure that nothing vital is left out.*

Outline of a Business Plan

Cover Page
Table of Contents
Statement of Purpose

Part One: The Business

- Description of the restaurant
- Background of the restaurant
- Company mission statement
- Unique concept
- Location
- Restaurant industry trends
- Other resources
- Management
- Objectives and financial expectations
- Product and service
- Pricing and profitability
- Product life cycle
- Market analysis
- Competition
- Customers
- Marketing strategy
- Personnel
- Risk
- Loan request and anticipated benefits
- Summary of Part One

Part Two: Financial Projections

- Start-up requirements
- Estimated annual sales
- List of furniture, fixtures, and equipment
- Leasehold improvements
- Sources and uses of funds
- Income statement for first year
- Projected income statement— month by month
- Cash-flow statement by month
- Daily break-even analysis
- Conclusion and summary of Part Two

Part Three: Supporting Documents

- All legal and professional documents and any other applicable documents that will strengthen the plan

Ideally, you will number the pages using chapter and page numbers, such as 1.1, 1.2, and 1.3. for Chapter 1; and 2.1, 2.2, and 2.3 for Chapter 2; and so on. This system allows you to add pages at the last minute without having to renumber the entire document.

For clarity and emphasis, always start new sections on a new page. Business plans will typically run 20 or more pages.

Statement of Purpose

The statement of purpose explains, in summary, what the rest of the report covers in detail. Essentially, it answers the who, what, when, where, and how much questions:

- Whom is the report about? Who is asking for the loan?
- What is your legal form of ownership: sole proprietorship, partnership, corporation, or limited liability corporation (LLC)?
- How much funding is sought?
- What will the funds be used for?
- What benefits will accrue to the restaurant from the use of the funds?
- How will the borrowed funds be repaid? If you are seeking outside funding, this information will be of great interest to a lender. If you are preparing the business plan for your own use, it should be of equal interest for you; you will want to know the restaurant's potential for achieving your profit objective.

Part One: The Business

In this section, you will describe the business, what it will do or sell, and how it will do it.

Description of the restaurant. Tell its name, intended starting date, the kind of menu and style of service it will offer, its days and hours of operation, the names of the investors, and their roles in the business.

Background of the restaurant. Explain how the idea began, describe your research findings from surveys and interviews, and indicate why the findings support your proposed business.

Company mission statement. Concisely state your overall goal for the restaurant, throughout its lifetime, as you now see it.

Unique concept. Explain the uniqueness of your restaurant. Describe it in detail, telling how it will fit into the marketplace. Focus on the desirability of your concept. Photographs and illustrations are useful in highlighting key items of interest. Lengthy exhibits should be placed in the appendix at the back of the document and referenced in the body of the text.

Location. Enumerate the reasons why you have chosen the proposed site and describe its salient features. This information can be obtained from your property analysis checklist.

Restaurant industry trends. Cite predictions by restaurant industry analysts for the next year or two. Reference the sources from which information was obtained, such as the National Restaurant Association; your state hospitality association; the National Licensed Beverage Association; the Bureau of Alcohol, Tobacco, and Firearms; trade journals; census data; etc.

Other resources. Financial: List your food and equipment suppliers and state their credit terms. Professional: List your lawyer, accountant, banker, insurance agent, and consultants.

Management. List your management team. Describe their personal histories, stating their training and experience in the restaurant field as well as anything else about them that will enhance the business's chances for success. Point out how they are suited to the duties and responsibilities they will be assuming. Their proposed salaries should be stipulated.

Objectives and financial expectations. Indicate your short- and long-term goals for sales, customer acceptance, growth, and expansion. Tell where you want the business to go—recount what you wish to achieve, stressing quality, profits, return on investment, and public service. Your objectives should be feasible, understandable, and realistic in terms of the resources you will have to work with.

Describe the benefits that investors and lenders may expect to realize when the restaurant's short- and long-term objectives are met. The point here is to convince potential investors or lenders that all aspects of the project have been carefully considered and that the idea makes sense. But be accurate and thorough, because the business plan is first and foremost for your edification.

Product and service. Tell what will differentiate your product and service from that of your competitors—explain its benefits. Here you inform the reader about how the restaurant will fill a market niche and how the menu and the style of service you offer are demanded by the target market. Stress the competitive advantages your restaurant will have. If your concept or product is based upon any proprietary secrets, such as recipes, you will want to protect them by asking prospective investors and lending institutions to sign a nondisclosure agreement.

Pricing and profitability. Describe your pricing strategy and its profit-generating potential. Explain how you set prices and their relationship to costs. Comment on the competitiveness of your prices. Relate the profit potential to the payback period for investors and lenders. Copies of menus, with prices, should be included in the appendix.

Product life cycle. Lay out the expected life cycle for your concept or product in the targeted marketing area. If your concept is one that has a high front-end acceptance, such as a trendy theme restaurant or a high-energy club, but has a limited life expectancy, point out the quick payback and lofty earnings potential.

Market analysis. This section describes your market as it currently exists. Define it clearly, and include charts where applicable. Your explanation must leave no doubt in the investors' or lenders' minds that the proposed business is appropriate for the market.

Discuss any economic conditions or market changes that may be taking place. Tell how they will benefit the business. Indicate the size of the marketing area and its potential for future growth. Detail your strengths and emphasize your marketing plans as much as your product. Point out any unexploited opportunities you may recognize.

Be realistic and identify any weaknesses that you or the business may have and describe how you plan to eliminate or improve upon those weaknesses. You want to deal in advance with objections that an investor or lender might bring up.

Competition. Identify your five or six nearest competitors. Elucidate the process by which you obtained information about your competitors to give your findings credibility. Tell what they offer and how they advertise (frequency, type of media, and size of advertisements). Show how their strategy compares with what you plan to offer. Indicate their strengths and weaknesses and explain how your marketing strategy is designed to meet and overcome the competition.

Customers. Give the demographics of your targeted clientele. Tell who your customers are, where they live, how educated they are, what income bracket they tend to be in, how they spend their money, what research shows their wants and needs to be, their motivation to patronize your establishment, what benefits they will receive from your restaurant, and why you expect they will be attracted to it.

Marketing strategy. This part of your business plan will guide you as you respond to business conditions and opportunities. It can make the difference between mediocrity, or even failure, and the achievement of your goals. It should tell how you intend to position your restaurant (how your customers will perceive you) and how, by contrast, you can reposition your competitors (make your customers think of them). Likewise, it should detail the segment of the market you plan to reach and the share of the market you expect to capture.

Describe the selling and advertising tactics you will use to accomplish your goals. List your outside resources, advertising and public relations agencies, the media you will use, and any sales promotional campaigns you intend to utilize. Tell who will be responsible for these areas.

Personnel. Describe your hours and days of business and your style of service. These factors will determine how many of each type of employee you will need and the skills required. An organizational chart accompanied by a proposed personnel schedule should be included here, along with estimated payroll costs.

Risk. Show in a convincing manner that you understand the risks of the restaurant business and have plans for managing them. These might include insurance programs, cost controls, and specialized training for employees.

Loan request and anticipated benefits. This section is used when seeking external funding. It should state the sum being applied for, contain an itemized list of the intended uses of the funds, and declare the benefits that will be realized from them. The display of sources and uses of funds will be restated in "financial projections" in Part Two.

Summary of Part One. The summary consists of a few paragraphs that encapsulate the contents of Part One. They should tell who you are, what you want to do, how you plan to do it, when and where, what it will cost, why it is feasible, what the benefits are, and (where applicable) how much you want to borrow.

Part Two: Financial Projections

The financial statements that compose Part Two of the business plan are illustrated in detail in Appendix A.

The supporting documents section may include market survey data, drawings, and layouts. It should include all legal and professional documents that support the information contained in Parts One and Two as well as credit reports, letters of recommendation, letters of intent, copies of leases, contracts, personal resumes of all principals and their personal balance sheets, and any other documents that will strengthen the plan.

Action Guidelines

☐ Firm up the concept of your proposed restaurant and be able to describe it clearly.

☐ Talk to business brokers and real estate agents to determine economic conditions in the market areas in which you are interested.

☐ Conduct a feasibility study for your proposed business. Investigate your target market. Know the wants and needs of your prospective clientele.

☐ Evaluate the opportunities and the competition.

☐ Use the outline of a business plan in this chapter and the sample business plan in Appendix A as a guide for writing your own business plan.

☐ Determine your financial needs.

☐ Present the business plan to prospective investors or institutional lenders, if desired, or use it for your own purposes as a management tool.

6

DEVELOPING MENUS THAT SELL

In today's climate of changing fads, fluctuating prices, occasional product shortages, and shifting lifestyles, menus must be flexible while still meeting diners' expectations. Think of them as a marketing tool that attracts people to your restaurant and has great potential to generate word of mouth advertising. Your menu should be tuned to emerging trends as well as current favorites and avoid being perceived as a "me too" menu. For example, studies show that health consciousness is a growing influence on people's dietary decision making. Restaurants can capitalize on this while serving the public good by promoting healthful foods that are also outstanding cuisine.

Menus should be exciting in both form and content but, above all, be realistic in terms of your production capabilities. The menu influences everything in a restaurant. For that reason, it must be planned with your staff's production skills, your equipment, inventory, style of service, decor, and image in mind.

WHO SHOULD PLAN THE MENU?

The planning of menus should be a cooperative effort between the chef and the manager. The chef, who knows the capabilities of the kitchen staff and the equipment as well as the availability of food products and their cost, is the principal creator of menus. However, the chef works within the parameters set by the manager, who is largely concerned with sales objectives, profitability, and image of the restaurant. Together, they cover all of the main concerns of a restaurant.

If a restaurant has a banquet department or a bar, it is wise to consult with the heads of those operations to determine any special needs of their clientele. Feedback from customer comment cards, if used, should also be factored in.

TYPES OF MENUS

Restaurants use a variety of menus—each appeals to a specific segment of the market. Once you know the wants and needs of your target market, you are ready to plan your menu. Following are the most common ones:

À la carte menu. Foods are listed separately, and each item is individually priced.

Table d'hôte menu. A complete meal is offered for one, all-inclusive price.

Du jour menu. Literally "the menu of the day," this is sometimes used for daily specials in conjunction with one of the other forms.

Limited menu. This menu offers a limited number of entrees that do not change often.

Function menu. This menu offers a group of specially designed complete meals or buffets from which function planners may choose for banquets.

VARIETY IS THE SPICE OF LIFE—AND YOUR MENU

A menu should have balance, variety, and an attractive composition. For example, an entree consisting of chicken à la king, mashed potatoes with light gravy, and cauliflower would be unappealing—it would have a pasty texture and monotonous colors while lacking distinctive tastes. The expression that, "People eat with their eyes," has much truth. All menu items should both appear and taste tantalizing to guests, regardless of their price. Following are some ways that a menu may be varied:

- *Type of protein.* Beef, lamb, veal, pork, poultry, fish and tofu
- *Method of preparation.* Broiled, boiled, baked, fried, barbequed, and poached
- *Colors of the components on the plate.* Red, yellow, brown, white, and green
- *Textures of the items.* Crisp, tender, soft, and al dente
- *Shapes.* Flat, mounded, round, shredded, and random
- *Serving sizes.* All foods should not be the same portion size.
- *Temperature.* Some items may be hot, while others, such as salad plates, are cold.
- *Cost.* Offer a price range that appeals to your target market.

Fusion Cookery Continues to Grow

As the American population continues to grow more diverse, new market segments are presenting fresh opportunities for restaurants. The combining of two or more dissimilar types of cookery, known as *fusion cookery*, reflects the American tendency to experiment and find new ways that ingredients may be used, prepared, and served. Influenced by the background or heritage of chefs, the culinary styles of other countries are merged with American-style cookery in distinctive ways that take advantage of our high-quality meat, poultry, fish, fruits, and vegetables. The result, fusion cuisine: new and exciting flavors, textures, and color combinations.

LIMITATIONS ON YOUR MENU

Does your menu match your customers' expectations, or will they come to your restaurant expecting one thing and find another? Here's where your market research pays off.

Challenge each item as you consider it for inclusion in your menu. Is it available all year or just seasonally? Is it worth promoting for only a short period of time? Some items are imported from other countries in the off-season, but their prices are considerably higher due to being flown in. How would such price increases impact your menu?

Consider your staff. Do your employees have the necessary skills to produce the item in a high-quality manner? Does the item require such intricate production skills that it would disrupt the flow of kitchen work whenever one was ordered?

Equipment must also be taken into account. You may have designed a great menu, but can you deliver it? Will the new item put additional pressure on equipment that may already be overused? Is it worth buying another piece of equipment just to produce this item for your menu, and if so, can it be installed where you want it?

This type of questioning must also be applied to your dining room staff and equipment. Suppose a restaurant wished to offer crêpes suzette, prepared at tableside. This would require a gueridon cart, chafing dishes, skilled waitstaff capable of preparing the flamed delicacy safely, and adequate aisle space to maneuver the cart throughout the dining room. Unless all of these conditions could be met, it would be unwise to include that item in the menu.

FORMAT IS IMPORTANT

Although no rigid rules exist, common sense dictates that menus should be easy for guests to handle while seated at a table and should be easy to read. The progression of items in the menu layout should be generally the same as that in which a guest would order them. For example, a dinner menu would list appetizers, soups, and salads first, followed by entrees and finally desserts. Menus should be neither cluttered nor so long as to make selection difficult for the guest.

In the case of ethnic restaurants, unless it is certain that most customers will understand the language of the restaurant, it is wise to add English descriptions beneath foreign names. English "subtitles" speed up ordering and make guests feel more comfortable.

Lighter foods or specialty items to which you may want to call attention may be listed separately. It is generally considered better to intersperse menu items, rather than list them in the precise order of their price. Mixing the items causes guests to focus less on the price and more on the qualities of an item.

Some restaurants will print everything but the prices on their menus, so that the menus will not have to be discarded whenever prices change. However, the practice of filling in prices with a pen is more common in lower-priced establishments and those whose prices change frequently. Unless the prices are written neatly in good handwriting, the menus tend to look messy.

Clip-ons featuring a new or special item may be attached to printed menus, and if used tastefully, they are not objectionable. However, they should be located carefully, so that they will not completely hide items on the menu.

Menus are made of a wide variety of materials. There is no end to the possibilities of what you can use, if you are creative. Some menus can be found on novelty materials such as wooden boards, leather aprons, miniature slates, and even painted on walls and objects such as frying pans. The only caveat here is that the physical menu should be practical and appropriate to your decor, theme, and style of service.

The most common menu materials are heavy paper or card stock, mainly because they are relatively inexpensive and easy to replace. Both of these materials should be coated to allow for cleaning when soiled or wear protective covers. Menus should be inspected daily to remove any that are messy or dog-eared from service. Attractive menu holders can be purchased in leather or plastic and can be filled with changeable inserts. Computers and laser printers have made a wide variety of type faces and sizes available. Print shop-quality menus can now be produced in-house quickly and inexpensively, and best of all, they can be changed as often as desired with a minimum of effort.

The typeface chosen for a menu is important, because it conveys messages about a restaurant, such as formal elegance or casual simplicity— whatever is desired. The main thing to consider when selecting a typeface is readability. Some fonts, such as Old English, are attractive but difficult to read and best used sparingly. If your restaurant caters to significant numbers of senior citizens, you might consider using larger type.

"Truth in menus" must always be kept in mind when designing your menu. Today, people are much more concerned about what they eat than ever, and they are very sensitive to being misled by menus. You must be careful about how you use words like *fresh, natural, homemade,* and *light.* Disgruntled guests may not complain to you, but they will tell others and will probably not return to your restaurant.

An interesting history of a restaurant, when printed on a menu, can provide entertaining reading for guests while they are waiting for service. If it is sufficiently interesting, it may also generate discussion and valuable word-of-mouth advertising among their friends.

CHILDREN'S MENUS SELL ADULT DINNERS

The main reason for having children's menus is to attract adults. Parents want to enjoy themselves when they go to a restaurant, and this can only happen when their children are happy.

Children's menus offer nothing more than adult foods served in smaller portions with a less formal presentation. For example, parents like to eat steak, but children often prefer burgers (ground steak). Children's menu items often have a higher food cost percentage than adult menu items, because they are considered a promotional item.

With a little creativity, children's menus can be used to entertain them until their food arrives. The reverse side of a disposable children's menu can be a connect-the-dots puzzle, a simple quiz, or a coloring picture. Many things can be done to make dining with children a pleasant experience for parents. For example, some restaurants offer them a chance to reach into a treasure chest from which they can pull out an inexpensive novelty gift, if they clean their plates.

Many establishments specify that their children's menu applies only to youngsters up to age 12, when accompanied by a parent ordering from the regular menu. This is done to deter adults who want a small portion from ordering from the children's menu. However, if a restaurant has a significant number of older customers who request smaller portions, it should consider adding a special light meal section to its regular menu.

MICRONICHES ADD UP TO GOOD BUSINESS

Health studies show that a growing number of people have allergies or chemical sensitivities and suffer various reactions when they eat certain foods or inhale certain odors that would not bother other people.

Some restaurants are reaching out to these people in various ways, such as by listing ingredients on menus, pointing out items such as peanuts and shellfish that are known to affect some people, and educating allergic and chemically sensitive people to come early, when it is not as busy and chefs can accommodate special requests. Some restaurants are also using odor-free or odorless carpet and floor cleaners and toilet-sanitizing agents.

When restaurants act proactively, they not only position themselves as socially conscious businesses in the eyes of the community, but they also win the patronage of the affected people and those who accompany them.

STANDARDS ARE NECESSARY

In the food and beverage business, people tend to be less forgiving of poor quality or service than in many other businesses. Customers want the assurance that every time they return to a restaurant and order their favorite dish, it will look the same and taste the same as it did the last time they ordered it. That assurance can only be achieved by having standards—standard recipes, standard portion sizes, and standard methods of preparation.

Few things will irritate a customer more than noticing that someone else with the same entree has received a larger portion or a better-looking product than they did. Cooks may vary their cooking methods and portion sizes according to their mood. Having standard preparation methods and portion sizes for all items these unwanted variances.

MENU PRICING—A MARKETING TOOL

A restaurant's prices influence the type of clientele it attracts. People of lower incomes usually patronize restaurants with economical prices, while people with higher incomes tend to patronize fancier restaurants. However, in economically depressed times, many people tend to move a step down on the pricing ladder. Higher prices are usually associated with superior service, elegant cuisine, and a special location or entertainment.

Management should test its prices frequently to ensure that they are appropriate to the style of service and the quality and quantity of the food served and are in-line with those of comparable competitive establishments. At any level of pricing, customers must perceive that they are receiving commensurate value. Few second chances are given in the food and beverage business when high prices are charged.

PRICING IN GENERAL

The total revenue from food and alcoholic beverages should be adequate to cover all the costs and expenses of the restaurant and produce a profit. Therefore, food and drink prices must be determined in relation to the costs, expenses, and profit objective of the restaurant.

It is critical to your success that your menu prices be appropriate for your type of operation. If they are set too high, they may drive away customers; if set too low, you may incur losses. This is an area where you should seek the assistance of an accountant with experience in the restaurant industry

METHODS OF PRICING A MENU

There are numerous ways to price menu items. Each has merit under certain circumstances, but care should be taken to select the one that is most appropriate for your restaurant.

Most importantly, a realistic food cost percentage must be used. Industry statistics, available from the National Restaurant Association, for similar operations can be helpful when planning, but your food cost percentage should be based on actual costs and expenses, as determined through research with vendors and providers in your specific locale. Otherwise, you may be deluding yourself. Four common ways to set menu prices are described below.

Method 1: Total Costs Plus Desired Profit

This method takes into account all of the costs of your restaurant as shown in your estimated income statement. It also considers the percentage of profit you desire. The desired profit should be realistic in terms of industry norms for comparable restaurants.

For example, if your estimated income statement revealed the following cost and profit percentages, and the raw food cost of the item you are pricing is $3.50, you can calculate its selling price by using the formula shown in Figure 6.1.

FIGURE 6.1 *A method for calculating selling prices*

Estimated Income Statement Data:
　　All costs other than food cost   56.7% of sales
　　Desired profit (% of total sales)   10.00% of sales

Formula:
Food Cost % + All other Cost % + Desired Profit % =
Selling Price (100%)

Step 1: Calculate what your food cost percentage (x) should be.
　　　$x + 56.7\% + 10\% =$ Selling Price (100%)
　　　$x + 66.7\%$　　　 $=$ Selling Price (100%)
　　　x　　　　　　 $= 33.3\%$ (100% − 66.7% = 33.3%)
　　　33.3% is your food cost percentage.

Step 2: Calculate the selling price of the item.

$$\frac{\$3.50}{0.333} = \$10.51$$

Round on menu to **$10.50 selling price.**

Method 2: Percentage Markup on Cost

Once a meaningful food cost percentage has been developed as described in Method 1, it may continue to be used on other items until significant changes occur in the restaurant's other costs.

To illustrate, assume that another entree to be added to your menu has a raw food cost of $4.05. You could calculate its selling price simply by dividing the raw food cost of that new item by the food cost percentage already established in Method #1.

$$\frac{\text{cost of ingredients}}{\text{food cost percentage}} = \frac{\$4.05}{0.333} = \$12.16$$

Round on menu to **$12.25 selling price**.

Unfortunately, some restaurants set their prices with an arbitrary food cost percentage. That can be risky, because the percentage has not been developed in relation to their other costs (as in Method #1) and can produce selling prices that are too high or too low.

Now, suppose it was arbitrarily decided to use a food cost percentage of 39.0 percent instead of the 33.3 percent developed by Method #1. In that case, a selling price of only $10.39 would have resulted, instead of $12.16. The new entree would therefore be underpriced by $1.75.

$$\frac{\text{cost of ingredients}}{\text{food cost percentage}} = \frac{\$4.05}{0.39} = \$10.38$$

Round on menu to **$10.50 selling price**.

The percentage method is easy to work with, but it is only reliable if verified periodically by an analysis of the actual costs of an operation, rather than used arbitrarily.

Method 3: Charging What the Market Will Bear

This method, often referred to as *skimming the market*, works best when you are the first one with a new concept that is in strong demand and you do not have any competition.

Essentially, this method involves testing the market for the highest price that people are willing to pay and "skimming the cream" until competitors come along and force you to lower your prices. For that reason, this is considered a short-term method of pricing.

It is essential when using this method to be aware of your *pricing points*. Those are limits in consumers' minds—prices above which they do not perceive your products or services to be worth what you are charging.

Method 4: Competition-Based Pricing

This refers to charging the same prices as your competitors. This can be chancy because they may be more efficient than you, or they may have greater purchasing power and buy at better prices. Consequently, you may not be able to produce a profit if you duplicate their prices. It is not a practice to be followed blindly but, rather, one that should be factored into your decision-making process when using the other methods.

OLD-FASHIONED SPECIALS STILL DRAW PEOPLE

Years ago, most restaurants offered what was known as the "blue plate special." Actually, very few restaurants used blue plates, but the specials were popular because they were recognized as a good meal that usually sold at a lower price. Today, the term *specials* most often refers to items that are not printed on the menu and, in contrast to the blue plate specials, are not usually lower priced.

Some restaurants, however, still maintain the old concept and have built a base of loyal customers by offering specials of the day that are both good and favorably priced. An example of how a complete luncheon special could be priced is shown in Figure 6.2.

WILL YOUR RESTAURANT SERVE ALCOHOLIC BEVERAGES?

If you are going to serve alcoholic beverages, you will need to create wine lists or beverage menus. Much of what has been said about food menus applies to beverage menus as well: they must be attractive, easy to read, have variety, meet the expectations of the target market, and be priced properly.

How to Design a Wine List

Wines sell much better when they are promoted, and your wine list is your best sales promotion tool. A good wine list should have enough

FIGURE 6.2 *Illustrates how a complete luncheon special may be packaged and favorably priced to build sales volume.*

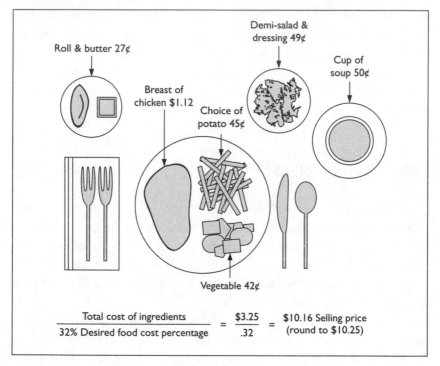

$$\frac{\text{Total cost of ingredients}}{\text{32\% Desired food cost percentage}} = \frac{\$3.25}{.32} = \begin{array}{l}\$10.16 \text{ Selling price}\\ (\text{round to } \$10.25)\end{array}$$

choices to be interesting and should complement your food menu, but it should not be so long as to be confusing.

The wines you carry should be consistent with your style of service and price structure. Small, modestly priced restaurants with a simple style of service may do well with lower-priced wines and a red and a white house wine, but an upscale restaurant will be expected to carry a reasonably extensive list of premium wines. It is good to search out new wines that your customers might enjoy, but be careful not to make your dining room a testing ground for new products.

Be sure to carry the items that are popular with your clientele. Check your wine inventory turnover periodically to weed out the slow movers—allowing, of course, for rarer wines that move slowly because of their high price but are maintained in stock for their prestige value.

When writing a wine list, choose descriptive words that are easy to understand. Avoid vague expressions like, "It has excellent nose and an extravagant taste that challenges the palate." Also, shun snobbish words that may send inappropriate messages to inexperienced wine drinkers. Try to use positive words that enhance the appeal of your wines and assist your customers in matching them with food items. Operate on the premise that all your wines are good, but some are better with certain foods. If a wine is not good, you should not carry it.

A logical order for listing wines is as follows:

1. Before-dinner wines
2. Red dinner wines
3. White dinner wines
4. Sparkling wines
5. After-dinner or dessert wines

Wine lists should be printed on substantial stock, and your restaurant name should appear prominently on the cover page. As with food menus, some items can be promoted by highlighting them with a different ink color or typeface or by boxing them to draw attention.

PRICING ALCOHOLIC BEVERAGES IN GENERAL

As with food menu prices, the selling prices of alcoholic beverages must be determined in a manner that relates to the total cost and profit structure of the restaurant. However, the methods by which the prices of wines, beer, and mixed drinks are calculated vary because of the differences in the products themselves. And unlike food products, the selling price of alcoholic beverages, once calculated, may be further adjusted to compensate for the high costs of liquor liability insurance, entertainment, free snacks, or other expenses associated with beverage alcohol.

Pricing Wines

Wines are most often bought by the bottle and are considered add-on sales. They are usually consumed during a meal and compete mainly with water, which is free. For these reasons, it is considered best to use a flexible markup system and sell a lot of wine than to price wines with the high markups of liquors, for example, and sell much less.

Under the flexible markup system, higher-cost wines are priced for resale with a smaller percentage of markup than lower-cost wines. This makes finer wines more affordable and increases their sales.

	Wine A	Wine B
Your cost per bottle	$12.50	$32.00
Percent markup	100%	50%
Price to customer	$25.00	$48.00
Gross profit per bottle	$12.50	$16.00

In the above example, the restaurant will earn an additional $3.50 of gross profit when it sells a bottle of Wine B ($16.00 – $12.50 = $3.50). Even though a smaller percentage of markup was used for pricing Wine B, it yielded a larger dollar amount of gross profit. Besides, customers will perceive Wine B as being a relatively good value and will buy more of it.

Pricing Beer

Three main factors determine the selling price of draught (pronounced *draft*) beer: the cost of the beer, the size of the glass used, and the size of the head poured. In general, the selling price of draught beer is calculated as shown in the following example.

Half-barrel keg costs	$75.00
Keg contains	1,920 ounces
Cost per ounce is $75.00 ÷ 1,920 =	$0.039
Cost per 14-ounce goblet (which actually holds about 12.2 ounces of beer, assuming a 1-inch head is poured) is $0.039 × 12.2 =	$0.48
Marked up 5 times to accommodate a 20% pouring cost percentage: $0.48 × 5 =	$2.40
R ound to get selling price	**$2.50**

Following is an illustration of how to calculate the profit potential of a keg of beer, assuming a one-inch head of foam is poured per glass.

14 oz. goblet (as described above)	12.2 oz.
Number of glasses in a keg (half-barrel)	157
Selling price per glass	$2.50
Total sales value of a half-barrel keg is 157 × $2.50 =	$392.50
Less: Cost of half-barrel keg	($75.00)
Profit on a half-barrel keg	**$317.50**

In the above example, the restaurant is selling draught beer at a 20 percent pouring cost, yet its price is very competitive. The four keys to selling a lot of beer are:

1. Carry the brands your customers want.
2. Keep your beer stored at the proper temperature (38° to 42° F) and gauge pressure (12–14 psi).
3. Keep your dispensing system meticulously clean.
4. Price beer competitively.

Some brewpub restaurants make their own beer. The recent popularity of premium microbeers illustrates that many discriminating beer drinkers are willing to pay substantially more for a bottle of their favorite premium beer, provided they can take their time drinking it in a pleasant atmosphere.

Most full-service restaurants now carry at least two premium beers. The secret to selling a lot of premium beers is to know the brands your customers want and carry them. Although microbeers cost more at wholesale, they command much higher prices at retail and can be very profitable.

Pricing Mixed Drinks

There are a number of approaches to pricing mixed drinks. Some are simple and others are more complex, but all are acceptable as long as they cover all costs and yield the desired profit. Prior to the advent of point-of-sale systems, restaurant owners were concerned that bartenders and servers would not be able to remember a great many prices and felt that mistakes would more than offset the benefits of pricing every drink individually. Consequently, a tiered pricing system was frequently used. Under the tiered system, all drinks that were made with one liquor would have one average price, all two-liquor drinks would have another average price, and so on for three-liquor drinks.

Today, POS systems can be programmed to handle as many drink prices as a restaurant needs, and they are easy for bartenders to use. There is little to remember—the bartender simply presses the touch screen button bearing the name of the drink, and the computer finds the price of the drink in its memory. The POS system tells the bartender how much change to give the customer, records the amount of liquor used, and keeps count of the number of each type of drink served—hour by hour if you wish.

Figure 6.3 shows one method for pricing drinks.

FIGURE 6.3 *Determining the selling price of mixed drinks*

Assume:
- A 750 milliliter (25.4 ounce) bottle of whiskey costs $13.50.
- Drink prices are based on a 20 percent pouring cost (20 percent of the price of a drink goes to pay for its ingredients).
- Your standard pour is 1.5 ounces (a pour is the amount of alcohol you put into a standard drink).
- You allow 1.4 ounces out of a 750 milliliter bottle for spillage.
- Therefore, 25.4 oz. − 1.4 oz. = 24 salable ounces, or 16 drinks made with 1.5 oz. of whiskey each.

Step 1:
cost of bottle ÷ pouring cost % = sales yield
$13.50   ÷ 0.20   = $67.50 (the sales yield of the bottle)

Step 2:
sales yield   ÷ # of pours   = selling price
$67.50   ÷ 16   = $4.22 (unadjusted selling price)

Step 3:
- Add a "kicker" of $0.25 to $0.50 to cover the cost of garnishes and mixers, etc.
- The selling price may be further adjusted to defray entertainment costs, an unusually high rent for a premium location, or a high liquor liability insurance cost.

Using the above method, the example drink might sell for $4.50 to $6.75 or more, depending on adjustments. The same pricing system could be used for larger drinks and drinks that require multiple liquors by factoring in the cost of the additional liquors to arrive at a higher drink price.

Action Guidelines

☐ Research your target market to determine their wants and needs.
☐ Visit other restaurants with a similar concept to examine their menus and style of service.
☐ Analyze the pros and cons of the various types of menus.
☐ Write a menu for your restaurant. If applicable write a wine list.
☐ Establish standard portions sizes for all items on your menu.
☐ Evaluate your menu for variety in the following areas and make adjustments as necessary:
  • Type of meat or other protein used
  • Methods of cookery
  • Colors of foods on the plate
  • Textures of the foods
  • Tastes of the foods
☐ Develop food and beverage prices for your menus.

C h a p t e r

7

THE FRONT OF THE HOUSE

"The taste of the roast is often determined by the handshake of the host."

Benjamin Franklin

Within minutes of their arrival, customers' perceptions of a restaurant are influenced by the manner in which they are greeted, the ambiance of the dining room, and the promptness with which they are looked after.

The term *front of the house* refers to all of the service areas in a restaurant; it extends from the front entrance to the kitchen door and includes the bar and lounge. It is the customer contact point—the place where customers are won or lost. Consequently, all activities in the front of the house should focus exclusively on satisfying customers.

AMBIANCE AND DECOR

Everything a customer sees, feels, smells, or hears in your establishment is a part of its ambiance and decor. The instant customers pull on your front door handle, they are getting a message. A massive front door with heavy hardware conveys one image, while a small, lightweight door with economical hardware conveys a totally different image.

So it is with everything in your establishment—colors, sizes, shapes, weights, and textures are all part of your decor and must be coordinated to produce the desired image.

YOUR MESSAGE MUST BE CLEAR

Customers should never be in doubt as to what your image message is. The items listed below should be coordinated to project the same message:

- Name of the business
- Building design
- Signs (colors, size, type of print)
- Style of tables and chairs
- Chinaware and flatware
- Tablecloths and napkins
- Carpeting or flooring

FIGURE 7.1 *A spectacular view of the dining room of Acorn's Restaurant at the New England Center, Durham, New Hampshire. (Photo courtesy of UNH Photo Services)*

- Wall hangings, pictures, and drapes
- Light fixtures
- Menus (the physical menu)
- Floor plan (table spacing)
- Uniforms
- Plants or other decorator objects

Aim to meet your patrons' expectations—define your target market before designing and decorating your restaurant. The wants and needs of your desired clientele should dictate the type and style of decor. With your customers clearly in mind, an appropriate theme should be developed and maintained throughout the front of the house.

ORGANIZATION AND TRAINING

Good service doesn't just happen; it must be planned. To operate smoothly, the front of the house must be properly staffed with well-trained waitstaff. Factors that affect the staffing of a dining room are the style of service, the menu, hours of service, and the size of the restaurant. Figure 7.2 depicts a typical dining room staff for a midsized, white

FIGURE 7.2 *A typical organizational chart for a dining room staff in a full-service restaurant.*

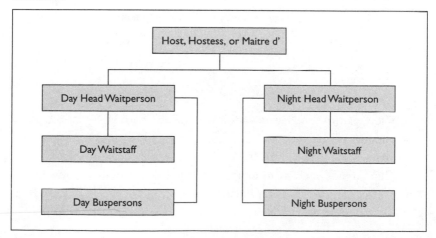

tablecloth restaurant that serves lunch and dinner. Upscale restaurants, depending on their size, may have additional ranks, such as captains and runners.

Normally, the host is in charge of the dining room. The host greets guests as they arrive, takes their name, calls them when their table is ready, escorts them to their table, issues menus to them, keeps an eye on their table to ensure that everything is going well, and thanks them on their way out. The host assigns a group of tables (called a wait station) to each waitperson and assigns parties of guests to the various stations throughout the shift. The wait station should include a variety of table sizes so that waitstaff, who depend on tip income, may all be assigned a relatively equal number of parties during a shift. The pace of a dining room is set by the speed with which guests are seated by the host.

ALLOCATING SPACE

Every style of service has its particular space requirements. Luxury dining implies large, comfortable seating; more space per place setting; and wider aisles than would be needed for lesser forms of service. The following space allocations are often referred to as a starting point when planning dining rooms:

Type of Dining	Square Feet per Person
Luxury dining	18 square feet
Regular table service	15 square feet
Cafeteria service	12 square feet
Banquet service	10 square feet

When planning a layout, additional space should be added for a lobby, coatroom, bus stations, restrooms, and a lounge, where applicable. Salad bars, storage space for infant seating, and special decorator items in dining rooms, such as fountains and hearths, will also require additional space. Figure 7.3 is an illustrative example of a preliminary floor plan.

FIGURE 7.3 *An example of a restaurant layout with a variety of seating accommodations*

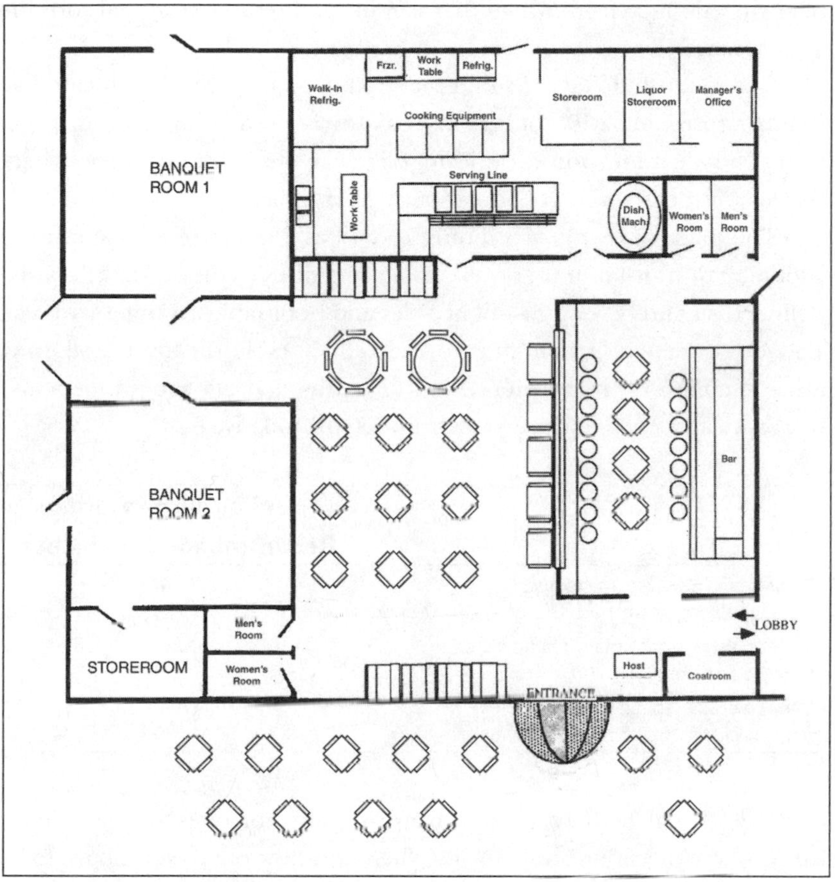

Another consideration is the cost of square footage. In high-rent situations, tighter seating and a more judicious approach to space allocation may be needed than where space is plentiful and more affordable.

LAYING OUT AN EFFICIENT FLOOR PLAN

Your layout should appear friendly and inviting. It should excite your guests when they arrive and make them want to stay. To ensure that guests get a pleasing view upon entering a restaurant, allow some free space near the entrance from which they can orient themselves and absorb the atmosphere.

If a restaurant has a lounge, it should be conveniently located so that bar customers will not have to walk through the dining room to get to it. The ideal location for a lounge is near the front entrance, where the host can easily reach people waiting for tables.

The physical layout of a dining room has a direct relationship to its profitability. Waitstaff must be able to move quickly as they take orders and deliver food and beverages—tight aisles and poor table arrangements can slow down service, irritate guests, and reduce table turnover. Following are the minimum recommended aisle widths that allow customers and servers to approach and leave their tables with relative ease.

Type of Aisle	Minimum Width Recommended (in inches)
Main traffic aisle (from host's stand through dining room)	54
Access aisles (from main traffic aisle to wait stations)	36
Service aisles (space around tables, from back of one chair to another)	18–24

If you plan to have a salad bar, a number of questions should be asked when allocating space for it. When and how often will it have to be restocked? From where will the supplies come? Will guest service be affected at those times? Will it impede the flow of traffic? The answers to these questions will influence the location of the aisles and the salad bar.

Shown below is a list of front-of-the-house equipment items common to most full-service restaurants.

Typical Front-of-the-House Equipment

Tables	Chairs	Booths
Service stands	Bus carts	High chairs
POS cash register	Host's stand	Coat racks
Lobby telephone	Restroom fixtures	Banquettes
Lobby seats	Servers' prep stations	

Guidelines for Restaurant Layouts

Following are some useful guidelines for laying out your establishment:

- Avoid congestion around doorways and traffic lanes.
- Divide large spaces into smaller, more intimate areas through the use of partial walls, planters, and decorator panels.
- Use contrasting colors or materials to give smaller areas an atmosphere of their own.
- Provide adequate aisles for waitstaff to deliver food and beverages.
- Vary your table sizes and arrangements, so that you can handle parties of various sizes.
- Folding doors may be used to create private rooms or to close off empty areas.
- Plan food and beverage pickup stations so that they minimally distract guests.
- Where possible, integrate POS systems and handheld digital devices with peripheral equipment in all locations to facilitate communications among the various departments.
- Fire exits and safety equipment should be readily visible.
- Provide adequate restroom facilities, including infant-changing stations where appropriate.
- Restroom signs should be visible from most points in the restaurant.
- In colder climates, ample facilities for coat hanging should be provided.
- Choose easily cleanable materials for floors, walls, and furniture.

HOW TO SELECT TABLE SIZES

It is important to have adequate table sizes that match the needs of your clientele. If a party of two must be seated at a table for four because there are too few small tables, the extra two seats are wasted. Similarly, if a party of five or six people has to wait an unusually long time for seating because a restaurant lacks large tables, they will be annoyed. To avoid these problems, it is essential to have an appropriate variety of table sizes to meet the needs of your clientele. Figure 7.4 illustrates a method for calculating your table needs. This example assumes that the restaurant

FIGURE 7.4 *In this example, 24 tables for two, 20 tables for four, and 6 tables for six would best accommodate the expected clientele. Additional flexibility can be achieved by substituting one or two tables for four with expandable fours, which have leaves that are stored underneath and can be folded out to become a table for six people.*

Calculating Table Needs					
Type of Table	Percent of Total Clientele	Total Seating Capacity	No. of Seats Needed	No. of Seats at Table	No. of Tables
Tables for 2	30% ×	160 =	48 ÷	2 =	24
Tables for 4	50% ×	160 =	80 ÷	4 =	20
Tables for 6	20% ×	160 =	32 ÷	6 =	6

will seat 160 people and the makeup of the clientele is: parties of one or two people, 30 percent; three or four people, 50 percent; and five or six people, 20 percent.

DESIGNING A DINING ROOM SERVICE SYSTEM

The easiest way to design a service system is to put yourself in your customer's shoes and walk through the process of entering a restaurant, being greeted and seated, and having your order taken and served. Then put yourself in an employee's shoes and walk through the process of greeting the customer, taking their order, turning it in to the kitchen, then picking it up and delivering it to the customer. In your mind's eye, you will envision every step of the service system from order taking to cashiering.

Answering the following questions will assist in the process of planning your service system:

- How will guests arrive? As pairs, singles, or in larger groups?
- What types of seating will you need?
- Will guests arrive by car? If so, do you have adequate and safe parking available?
- Where will guests enter, and how will they be greeted? By whom? When? Where?

- Will your lounge be used to accommodate guests while they wait to be seated in the dining room?
- Where will your lounge be located in relation to the main entrance and to the dining room?
- How will waiting guests be notified when their dining room table is ready?
- Will the lounge check be transferred to the dining room, or must guests pay for their drinks before leaving the lounge?
- Will your dining room have smoking and nonsmoking areas?
- How large will each area be?
- Who will take the guests' cocktail orders and dinner orders?
- What kind of uniforms will your waitstaff wear?
- How will food orders be delivered to the kitchen? Wirelessly? Verbally? Via written slips?
- How will servers be notified when their orders are ready to be picked up?
- Who will set up and bus tables?
- Who will correct mistakes and void guest check items?
- Who will handle any complaints that might arise?
- How will the guest check be presented to the guest?
- Who will cashier the guest check?
- Where will charge card sales be processed?
- Will there be a coatroom for guests' wraps? Free? Coin operated? Coat checks?
- Where will your restrooms be located?
- Where will your telephone be located?

The Buddy System

To assure better service, the host will keep track of the parties that are seated at each station. This helps to prevent overburdening any one station. Still, overload situations may occur on occasion. To alleviate such dilemmas, waitpersons should practice the *buddy system*, which simply means that in an emergency, waitpeople will assist the station on either side of their station. In Figure 7.5, the waitperson in Station 2 is the buddy of the waitperson in Stations 1 and 3 and will assist those people in times of special need. They, in turn, will reciprocate when needed.

FIGURE 7.5 *Typical wait stations in full-service restaurants have about 18 seats.*

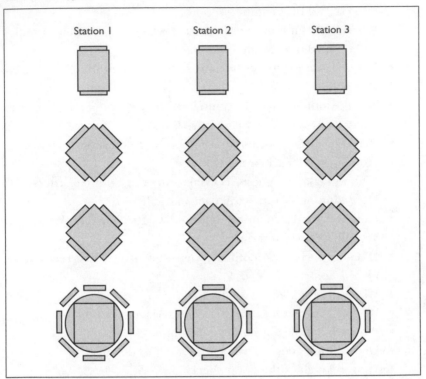

The head waitperson supervises the *side work*, which includes the preliminary setup of the dining room and the changeover between meal periods. A variety of tasks, ranging from filling salt and pepper shakers to folding napkins, must be done to make the dining room ready for guests. The head waitperson typically makes up the dining room work schedules.

Depending upon the hours of service, waitstaff may work one or two meal periods straight through, such as breakfast and lunch. In the case of lunch and dinner, they will sometimes work a split shift because of the length of time between the two meals. The scheduling of employees is largely an accommodation between the restaurant and the individual. Some restaurants have found that using flexible schedules and working closely with their employees when scheduling serves both parties well.

Taking the Order

Waitstaff must be salespeople and ambassadors of goodwill, because they are in the position of greatest contact with customers. As such, they must be alert to customers' needs and respond with ingenuity when things go wrong. A skilled waitperson can often salvage a bad situation simply by displaying a pleasant and caring attitude.

A traditional way to take guests' orders is to call upon ladies first, followed by elders, then children, and finally men, moving counterclockwise around the table.

Abbreviations Reduce Chaos

Using standard abbreviations on guest checks speeds up the order-taking process. More importantly, however, abbreviations are very helpful to cooks and bartenders because they are consistent and easy to read.

Although there are no universal abbreviations, some make more sense than others. You can make up your own, as long as everyone understands them and uses them consistently. Figure 7.6 shows some possible abbreviations.

Where POS systems with touch screens are used, the abbreviations will be displayed on the screen.

FIGURE 7.6 *Some examples of abbreviations for food and drink items*

Food Abbreviations
Bk Chk/OB/Asp = Baked chicken with O'Brien potatoes and asparagus
Veal Salt/Sp Fet = Veal saltimbocca with spinach fettucini
Mx Gr/OR/FF = Mixed grill with onion rings and french fries

Drink Abbreviations
V Mart r tw = Vodka martini, on the rocks, with lemon twist
Sing Sling = Singapore sling
Bour Man ↑ = Bourbon Manhattan, straight up

CUSTOMER SERVICE

No matter how well employees are trained and systems are improved, service will deteriorate if it is not monitored constantly. Undesirable conditions should not be allowed to continue to the point that a customer has to complain, because by that time other customers who did not bother to register their displeasure undoubtedly have already left and will not come back. Management should be the first to know when things are not right. Following are common situations that disturb customers:

- A restaurant opens late or closes early.
- A guest is greeted impatiently, rather than with a smile.
- Empty tables, in view of waiting guests, are not bussed quickly.
- The restaurant floor, tables, or chairs are not clean.
- Tablecloths have holes or tears.
- Menus are tattered or smudged.
- Glasses or tableware are chipped.
- Flatware is spotted, or coffee cups are stained.
- Guests have to wait to place their drink or food order.
- Guests see their food sitting under a warming lamp on the serving line waiting to be picked up.
- Beer or carbonated drinks arrive flat.
- Baked items are stale or salads are limp.
- Restaurants run out of advertised items prematurely.
- A waitperson does not know who ordered an item.
- A waitperson disappears for long periods of time.
- Salads are not chilled and hot foods are barely warm when delivered.
- Empty water glasses are not refilled promptly.
- A guest check has been handled with greasy fingers.
- No one says, "Thank you for your patronage."

HOW TO DEAL WITH DIFFICULT CUSTOMERS

Under the best of circumstances, it is not easy to deal with a difficult customer, and when conflict happens during a rush, it can be a challenge for a manager or host. From the time you are notified of a problem to the moment you approach the disgruntled person, you have little time to decide how to handle the situation.

What you *can* do on your way to the table is to put aside any preconceived notions that will prevent you from really hearing what the guest has to say. You must also dispel any thoughts that you are being harassed.

Approach the person calmly and diffuse the guest's negativity by introducing yourself and letting the person know that you value their patronage and want them to be pleased. Keep the atmosphere civil and avoid displaying anger with your verbal or body language.

Keep in mind, the person may represent hundreds, if not thousands, of dollars of future business and try to come up with a solution that will salvage the situation. Sometimes, replacing the item in question will do it; other times, a drink on the house or not charging for the replaced item will handle it. Do what it takes and consider it an investment in the future.

Following is an example of an actual solution that converted a difficult customer into a regular customer:

When the guest complained brusquely that his steak was awful, the server apologized and brought him another one. Minutes later, he called her back and insisted that the second steak was just as bad. The server took it back but this time reported it to the manager.

The manager told her to have a cook line a tray with aluminum foil and fill it with six raw steaks and put a sprig of parsley on them. The manager accompanied the server as she carried the tray to the table, introduced himself, and explained that he was sorry they had not pleased the customer. He asked the customer to choose any steak he liked from the tray. The man smiled at the woman who was with him, obviously pleased by the special attention he was getting, then chose one.

Not another complaint was heard from him that night. He left a good tip, became a regular customer. and never complained again.

In the rare instance when all reasonable efforts to please a customer have failed, it is justified to tell a constant complainer who is unsettling the staff or who uses abusive language, "I'm sorry we can't please you, but under the circumstances, it would be best for everyone if you took your patronage elsewhere." It is important to confront harassing customers calmly and politely to prevent disturbing other guests.

THE TAKE-OUT BUSINESS: ANOTHER FRONT-OF-THE-HOUSE PROFIT CENTER

No concept in food service is more closely identified with the fast-paced lives of hardworking, multitasking Americans than is take-out food service, whether it be picked up at curbside or at the host's stand or delivered to a caller's home. Its growing popularity has caught the attention of all restaurants, and it now represents a significant slice of the commercial food service market.

The delivery concept has enabled many pizza shops to flourish, even those in a less desirable location. Asian restaurants have for a long time used the call-in/pick-up form of service. Both types of food products retain their temperature and texture very well and, consequently, are well suited for packaging and travel.

Today, even some upscale restaurants, which formerly frowned on the notion of takeout are engaging in it, using elegant packaging and bows and adding extravagant touches, such as a long-stemmed rose, to their gourmet dinners to go.

Take-out and pick-up service is now being extended to all types of foods, as lifestyle changes and a growing demand for convenience drive the trend, pointing to a bright future for the concept. The beauty of it is that it can add significant volume to a restaurant's daily receipts without a great investment or disruption of the existing production system for the dining room. Moreover, it attracts new customers, offsets sluggish table turnover on busy nights, and gets better utilization out of present facilities.

Action Guidelines

☐ Decide on a style of service for your restaurant.

☐ Choose a theme for your decor.

☐ Analyze your clientele: when they will arrive, numbers in party, etc.

☐ Determine your desired seating capacity.

☐ Lay out a preliminary front-of-the-house floor plan.

☐ Design a service system for your restaurant.

☐ Make a list of the equipment that will be needed in the front of the house.

8

THE BAR AND LOUNGE

To have a bar or not to have a bar? That is the question many restaurateurs must answer when starting up a restaurant. In some cases, the liquor law requirements will dictate the answer; in others, the targeted clientele's expectations and the owner's personal wishes will determine it. Not every restaurant needs to have, or should have, a bar.

If you do decide to have a bar, the next question is what will it serve—beer and wine, or all alcoholic beverages? A different type of license or permit is required for each, and the cost and provisions of each will vary from state to state.

What kind of a bar will best serve your restaurant? You have some choices:

- *Full bar.* Usually located near the front of the restaurant, a full bar serves all types of alcoholic beverages with stools at the bar and, usually, seating in a lounge area. Bartenders deal with customers and handle payments and fill in as lounge servers when it's slow. Typically, a full bar will include a service window or station at one end of the bar, which functions as the service bar for the dining rooms.
- *Wine and/or beer bar.* This kind of bar may appear physically similar to the full bar, but it does not sell spirituous liquors, instead selling only wine and/or beer.

- *Service bar.* Located in the back of the house to prepare drinks only for dining and banquet room guests, it does not have any seating; consequently, service bartenders do not deal directly with guests or handle payments. Its purpose is simply to fill drink orders for the waitstaff, who deliver and handle payments for the drinks. The service bar may serve all alcoholic beverages allowed under its license.
- *Banquet bar.* Often a satellite of the full bar, a banquet bar is often a portable bar dispatched to a function room. It operates only for the duration of a specific function, after which it is broken down, the cash is reconciled, the remaining liquor is stored away, and the portable bar is put away until needed again. Where a high-volume function room justifies it, a small bar may be built in the room specifically to serve functions. Those bars are designed to be closed and locked up when not in use for a function.

Liquor laws vary from state to state. Permission to proceed with plans for a bar should be obtained from the liquor control agency in your jurisdiction before entering into any binding agreements. The requirements and limitations of each type of license dictate the specific rooms and outside spaces, such as sidewalk and courtyard patios, where alcoholic beverages may be sold. Until a restaurant actually receives its liquor license, or beer and wine permit, it is prohibited from selling any alcoholic beverages. Licensing sometimes requires special hearings; an attorney familiar with the process can be of great assistance.

LOCATING THE BAR

If a bar is to serve as an optional waiting room for people before they are seated in the dining room, it should be near the entry by which most guests will arrive. And because bars are typically more active and noisier than dining rooms, care must be taken to insulate dining guests from bar traffic, smoke, TV blare, and loud music.

BAR LAYOUT

First and foremost, the bar should appear welcoming and present choices to entering guests—sitting at the bar, sitting in the lounge area, sitting in a brighter spot, or sitting in a more private spot with lower light. It should also be laid out as conveniently as possible for guests and provide the best functionality for production and service.

Individual consideration should be given to the four elements of a bar:

1. The front bar
2. The back bar
3. The guests' seating arrangements
4. The traffic flow for both guests and servers

The *front bar* consists of the bar counter, in front of which guests sit on stools, and the bar top on which guests' drinks are served. If food will be served at the bar, ample space should be allowed between bar stools to provide elbow room for diners.

The *back bar* is the production area, traditionally consisting of an array of sinks and bar equipment installed on the back side of the bar counter as well as the work aisle, the liquor storage cabinets, and the display shelves above the cabinets. The work aisle should be wide enough for two bartenders to pass each other without interference, and the aisle floor should be covered with rubber mats to ease the impact of hard floors on a bartender's feet and back.

Guest seating should be sturdy but comfortable, and it should be grouped to accommodate parties of various sizes. The number and types of seats in each grouping are determined by the makeup of the clientele. Do they usually arrive as parties of two, three or more? Flexibility may be achieved by purchasing furniture that can be butted against, or separated from, other furniture to form interesting groupings. Customer and service aisles should be wide enough for the traffic to flow freely, without disturbing other guests.

DESIGNING YOUR BAR

In most full-service restaurants, the lounge is an integral and important part of the front of the house, and as such, its theme should blend with that of the restaurant.

Two basic questions must be answered when designing a bar, because your answers will form the basis of any bar layout.

1. *What types of beverages will be served?* The types of beverages dictate what equipment is required, the styles of glasses needed, what is needed to prepare specialty drinks (ice cream, coffee, slush), the amount of refrigerated storage needed, and whether to dispense draught beer or serve bottled beer.

2. *How many customers will have to be served at one time?* The number of customers determines the quantity and size of the equipment, the amount of ice required, the number of glasses needed, how much glass storage space is necessary, and how many serving stations are required. And because every drink begins with a clean, sterile glass, appropriate glass-washing equipment is necessary.

After equipment sizes and quantities have been determined, the equipment must be arranged to conform to the flow of the beverages and glasses to and from the serving stations. A *serving station* is the area and equipment used by a bartender to mix and dispense beverages. A small restaurant bar can have a single serving station, staffed by one server, while a large bar may have several. The greater the number of customers, the larger the bar must be and the more stations are required for efficient operation.

It is important to think of a bar in terms of efficiency and ask questions. How can a beverage order be prepared with the fewest number of steps? Where should the cocktail-mixing station be in relation to the beer-dispensing stations and in relation to the POS register? Will any specialty drinks have to be prepared, and what is needed for them? How much floor space, in relation to the total space available, can be dedicated to the bar operation? What is the budget? Will equipment cutbacks be necessary to meet budget constraints?

When a bar designer uses common sense and "acts out" the workings of an operation—pretending to take an order, make the drinks, deliver the drinks, and take payment for the drinks—what equipment is needed and where it should be placed becomes clear. In essence, a good bar layout is no different than an efficient kitchen or office layout.

Because service bars make drinks for dining room guests only and do not handle cash or wait on customers, they only need essential production equipment.

CONSTRUCTION OF THE BAR

Unless an individual has the time, experience, and skills to act as a general contractor, it is wiser to select an architect who can research the best products for your needs and subcontract the carpentry, plumbing, electrical, and decorating work to experienced trade specialists.

Some firms specialize in supplying complete bar interiors in various motifs, such as Irish pubs and Western saloons. The interiors are built in modular form in factories and shipped to the buyer's destination, where they are installed and, if desired, outfitted with wall hangings and decorative memorabilia.

ACQUISITION OF EQUIPMENT

What brand of equipment you choose depends on what will best satisfy the requirements of the bar. Equipment may be custom manufactured, but custom manufacturing takes longer and is often more costly than buying standard production items.

The benefit of the modular concept is that a manufacturer's component products can be mixed and matched to satisfy a customer's specific requirements. Serving station modules can be mated with freestanding pieces— such as cabinets, glass frosters, bottle coolers, and glass washers—to create a customized total beverage center and a coordinated appearance.

Bar equipment is available from many manufacturers. However, dealing with numerous suppliers entails greater coordination of purchases to ensure that everything arrives at the desired time, fits where it is supposed to go, and looks uniform. Professional buyers prefer to buy as much equipment as possible from a single source. By doing so, they have to deal with only one purchase order, receive one freight shipment, and cut one check.

A typical list of bar equipment includes:

Bar sinks (three-compartment)	Blenders and slushers
Speed racks	Cocktail stations
Workbenches (stainless steel)	Beer tap system
Glass chiller or froster	POS system, cash drawer
Glass racks	Ice cube maker

FIGURE 8.1 *An array of bar equipment designed to serve the clientele of a high-volume casual restaurant. (Photo courtesy of Perlick Corporation, Milwaukee, Wisconsin)*

Keg beer cooler	Ice crusher or flaker
Bottled beer cooler	Glass storage racks
Bottle wells	Speed-gun soda system
Ice chest with cold plate	Ice cream cabinet
Underbar refrigerator	Underbar glass washer

STOCKING THE BAR

It is not necessary to carry every brand of liquor, beer, or wine on the market. However, you do need an adequate representation of all categories of alcoholic beverages that your targeted clientele will expect from your type of restaurant. Most bars carry "bar brands" (lower-cost) liquors of each type in their speed racks or wells for when a specific liquor is not requested. Typically, at least two popular call brands of each type of liquor are carried on the back bar shelves to give customers a choice, and a few more premium brands of certain types are carried on the top shelves.

The main types of spirituous liquors to be stocked are:

Blended whiskey	Gin
Scotch whiskey	Vodka
Canadian whiskey	Tequila
Bourbon whiskey	Light rum
Irish whiskey	Dark rum
Liqueurs	Brandy

The size and kinds of wine and beer inventories you carry will depend on the menu, the size of the bar, and the clientele. Beer and wine distributors are familiar with local tastes and drinking patterns and can be very helpful in assisting restaurant start-ups plan their initial inventories.

BAR GLASSWARE

Attractive glassware, suited to your decor, will sell more drinks than plain glassware. Glasses have become an important merchandising tool for drinks such as martinis and margaritas. When purchasing glassware, consider the types of drinks that will be sold and the volume of guests you expect at peak times. Also, keep in mind that some glasses will be in use by guests, while others may be waiting to be washed, so in extremely busy periods, you will need to dip into your backup stock. It is prudent to have at least a 50 percent backup stock on hand. Besides that, you should plan on at least 25 percent breakage every year. Following is a sample initial inventory for barware; actual sizes and quantities will vary according to the drink sizes that you plan to serve and the maximum number of patrons you may have to serve at any one time.

Type of Glass	Quantity
5-ounce rocks	13 dozen
7-ounce highball	12 dozen
10-ounce Collins	12 dozen
4-ounce cocktail	13 dozen
4-ounce sour	6 dozen
5-ounce brandy snifter	2 dozen

Type of Glass	Quantity
12-ounce beer	13 dozen
6-ounce wine	12 dozen
2-ounce sherry	3 dozen
4-ounce champagne	3 dozen
1-ounce cordial	3 dozen

STAFFING THE BAR

The drinks a restaurant serves are just as important to guests as its food. Poorly made drinks can discourage a guest from returning as much as a disappointing entree. Hiring well-trained bartenders is essential.

Many bars sponsor a responsible alcohol service program for their bartenders and servers of alcoholic beverages. Two prominent programs are Training for Intervention ProcedureS (TIPS program) offered by Health Communications, Inc. and the ServSafe Alcohol program developed by the National Restaurant Association. Hiring certified bartenders and offering continuing training is the best way to achieve a high level of professional service.

INVENTORYING AND CONTROL OF THE BAR

A *par stock* should be established for the bar. This number is the combined total of all bottles that will be placed at the bar. Management determines how large or small the par stock should be. Theoretically, it should be an amount of stock adequate to carry the bar through a full day of business without having to restock during the day.

Once the par stock number is established, empty bottles are saved in a box under the bar. Every morning, the empty bottles from the previous day are turned in to the liquor storeroom in exchange for full bottles of the same kind and size to restock the bar.

With this system in place, management can audit the bar at any random time, and the total number of bottles at the bar—full, in action, and empty—must equal the par stock number. If it doesn't, the variation must be explained. Only management need know the par stock number, and it may be changed periodically for security purposes.

FOOD SERVICE IN THE BAR

Some bars serve food in their bars; others do not. This decision should be made after serious consideration of some questions:

- What would be your main reason for serving food in the bar?
- Would you offer a limited menu in the bar?
- Who would take the food orders?
- How would the food orders be communicated to the kitchen?
- Who would pick up the food order and deliver it to the guest?
- Would utensils and napkins be kept at the bar or brought with the food?
- Who would bus the soiled dishes and utensils?
- Would you serve food just at the bar counter or at the booths and tables in the lounge as well?

If you decide to serve food or snacks in the bar, be prepared to clean the floors and carpets more often. Spillage and fallen food fragments will invite insects if not removed quickly. This work can be done in slack periods between rushes.

SALES PROMOTION

Unless the intended purpose of a restaurant bar is to function solely as a waiting room for people headed to the dining room and to serve drinks to dining guests, an ongoing promotional program should be maintained to maximize the bar's sales potential. Promotions may be done both in-house on table tents and menus and externally in newspaper advertisements and radio and TV commercials. This subject is covered in detail in Chapter 14 on restaurant marketing.

WINE AND THE DINING-OUT EXPERIENCE

Many people consider wine an important part of their dining experience, a component that goes together with food as naturally as butter does with bread. But for others, the mystique that surrounds wine is intimidating and deters them from ordering it.

Restaurants that have bars can expect to sell a lot of wine—if they do it right. That usually requires staff training. Wine brokers and company representatives are happy to assist with staff training, because if you build a successful wine-selling program, they benefit, too. Besides, they have the promotional tools and techniques to do it effectively.

The secrets to selling wine are to:

- demystify it;
- make it easy for guests to order; and
- make sure your guests are satisfied.

Wine can be demystified by giving guests useful information on your menus and wine lists, suggesting pleasing pairings with foods, and describing wines with words that are easy for guests to understand. This approach can be a great help to servers as well.

A bartender or server need not be an expert on wines, but they should have a basic knowledge of them to do their job properly and answer the questions guests are likely to ask. A bartender should know the classes of wines, how they relate to a meal, how they should be stored and served, how to open wine bottles, and how to judge wine.

How Wines are Classified

Wines are usually named after the variety of grape from which they are produced or the geographic region where they are produced. When named after a variety of grape, they are referred to as *varietal* wines; when named after a region, they are called *generic* wines.

Examples of varietal wines are cabernet sauvignon, pinot noir, and chardonnay. Examples of generic wines are Burgundy, Rhine, and Napa Valley.

The choice of a name is decided largely by the relative popularity of each option. If the region is well recognized, the generic name is most likely to be used, but if the variety of grape is more prestigious, the producer is apt to use the varietal name.

Wines may also bear the proprietor's name, if it gives the wine greater value. An example is movie producer Francis Ford Coppola's wines.

Controls are associated with the use of certain names. To use those names, winemakers must adhere to strict standards.

Five General Classifications of Wines in Relation to a Meal

Class	Examples
1. Appetizer	Dry sherry, vermouth, Madeira
2. Dinner Wines	
Red	Cabernet sauvignon, Burgundy, Chianti, Beaujolais
White	Chardonnay, Chablis, riesling, pinot blanc
3. Dessert Wines	Port, cream sherry, muscatel
4. Sparkling Wines	Champagne, sparkling Burgundy
5. Blush and Rosé	White zinfandel, rosé

Which wine should be consumed with which food? This is an often-asked question. Generally, most people find red wines more compatible with red meats, because both tend to have more body and stronger flavors, and white wines pairing best with light meats, fish, and poultry because of their more delicate flavors. Because of their unique verve, sparkling, blush, and rosé wines may be paired with any food. But in the end, the selection of a wine is a personal choice for each person. The professional server's role is to convey basic information that helps guests make their choice.

How to Store and Serve Wines

Wines should be stored in a dark, cool environment. Bottles with corks must be stored on their sides to keep the corks moist and prevent them from drying and rotting. Bottles with plastic or metal caps may be stored upright.

Red wines should be served at cool room temperatures; the ideal temperature for a storeroom is about 60 degrees Fahrenheit. White wines should be refrigerated before serving to be enjoyed at 40 to 45 degrees Fahrenheit. The reds will develop a fuller aroma if opened and left to stand uncorked for an hour before serving, but this technique is impractical in a busy restaurant setting. An alternative when expensive wines are ordered, if the guest wishes, is to decant the bottle at tableside. This allows oxidization to occur more quickly than in an open bottle.

Many lower-priced restaurants offer bulk packaged wines by the glass or carafe. Figure 8.2 shows two dispensing systems for bulk wines.

FIGURE 8.2 *Two systems for dispensing bulk packaged wines are illustrated. One by using a refrigerator box, the other by using a cold plate positioned at the bottom of an ice bin.*

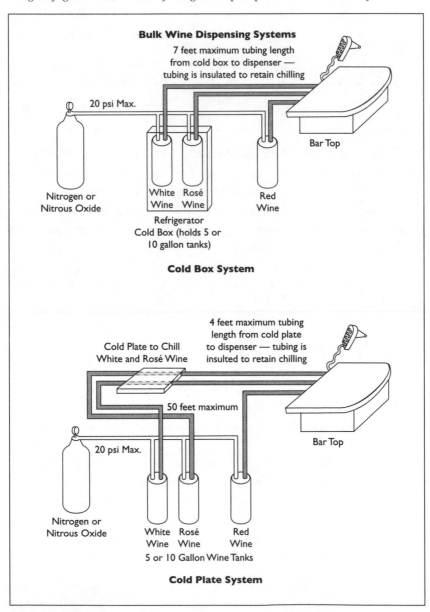

This practice is very acceptable when the target market seeks a value-based dining experience. It can also be quite profitable in high-volume, quick-serve table restaurants.

How to Judge Wines

In the restaurant business, three situations require knowledge about how to judge wines. They are:

1. When buying wines
2. When handling a customer complaint
3. When hosting a wine-tasting session

Basically, wines are judged on color, taste and aroma.

The *color* of a wine should be clear and shiny, regardless of whether it is a red wine or a white wine. Any wine that appears dull or cloudy when held up to a light is inferior.

The *aroma* of a good wine should be pleasing, not overwhelming and never pungent. It should be faint, yet noticeable enough to be exciting.

Finally, the *taste* of every wine should be pleasing to the palate, in its own way. Some wines are intended to be sweet, others dry (i.e., they lack sweetness). Vinegar-like flavors are a sign of poor wine. Figure 8.3 describes the zones of the tongue that respond to particular tastes.

FIGURE 8.3 *The zones of the tongue that perceive different wine characteristics*

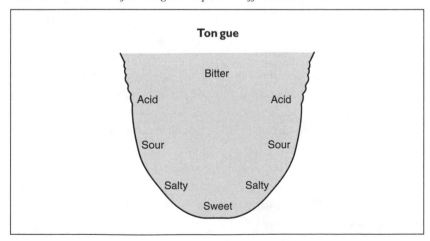

The best way to taste wine is to sip a small amount, then suck a bit of air into your mouth to oxygenate it, circulate the wine in your mouth, and swallow it. Focus on the various parts of your tongue as you do this to isolate the characteristics of the wine.

THE SECRET TO SELLING A LOT OF BEER

Beer drinkers can be very selective—they are brand conscious and perceptive about the qualities of the beer they like to drink. They will order their favorite beer, but if it is not available, they will expect one of similar quality. Most bars offer choices among premium beers, mass-market beers, microbeers, and nonalcoholic beers. The secret to selling a lot of beer is to carry the brands that are most popular in your region and serve them in a sparkling clean, chilled mug or glass at the right temperature and pressure.

Rules for Handling Beer

1. Serve fresh beer. Rotate your stock using the first-in, first-out method.
2. Store bottled beer in a cool, dark, and dry room. Keg beer must be refrigerated at all times, because it is not pasteurized and will start to turn sour very quickly if not refrigerated.
3. Avoid exposing beer to freezing temperatures. It will not be servable if it freezes; thawing will not return it to its original condition.
4. Store beer at 38 degrees Fahrenheit and serve it at 40 degrees Fahrenheit.
5. Always serve beer in a *beer-clean glass.* A beer-clean glass is one that has no trace of soap, fat, or grease on it. Even a light film of those substances on an improperly washed glass can cause beer to go flat. Glasses should be washed, rinsed, sanitized, and air-dried.

Beer distributors are extremely helpful with staff training and equipment maintenance, because they want their products to sell well.

See Chapter 15 for information on responsible service of alcoholic beverages and legal liability.

Action Guidelines

___

☐ Make up a wine list to complement your dinner menu.
☐ Make up a beer list that includes draft beers and bottled beers.
☐ Select liquors to be carried in your bar.
☐ Create a rough drawing of your bar layout as you envision it.

9

THE BACK OF THE HOUSE

The workings of the back of the house are usually unseen to guests, but the products that come out of the kitchen tell a great deal about it. People may be forgiving of some things, if the food is very good, but rarely will they forgive disappointing food.

The *back of the house* encompasses all of the production-related areas of a restaurant, from the receiving door to the swinging doors that open to the dining room from the kitchen. When the back of the house runs smoothly, customers are usually happy in the front of the house.

A key contributor to a smooth-running kitchen is a good layout—and the best time to design one is before you start signing binding agreements with contractors and vendors. It is much easier and less costly to make changes before construction has begun and equipment has been ordered.

ANALYZE YOUR NEEDS

Your menu determines your equipment. Every item on it should be analyzed in terms of what equipment will be needed for its preparation. The equipment should then be arranged in a configuration that moves food products steadily from the receiving and storage area, through the

FIGURE 9.1 *A state-of-the-art kitchen, equipped with modularized equipment capable of high-volume production (Photo courtesy of the Hobart Corporation, Troy, Ohio)*

preparation and cooking stations, and then to the serving line, from which they go directly to the dining room with a minimum of backtracking and crisscrossing. The flow may be in a straight line, in a circular flow, or even a horizontal "E flow," as long as it moves products from the point of receiving toward the point of service continuously. The size and shape of the available kitchen space ultimately dictates which flow scheme is the best in the given circumstances.

WORKING WITH VENDORS

Certified food facilities consultants are qualified to calculate the equipment needs of a restaurant and draw up working plans, for a fee. They have expertise and are acquainted with the latest food service products on the market. Moreover, you can benefit from the experience they bring from other projects. If your funds are tight, they can help you work within budget by suggesting alternatives.

Many equipment vendors also have staff that can assist with smaller, less complicated renovations. For vendors to work successfully with you, however, they must have exact data regarding the size and shape of the rooms involved, the utilities available, and the menu you will be producing.

On large or complex projects, an architect who is experienced in restaurant design should be engaged to construct your facility. The architect will, in turn, engage a food equipment consultant and subcontractors for each of the specialized areas of the project.

When selecting consultants, contractors, or architects, ask for a list of their previous clients and check their references carefully to determine how satisfied those clients are.

ALLOCATING KITCHEN SPACE

The amount of kitchen space needed to produce your menu will depend on the extent to which you use convenience foods. Restaurants that make extensive use of convenience foods require much less equipment and work space than do those that cook almost entirely from scratch. Restaurants in the nonconvenience foods category must refrigerate, wash, prep and process many foods that would otherwise be ready to use. The following relationships can serve as a starting point when planning a kitchen.

Extent to Which Convenience Foods Are Used	Approximate Size of Kitchen in Relation to Dining Room
Little or no use of convenience foods	50%
Moderate use of convenience foods	40%
Extensive use of convenience foods	33⅓%

Additional space should be added for storerooms, locker rooms, trash rooms, employee restrooms, and such other facilities that might be desired.

SELECTING EQUIPMENT

Your budget will influence the type, size, and quantity of equipment you select, but purchases of equipment should be made mainly on the basis of how you answer the following questions:

- Is it essential to your operation? Will it improve your production or service systems?
- Is it the right size? Will it do the job you expect of it in terms of volume, speed, and quality?
- Does the equipment bear the appropriate NSF (sanitation), AGA (gas), UL (electric), or ASME (steam) approval seals? Is it safe and sanitary?
- Will it blend in well with the rest of your equipment? Does it have a good appearance, and is it easily cleanable?
- Can it be serviced easily, and what type of warrantee does the seller or manufacturer offer? Is a service agency located reasonably nearby?
- Will it fit in the space you have available?
- How much will the utility hookups and installation cost? Do you have the required water pressure, electrical phase, and voltage?
- Is it cost-effective in relation to alternative ways of getting the job done?

Typical Back-of-the-House Equipment

Range	Racks	Hand Sink
Gas Broiler	Slicer	Time Clock
Charcoal Broiler	Mixer	Waste Disposal
Deep Fat Fryer	Attachment Rack	Dish Heater
Roast Oven	Tenderizer	Meat Grinder
Steam Kettle	Three Compartment Sink	Tenderizer
Compartment Steamer	Scale	Breading Table
Hoods and Vent	Peeler	Pot Sink
Work Tables	Tilting Skillet	Desk
Bain-Marie	Ladder Rack Carts	File Cabinet
Griddle	Proofing Cabinet	Computer
Grill	Soiled Dish Table	
Toaster	Dish Washer	
Reach-in Refrigerator	Clean Dish Table	
Reach-in Freezer Pot and Pan		

Analyzing Equipment Needs

A chart that follows the production process needed to prepare your menu can be constructed as shown to identify the equipment required. Only major equipment need be considered in this analysis.

Equipment Analysis

Menu Item	Method of Preparation	Equipment Necessary
Homemade soups	Stockpot cooking	Range
		Work table
		Refrigerator
Salads	Fresh	Refrigerator
		Work table
		Sink
		Disposer
Fried chicken	Deep fried	Deep fryer
Steaks	Broiled	Broiler
Hamburgers	Grilled	Griddle
Ham steak	Baked	Conventional oven
Baked potatoes	Baked	Convection oven

It is helpful to visualize the process by which each item is made, from the starting point where its ingredients are gathered until the product is cooked and served.

THE PRODUCTION SYSTEM

A commercial kitchen is made up of a number of work centers that together comprise a *production system.* A good production system does not have congested areas and dangerous intersections that may cause accidents. Its layout may be linear, circular, or E-shaped (three legged) to fit a limited space, but it should move steadily toward the point of service. Typical work centers in a restaurant kitchen are the following:

- Receiving and storing
- Pre-preparation and salad making

- Sandwich and cold food preparation
- Cooking and baking
- Serving line
- Dish washing and pot washing

Work Center Layout

A *work center* is one section of a production system that is devoted to a particular function, such as baking, salad making, cooking, or dish washing. Each center must be designed to perform its function efficiently and to interface smoothly with the other centers.

Three key issues should be considered when planning a work center:

1. What is the intended purpose of the work center?
2. What equipment will be needed to accomplish the intended purpose?
3. What are the special needs of the employees who will work in the center?

The first step in the process is to define the primary functions of the center. The second is to break down the functions into the tasks required to accomplish them. Finally, the equipment needed to perform the tasks must be identified and laid out in a logical arrangement, with adequate space for employees to do their jobs safely and efficiently. Figure 9.2 illustrates how a bakery work center might be designed.

Efficiency Doesn't Happen—It Must Be Planned

When designing your floor plan, the efficiency of your operations must be considered. The flow of foot traffic should be smooth and free of dangerous blind corners where collisions might occur. Aisles must be wide enough for workers to perform their duties freely and to pass each other safely with hot or heavy pans.

FIGURE 9.2 *Breaking down the tasks and the equipment needed for each task can help ensure an efficient design for a food production area.*

Example: Laying Out a Bakeshop Work Center

Step 1: List the main functions of the bakeshop: to bake breads, pies, cakes, and other pastries.

Step 2: Break down the tasks required to perform these functions and identify the equipment needed.

Tasks	Equipment Needed
Gathering ingredients	Dry storage and refrigerator
Weighing	Baker's work table and scale
Mixing	Mixer and sink with water hose
Kneading	Work table
Panning	Work table
Cooking fillings and icings	Trunnion kettle
Proofing	Proof boxes
Baking	Deck ovens
Landing and cooling	Work table and ladder rack carts
Slicing	Bread slicing machine
Decorating	Work table
Storage and delivery	Ladder rack carts

Step 3: Lay out the equipment in a functional manner:

1. Refrigerator
2. Mixer
3. Baker's table
4. Sink w/spray arm
5. Stainless steel worktables
6 Steam-jacketed kettle
7. Proof boxes
8. Deck ovens
9. Ladder rack carts
10. Bread slicer and table
11. Decorating table
12. Delivery carts

Type of Kitchen Aisle	Minimum Width Recommended
Main Aisles (through kitchen)	72"
Work Aisles (between lines of equipment)	48"

Additional space should be allowed near hazardous equipment, such as slicing machines and ovens with doors that swing into work aisles.

HOW TO SIZE EQUIPMENT

The sizing of equipment is done by calculating the volume of output required to satisfy your peak periods of business and finding a model that will produce the desired volume of output. The following example illustrates the steps that might be followed when selecting a conveyer-type dishwasher:

1. Determine the average number of pieces of chinaware used per patron in your restaurant.
2. Estimate the total number of patrons you will serve in a peak hour and multiply that number by the average number of pieces of chinaware used per patron.

   # of customers × avg. # of pieces of chinaware = total # of pieces of chinaware

3. Divide the total number of pieces of chinaware by the number of pieces that will fit into a dish rack, in this example 20.

   $$\frac{\text{Total \# of Pieces of Chinaware}}{20} = \text{of Racks Required per Hour}$$

4. Refer to dish machine specifications in equipment catalogs and find a model that matches your desired capacity for a peak hour.

Be aware that on some types of equipment, such as dishwashers, the capacities stated in manufacturers' catalogs are determined under the most ideal circumstances possible. To compensate for that, it is wise to reduce the manufacturers' claimed capacity by 30 percent when matching equipment with your needs.

SHOULD YOU BUY OR LEASE EQUIPMENT?

There are valid reasons for both leasing and for buying equipment, but the reasons vary from business to business and from time to time due to fluctuating interest rates and alternative uses of funds.

Although no single answer applies to all cases, it is important to understand the advantages and disadvantages of each course of action under varying circumstances. The pros and cons of buying and leasing are listed in Figure 9.3.

Perhaps the most important realization when considering leasing equipment is that old adage: nothing is free. Everything you lease has a price that includes all expenses, plus a profit for the lessor. The main reason that many people lease equipment is they just don't have the money to buy it.

FIGURE 9.3 *Buying and leasing each have advantages and disadvantages.*

Pros and Cons of Buying and Leasing

Buying

Advantages	Disadvantages
Buyer acquires a valuable asset.	Equipment wears out and must be replaced by the buyer eventually.
Buyer can depreciate a portion of the cost each year.	Buyer assumes the responsibility of maintaining and servicing the equipment.
Interest expense for installment payments is tax deductible.	

Leasing

Advantages	Disadvantages
Lease payments are tax deductible as business operating expenses.	Loss of depreciation write-off.
Lessor may maintain and service the equipment for the lessee.	At the end of the lease, you do not own the equipment.
Service calls on leased equipment are usually given priority over others.	The built-in charge for service may be more than you would otherwise have paid for it.
Lessor usually supplies brand-new models and updates equipment periodically.	

Another reason for considering leasing is that it is a way to hedge if a new business is uncertain of its future. If a short-term lease is signed, a lessee can terminate business with minimal losses, as opposed to a business that buys everything and gets stuck with a lot of money tied up in used equipment. It should be noted that used food and beverage equipment is plentiful and brings very little money at auction.

SPECIALIZED KITCHENS

Cafeteria kitchens differ from typical restaurant operations in that customers pass along a serving line, selecting items as they move along, and pay at the end of the line. Production tasks are performed on the back side of a wall that separates the kitchen from the serving line.

Food supplies for the serving line may be passed through a window or carried out through a doorway. However, newer installations tend to have pass-through refrigerators and hot food cabinets that are built into the wall. Food is inserted into them from the kitchen side and is removed, as needed, from the serving side. This arrangement is

FIGURE 9.4 *The popular Starlite Diner in Daytona Beach, Florida, has a '50s decor, including a large jukebox and a diner menu, that brings back memories.*

highly desirable, because it cuts down on kitchen traffic and reduces disruptions on the serving line when restocking. The hot and cold pass-through units hold foods at the proper temperature and humidity until they are ready to be put on the serving line.

Diners also have a hybrid arrangement that is very efficient. Short-order cooking and grilling is commonly done in view of customers on the counter side of the wall, while prep work, bulk cooking, and baking are done on the reverse side of the pass-through or walk-through wall.

TABLEWARE

Table settings are a key part of a restaurant's decor; therefore, the style should be based on your desired image and the kind of food you will be serving. You can choose from many types of ware—some work better with certain kinds of food and decor than others. Five main features to look at when selecting tableware are:

1. Style
2. Size
3. Strength and materials
4. Usefulness
5. Cost

Tableware should be easy to clean and should coordinate well with the overall theme of the restaurant. Plate sizes should be appropriate for the portions you plan to serve, and that, of course, will be related to the prices you plan to charge. The strength and chip-resistence of chinaware and glassware is important. Vitrified china and chip-resistant glassware are made especially for the hotel and restaurant trade; while they cost more at the outset, they save you money over the long run.

HOW MUCH SHOULD YOU BUY?

This depends upon your estimated sales volume. Keep in mind that some items will be in use at tables, while others will be soiled and waiting to be washed. You should have a large enough reserve inventory of chinaware and glassware to handle all contingencies. Most establishments keep a minimum of 25 percent reserve stock to be used for breakage replacements and very busy occasions. Once tableware is chipped, no matter how slightly, it must be removed from service.

Think very carefully before ordering chinaware with your name or initials on it. Even though monogrammed chinaware may be appealing to the ego, it costs more money when you buy it, it requires a long lead time for delivery—up to six months—because it has to be specially made, and dealers will not keep it in stock. Lastly, unless someone else wants to use your name or has the same initials as you, it is virtually worthless for resale.

Action Guidelines

☐ List the work centers that will be necessary to produce your menu.
☐ Determine the main function of each work center and determine the tasks that need to be performed there.
☐ Identify the equipment needed to perform the tasks.
☐ Develop a floor plan for each work center and design your kitchen by arranging the work centers in an efficient layout.

C h a p t e r

10

BANQUETS AND OTHER CATERED EVENTS

Enormous sums are spent annually to attract individuals to restaurants for their first time or to win them back after a bad experience. At the same time, function guests go to restaurants at no additional marketing cost to the establishments, and their potential is often overlooked. They come with an open mind, hoping to be impressed and giving you an occasion to strut your stuff, so why not take advantage of this ready-made opportunity to woo them back.

FUNCTION GUESTS MAY BECOME REGULAR CUSTOMERS

If a function guest is impressed with your food and service, that guest may patronize your restaurant often. Suppose such a person comes to your restaurant on average once a month with a friend and spends $70. That amounts to $840 of extra sales per year.

Now to get the full impact, assume that your restaurant does an average of one banquet a week with a typical head count of 30 guests:

30 guests × 52 weeks = 1,560 function guests per year
1,560 guests × $840 a year = $1,310,400 potential extra sales per year

129

Obviously, every satisfied guest will not become a regular customer, but the point of this example is that function guests can be very valuable if you please them. To convert them into regular guests, you must give them the best food, beverages, and service that you can for the price that they are paying. Best of all, they will tell others about the wonderful dining experience they had.

BUSINESS/LUNCHEON FUNCTIONS

Businesses and organizations often seek the stimulation of a restaurant function room for luncheon meetings that seek to enhance productivity with a social atmosphere. The size, type, and length of such meetings dictate their needs. Larger groups, for time efficiency, frequently prefer a buffet lunch that offers a variety of meat, fish, and chicken as well as salad items served in the function room. Buffets work well for restaurants, too, because most items can be prepared in advance and a mobile serving line can be wheeled into a function room and set in place quickly. Small groups typically are given a choice of two meat entrees plus a vegetarian choice, served in the function room. Depending on the size and type of group, bar service, if requested, may be offered in the function room or at the main bar.

Room setup is important to the success of luncheon meetings. Function managers must anticipate various problems that a client may overlook such as traffic flow, service needs, and presentation equipment. Business and organizational groups will usually require a microphone and speaker system, a projection table and screen or a viewing wall, and room-darkening capability. In addition, a lectern or podium, a fresh coffee station, and drinking water setups at each table are often requested.

It is important when originally planning the layout of a restaurant to identify what amenities will be offered in function rooms and to allocate adequate space for them.

EVENT CATERING

Wedding receptions, awards dinners, company parties, and social events constitute a large part of traditional catering. Such business is highly sought after and the market is competitive.

Banquet catering is highly desirable because it is done by reservation and can be preplanned to avoid waste and excessive leftovers as well as overstaffing and understaffing. It is, therefore, quite profitable. But it must be conducted with excellence to reap the rewards of good word-of-mouth advertising from satisfied guests. And above all, a banquet system must be designed to avoid interference with the production flow and service of food to the regular dining rooms.

When bar service is requested for a banquet, the size of the party will usually dictate whether a portable bar should be setup in the banquet room or a cocktail server should be assigned to the function.

The distance between the function rooms and the kitchen and bar should be as short as possible and not conflict with customer traffic patterns. Careful preplanning can minimize the occurrence of such problems.

Social functions, awards dinners, and wedding receptions typically require a lengthy head table for honored guests, gift or awards display tables, and a dance floor. The latter may be installed, or it can be collapsible and assembled when needed. Decorations are usually left to the client.

IN-HOUSE VERSUS EXTERNAL FUNCTIONS

In-house banquets are catered in function rooms, and where possible and requested, they may be catered in a courtyard, a showplace garden, or in elegant party tent on the restaurant premises. External functions may be catered at a rented facility or at a client's venue.

It should be understood, however, that regardless of whether a function is catered in a tent on the restaurant's premises, in a rented venue, or at a client's facility, all applicable food safety, public health, liquor, and fire safety regulations must be satisfied. Check with the regulatory agencies in your locale to ascertain what is and is not allowed.

A restaurant's regular liquor license does not extend beyond the prescribed rooms and location for which it was issued. Some states or jurisdictions may issue special one-day licenses (for a specific function, date, and place) with certain requirements that must be met.

OUTDOOR FUNCTIONS

Weather is highly unpredictable in some parts of the country, especially at certain times of the year. Yet enthusiastic clients sometimes insist on having an event outdoors or in a tent. The importance of having a backup plan must be explained to the client, and together an alternative can be agreed upon.

When planning outdoor functions, special concerns such as the following must be addressed:

- Violent storm conditions and alternative plans
- Does the tent have walls that can be lowered if unexpected wind or rain occurs?
- Is the proposed site level and not apt to puddle from rain?
- Will a ground cover be necessary?
- Is the site free of insects, smells, and other objectionable characteristics?
- Will a portable dance floor be required?
- Where will the food be cooked, plated, and served?
- Will food have to be transported? Are adequate hot and cold thermal cabinets available?
- Will special tables, chairs, flatware, and table coverings be required?
- Are electrical, water, and gas hookups handy?
- Is ample parking available close to the site?
- Are adequate sanitary facilities located nearby?

In any off-premises situation, the function manager should physically check out the site in advance to be certain of its cleanliness and appearance

as well as the food safety, fire safety, and special liquor license requirements required. This is imperative, because the restaurant's reputation
is at risk.

In addition, insurance coverage should be reviewed with the appropriate insurance agent to ensure that such external functions are covered adequately by the restaurant's policies.

GOOD COORDINATION IS KEY TO SUCCESSFUL FUNCTIONS

Coordination among all departments affected by scheduled functions is critical. Each department head must be aware of the needs and
concerns of every other department involved.

Weekly meetings to discuss forthcoming functions should include the
head chef, whose concerns would be purchasing the necessary food in
sufficient quantities; the scheduling of adequate kitchen staff; and the availability and timing of the kitchen equipment needed to produce the menu,
so that everyone is not rushing to use the same piece of equipment at once.
Potential conflicts between dining room needs and function event needs,
especially during peak hours, can be resolved at these meetings.

The bar manager would be concerned with stocking a portable bar
for the functions, scheduling an extra bartender, and possibly bringing
out more glassware from the storeroom for a large banquet.

The function manager would also coordinate with the dining room
manager about serving staff needs. On slow nights, some dining room
servers can be scheduled to work functions, but on busy nights, such
scheduling may not be possible. For that reason, many function managers develop a separate list of part-time servers who want to work only at
functions and are willing to work on a week's notice.

THE COMPETITION IS KEEN

Prospecting for new business is one of the function manager's
principal responsibilities. The function manager, or an assistant, should
search local newspapers every day for announcements of engagements,
promotions, anniversaries, and awards; these can lead to bookings for

wedding receptions and shower parties. Sporting and graduation banquets and service club luncheon meetings are also lucrative prospects for function business. Prospecting is so important that some restaurants pay the function manager a commission based on sales production on top of a salary.

An effective sales promotion program must be ongoing and may include a number of marketing tools, including:

Sales letters	Function menus
Color brochures	Photo albums
Telephone contacts	Table tents
E-mail communications	Posters
Press releases	Web sites
Newspaper ads	"Bird-dog" incentives
TV commercials	Blogs

BOOKING FUNCTIONS

It is critical that functions be booked systematically and clearly and that everyone concerned be familiar with the process and abide by it. Every decision about a function should be documented and confirmed with the client at each step of the process. A good practice is to have the client initial their understanding and agreement with the decisions when they are made. The written record of decisions form the basis of the contract, which the client will sign when paying the deposit and confirming the booking. There are numerous ways to book a function. Following is a typical process.

When someone calls to inquire about booking a function on a certain date, a *tentative-booking* form is filled out on the restaurant's computer or in a three-ring binder. The purpose of this record is temporarily to reserve a particular room at a certain time, on a certain date, for a certain function. The estimated number of guests, the arrival and departure time, the nature of the function, the name of the group and the person inquiring, and their telephone number and e-mail address should be recorded.

The inquirer is invited to come to the restaurant as soon as possible to view the facilities and discuss the menus and other details.

An information packet is mailed immediately after the call to the inquirer to facilitate action when they arrive. The inquirer is told a date by which a deposit must be made to continue to hold the reservation. In the meantime, if someone else calls about the same date, time, and room, the first inquirer is notified and asked for a decision. The idea is to keep the process moving toward a conclusion.

When the potential customer comes to the restaurant, the function manager shows them the physical facilities, pointing out such features as convenient parking, new renovations, and the fine reputation of the restaurant (as extolled in letters from satisfied customers, if available). The menus, prices, and contract terms are explained, particularly the payment terms and the restaurant's policies on changes, alcohol service, cancellations, and no-shows.

On receipt of the down payment, a detailed contract is signed, and the function is now confirmed. The customer is then told the deadline by which the final headcount must be received.

All of the final details of the transaction are now entered into a confirmed bookings form in the computer system or in a three-ring binder labeled "Confirmed Bookings" for all concerned parties to see.

CULTIVATE REPEAT FUNCTION BUSINESS

Service clubs such as Rotary and Kiwanis and business organizations such as chambers of commerce have longstanding relationships with restaurants and hotels for their luncheon meetings. They are highly sought-after accounts and should never be taken for granted, because you can be sure that another establishment is wooing them.

An ongoing prospecting program for such repeat business can turn up new accounts for your function facilities and is worth instituting. Inviting function planners for a complimentary lunch and an opportunity to view the facilities can be a productive strategy, as can being a member of one or more of these organizations.

Action Guidelines

- ☐ Set up a tentative reservation book.
- ☐ Set up a confirmed reservation book.
- ☐ Assign or hire a person to be function manager.
- ☐ Develop a prospecting program to build banquet and function business.
- ☐ Design a food preparation and serving system for banquets and functions that will integrate smoothly with regular kitchen activities.

C h a p t e r

11

OPERATING PROFITABLY

The restaurant business is largely made up of many small transactions and diverse activities—it is not a business of big deals and long lead times. Transactions are conducted rapidly and often under rushed circumstances. For that reason, it is important to keep tight control over all of your profit centers.

A *profit center* is an activity that, by its efficiency or inefficiency, can increase or decrease the profits of an operation. Typically, there are nine profit centers in a restaurant:

1. Menu planning
2. Purchasing
3. Receiving
4. Storing
5. Issuing
6. Pre-preparation
7. Cooking and production
8. Serving and bartending
9. Cashiering

THE MENU

Because the menu of a restaurant is the hub around which every-thing else revolves, planning it carefully is essential. Cross-utilization of ingredients, equipment, and personnel should be considered so as to minimize the size of the inventory that must be carried and prevent delays in service. Leftovers should be given careful thought—wherever possible, a secondary use for every item on the menu should be planned. For example, one day's leftover roast pork could go into the next day's American chop suey.

CONTROLS

Purchasing the right products in the proper quantities is important; of equal importance is keeping them securely stored until they are used. Food and alcoholic beverages are tempting products that may be pilfered easily if not controlled adequately. In a small restaurant where the owner or a supervisor is always present, it is not necessary to have the level of controls that are required in a large restaurant where, because of its size, things are not always under the watchful eye of the boss.

In large restaurants, where a formal food cost control program is maintained, incoming products are keyed into the computer system or logged into an inventory book as soon as they are put away. The storeroom should be kept locked, only authorized persons should make withdrawals, and all withdrawals should be recorded.

Waste can be reduced significantly in the pre-preparation and cook-ing stages by instituting *standards*. An example of a standard might be to cut eight slices or wedges out of every tomato, or it might be a standard recipe that specifies all of the ingredients and a step-by-step method for producing a menu item. When followed carefully, standard recipes ensure a consistent taste and portion size for all menu items.

Finally, to close the control loop, all money received should be accounted for. The totals of food and beverage items sold, as recorded in the POS system or on a register tape, should match the sum of the money in the cash drawer (after the opening bank is deducted) and the card charges.

PURCHASING WISELY

Purchasing dollars are high-powered dollars because they strongly impact the bottom line of an income statement. For instance, if a restaurant is netting 10 percent profit on sales before taxes, it must take in ten dollars of additional sales to make up for every dollar lost through poor purchasing practices.

Wise purchasing not only involves buying at the right price but buying the right quantities and grades, buying at the right stage of ripeness, and making sure that you receive what you ordered. In general, slow-moving items should be avoided, because money tied up on storeroom shelves gathers dust, not interest, and a restaurant cannot afford to carry dead stock.

Inventory Turnover Rate

It is important to know how your inventory is moving—does it turn over once a week, once a month, or less often? It is imperative to rotate your stock and to turn it over as frequently as possible, because few products improve with age. Following are four reasons why slow-moving or dead stock occurs:

1. Too much of a product was purchased.
2. Ingredients were bought for a product that did not sell well and were never used again.
3. Inventory is not taken regularly, and dead stock goes unnoticed until it spoils.
4. A system of "forced issues," which requires the chef to use up old items, is not practiced.

There are instances when a low turnover rate of an item is intentionally tolerated, such as when fine wines are carried in inventory for their prestige value on the menu. In these cases, a high degree of inventory control can still be maintained simply by removing those items from the calculations and focusing on the vast majority of the stock, which should turn over rapidly.

FIGURE 11.1 *Inventory turnover rate calculation*

Step 1: Calculate the cost of the food consumed.

Beginning food inventory 1/1/07	$ 5,200
Plus: Food purchases 1/1–1/31	13,500
Total food available	$ 18,700
Less: Ending food inventory 1/31/07	(4,300)
Cost of food consumed	$ 14,400

Step 2: Calculate the average food inventory.

Beginning food inventory 1/1/07	$5,200
Plus: Ending food inventory 1/31/07	$4,300
Total	$9,500
Divide by 2 to get average food inventory	$4,750

Step 3: Calculate the inventory turnover rate.

$$\frac{\text{Cost of Food Consumed}}{\text{Average Food Inventory}} = \text{Food Inventory Turnover Rate}$$

$$\frac{\$14,400}{\$4,750} = 3.03 \text{ times}$$

Your *inventory turnover rate* indicates how long it takes to sell the goods that you buy. Put another way, it is the number of times your inventory turns into cash within a given period. The period can be whatever you wish— a week, a month, or longer. However, no longer than one month is recommended between inventories, because it becomes difficult to analyze reasons for discrepancies and take timely action. Figure 11.1 illustrates a three-step method for calculating an inventory turnover rate.

In the preceding example, the food inventory was turned over about three times a month, or every ten days. Turnover rates may vary throughout the year, particularly for seasonal businesses. The optimum rate is the highest number of turnovers you can achieve that still allows you to cover your needs adequately between reorders and gives you a safety margin for emergencies and unexpected increases in sales volume.

Planning Your Initial Inventory

The size of your initial inventory will be based on several factors— the *frequency* with which you plan to reorder, the amount of *storage space* you have (dry storeroom, refrigerator space, and freezer space), your vendors' *delivery schedules,* your *expected sales volume* and the amount of *money* you can afford to tie up in inventory. The inventory of most full-service restaurants is made up of six categories of products:

1. Meats, fish and poultry
2. Fresh fruits and vegetables
3. Dairy products
4. Bakery products
5. Groceries (canned, jarred, and packaged products)
6. Beverages (soft drinks and alcoholic beverages)

Some restaurants buy meats and poultry from one purveyor, while others have specialized purveyors for each type of item. Some meat companies distribute frozen seafood products, but as a rule, fresh fish are sold by specialized seafood vendors. From whom you buy is largely a matter of the availability of vendors and the quantities you purchase.

Nonalcoholic beverages are purchased directly from soft drink bottlers, and alcoholic beverages are purchased from liquor companies (in open states) and from state liquor stores or warehouses (in control states).

Your initial inventory should be based on the production needs of your menu, which in turn should be based on your target clientele's wants and expectations. Care should be taken to avoid stocking many items that have only a one-time use, and when that happens, a plan for using up the leftover quantities should be instituted. The practice of making a chef find a use for the product within a certain period of time is called *forced issues.*

After you have been in operation for a while, you can establish reliable maximum and minimum inventory levels for all items, based on their actual sales history. But until sales trends develop, you must work from estimates.

Most vendors will work closely with new restaurants during their start-up period and try to stock them properly. However, an overzealous salesperson will occasionally overload an account by offering a deal or a volume discount. There is little point in buying more than you need simply to obtain a discount, if you have a tight budget or an alternative use for the money that might yield a greater return.

FIGURE 11.2 *Daily Quotation Market Sheet*

DATE					No. 1185

The Harborside Restaurant and Lounge
Daily Market Quotation Sheet

Date _____

On Hand	Item	Quantity Wanted	Telephone Quotes		
			Vendor	Vendor	Vendor

How to Buy Right

The goal of inventory management is to carry the products that are needed to produce your menu and keep your customers happy, while not tying up your money needlessly. Establishments with a limited menu have a much easier task of selecting their initial inventory than do restaurants with an extensive menu. But even in the case of the extensive menu, over 80 percent of the items in inventory are constant.

Competitive buying is practiced by many restaurants. This entails telephoning two or three vendors early in the morning to get current market prices on items needed for that day and recording them on a quotation sheet like the one shown in Figure 11.2. When all of the desired price quotations have been obtained, the restaurant calls back the vendors from which it has decided to buy and places its orders.

The practice of buying solely because of a lower price is referred to as *cherry picking*. Most buyers cherry pick some items, but choose others on the basis of the vendor's dependability, level of service, and product quality— especially its grade. It is important when cherry picking to compare like items, because a lower price may be attributable to a lesser grade.

It is recommended that restaurants keep some sort of written record of items ordered from distributors—such as a copy of the purchase order shown in Figure 11.3—because the person who receives shipments is not usually the person who placed the order. A written record allows the

FIGURE 11.3 *A typical purchase order used by larger restaurants*

DATE				No. 1185
The Harborside Restaurant and Lounge PURCHASE ORDER				
Please furnish the following—All carriers' charges prepaid				
Qty.	**Unit**	**Description**	**Unit Price**	**Amount**
Received by_____ Purchasing Agent_____				
INVOICE MUST ACCOMPANY MERCHANDISE				

receiver to compare the items shipped with the items ordered and quickly spot substitutions or incorrect items. It also avoids controversy about what was ordered and serves as part of an audit trail for cost control purposes.

Taking a physical inventory periodically is critical to any food control system; it is the basis for calculating your "cost of food consumed" and your "food cost percentage." Unfortunately many small restaurants do not take inventories regularly, because doing so can be time consuming. The process need not be painful, however, if a good inventory sheet is designed such as the one shown in Figure 11.4. A great deal of time is saved if the inventory sheet flows in the same order as the food products

FIGURE 11.4 *A typical food inventory sheet*

<table>
<tr><td colspan="10">The Harborside Restaurant & Lounge
INVENTORY SHEET
Date _____   Taken by _____</td></tr>
<tr><td rowspan="3">Name of Product</td><td rowspan="3">Unit Size</td><td colspan="4">Storage Location</td><td rowspan="3">Total Units</td><td rowspan="3">Unit Cost</td><td rowspan="3">Total Cost</td></tr>
<tr><td>Store Room</td><td>Walk-in Refrig.</td><td>Freezer</td><td>Serving Station</td></tr>
<tr></tr>
<tr><td>FISH</td><td></td><td></td><td></td><td></td><td></td><td></td><td></td><td></td></tr>
<tr><td>MALIBUT</td><td></td><td></td><td></td><td></td><td></td><td></td><td></td><td></td></tr>
<tr><td>MADDOCK</td><td></td><td></td><td></td><td></td><td></td><td></td><td></td><td></td></tr>
<tr><td>LOBSTERS</td><td></td><td></td><td></td><td></td><td></td><td></td><td></td><td></td></tr>
<tr><td>SALMON</td><td></td><td></td><td></td><td></td><td></td><td></td><td></td><td></td></tr>
<tr><td>SOLE FILLET</td><td></td><td></td><td></td><td></td><td></td><td></td><td></td><td></td></tr>
<tr><td>SHRIMP</td><td></td><td></td><td></td><td></td><td></td><td></td><td></td><td></td></tr>
<tr><td>MEAT</td><td></td><td></td><td></td><td></td><td></td><td></td><td></td><td></td></tr>
<tr><td>RIB-EYE STEAKS</td><td></td><td></td><td></td><td></td><td></td><td></td><td></td><td></td></tr>
<tr><td>TENDERLOIN</td><td></td><td></td><td></td><td></td><td></td><td></td><td></td><td></td></tr>
<tr><td>SIRL. TOP BUTTS</td><td></td><td></td><td></td><td></td><td></td><td></td><td></td><td></td></tr>
<tr><td>PORK CHOPS</td><td></td><td></td><td></td><td></td><td></td><td></td><td></td><td></td></tr>
<tr><td>BRISKET</td><td></td><td></td><td></td><td></td><td></td><td></td><td></td><td></td></tr>
<tr><td>GROUND BEEF</td><td></td><td></td><td></td><td></td><td></td><td></td><td></td><td></td></tr>
<tr><td>POULTRY</td><td></td><td></td><td></td><td></td><td></td><td></td><td></td><td></td></tr>
<tr><td>TURKEY BREASTS</td><td></td><td></td><td></td><td></td><td></td><td></td><td></td><td></td></tr>
<tr><td>CHIX. BREASTS</td><td></td><td></td><td></td><td></td><td></td><td></td><td></td><td></td></tr>
<tr><td>PRODUCE</td><td></td><td></td><td></td><td></td><td></td><td></td><td></td><td></td></tr>
<tr><td>BAKE POTATOES</td><td></td><td></td><td></td><td></td><td></td><td></td><td></td><td></td></tr>
<tr><td>LETTUCE, ICEBERG</td><td></td><td></td><td></td><td></td><td></td><td></td><td></td><td></td></tr>
<tr><td>TOMATOES</td><td></td><td></td><td></td><td></td><td></td><td></td><td></td><td></td></tr>
<tr><td>CELERY</td><td></td><td></td><td></td><td></td><td></td><td></td><td></td><td></td></tr>
<tr><td>CARROTS</td><td></td><td></td><td></td><td></td><td></td><td></td><td></td><td></td></tr>
<tr><td colspan="6">Page 1 of _____Pgs.</td><td colspan="3">SUB TOTAL _____</td></tr>
</table>

are arranged on the storeroom shelves. It is also helpful if the number of locations where food is stored is kept to a minimum.

RECEIVING, STORING, AND ISSUING

The person who receives shipments of food and beverages should check all products to make sure that the proper items were delivered. Cases should be opened; weighed or counted; and at least spot-checked for spoilage, inferior quality, or damage before the receiving clerk signs the delivery slip. Products should be checked while the delivery driver is present and recorded on a receiving clerk's report (see Figure 11.5). A commercial scale should be used for weighing incoming products, and everyone should stand back from the scale when it is being read. Delivery drivers soon get to know who checks their incoming products and who doesn't.

FIGURE 11.5 *A receiver's sheet used for recording incoming deliveries*

The Harborside Restaurant & Lounge No. _____

RECEIVER'S REPORT Date _____

Received by _____

| | | | | | | | | Distribution to | | |
| | | | | | | | | Kitchen | | |
Purveyor	Qty.	Unit Size	Description	√	Unit Price	Amount	Total Amount	Refr	Frzr	Storeroom

FIGURE 11.6 *A form like this one should be used when merchandise is received without a bill.*

					BI1860

The Harborside Restaurant and Lounge
MERCHANDISE RECEIVED WITHOUT BILL
Please send us a bill for the following items.

From: _____   Date: _____

_____

Quantity	Item	Amount

Total

Delivery Driver: _____   By: _____

From time to time, a shipment may arrive without the appropriate delivery slip. In such an event, a Merchandise Received without Bill form (Figure 11.6) should be filled out and signed by the delivery truck driver and the receiver. This acknowledges the quantity and type of goods that were actually received and avoids the possibility of confusion at a later date.

If incorrect merchandise must be returned, a Request for Credit Memo (Figure 11.7) should be signed by the truck driver when you relinquish the goods. In the past, when delivery slips were written by hand, it was possible to scratch out a returned item and retotal the slip. Today, with computerized billing, it does no good simply to change a delivery slip; the data must be entered into the vendor's computer. The Request for Credit Memo is proof that an incorrect item was indeed returned for credit and serves as a source document for a credit entry into the vendor's computer. It also serves as a reminder to the buyer's accounting department to make sure that the credit comes through at the end of the month.

FIGURE 11.7 *Credit memos stipulate the reason for a return of merchandise and serve as a follow-up reminder to check on credits.*

		B11860
	The Harborside Restaurant and Lounge	
	REQUEST FOR CREDIT MEMO	
	Please send us a credit memo for the following	

To: _____   Date: _____

_____

Quantity	Item	Amount
	Total	

Delivery Driver: _____   By: _____

Incoming shipments should be put away immediately after the products are received. For best shelf life, raw meats should be put into refrigerated storage of about 32°F to 34°F, and perishable vegetables should be put into refrigerated storage of about 40°F. Frozen foods should be placed quickly into a 0°F (or sub-zero) freezer. Nonperishable canned, jarred, and packaged products (known as *dry stores*) should be placed into a dry storeroom and keyed into the computer system, logged into an inventory book or on stock record cards (see Figure 11.8).

A storeroom should have a moderate temperature and be well lit, ventilated, and dry. It should also have a secure door lock. All food items should be placed on shelves or on pallets, as appropriate. Many small restaurants operate with an open storeroom, but large ones commonly have a controlled storeroom.

Liquor storerooms should always be locked. The issuance of liquor storeroom keys is a matter of company policy, but the fewer the keys, the

FIGURE 11.8 *Stock record cards are hung on bins or shelves. They indicate additions and withdrawals to stock as well as the current balance.*

The Harborside Restaurant and Lounge STOCK RECORD CARD											
Item: _____											
Purveyor: _____											
Max: _____ Article: _____ Size: _____ Unit Cost: _____											
Min: _____ Location: _____ Unit: _____ Cost per Oz.:_____											
Date	In	Out	Bal.	Date	In	Out	Bal.	Date	In	Out	Bal.	

less risk of misuse. Usually, liquor storeroom keys are issued only to one or two employees who need to access it regularly.

Storeroom shelving should be varied and spaced well enough to accommodate all the items. Modular shelving offers flexibility to change shelf spacing as needed with relative ease. The uppermost shelves should be easily reachable and used for lighter-weight products, while lower ones are best used for heavier or hard-to-grasp items. Every product carried should have a specific storage location on the shelves that matches its location on the inventory sheet. This practice significantly reduces the time required to take inventory.

A record should be kept of all products removed from the storeroom. This may be done with a requisition form (Figure 11.9), which the ordering department fills out and turns in to the storeroom whenever something is needed. This procedure helps to control both the food storeroom and the liquor storeroom. In the case of alcoholic beverages, it also helps to keep the par stock at the bar at the desired level. (The term *par stock* is described in detail in Chapter 8.) A *bottle-for-bottle*

FIGURE 11.9 *Requisitions provide a record of the items issued from the storeroom and the person who ordered them.*

The Harborside Restaurant and Lounge
REQUISITION

Date: _____ , 20 ___

_____Department

Issued to the undersigned.

No. 1234   Signed _____

                                                   Department _____

exchange system, whereby empty bottles are replaced with full ones of the same brand and size, should be practiced in conjunction with the use of requisition slips.

USING STANDARDIZED RECIPES

Customers want consistency every time they order an item. Variations in taste, portion size, and plate presentation are not infrequent occurrences in many restaurants. Such inconsistencies can annoy customers and can also be costly to the restaurant.

Such problems may be avoided, however, by developing standardized recipes for all items served on your menu and making sure that all employees adhere to them. A *standardized recipe* specifies the ingredients to be used, the step-by-step method by which a product will be produced, the portion size, and the way it will be presented on the plate. The main advantages of using standardized recipes are:

- They ensure high-quality products all day, every day.
- They are helpful when training new employees.

- They reduce overproduction and waste.
- They allow for more accurate accounting of costs and sales.

FOOD PRODUCTION PLANNING

Overproduction is wasteful and costly and results in excessive left-overs. For those reasons, it is important to plan the quantities of food to be produced each day. A production-planning system involves only three things, all of which can be programmed into a computer system or maintained manually:

1. A sales history
2. A forecast of the quantities of each item to be produced
3. A comparison of the forecasted amounts with the actual results of the day

A *sales history* is a count of how many of each item on the menu was sold on a given day. The count is related to the total customers who were served that day. A *popularity index* is then calculated, based on the average number of the item sold over the last 60 days, as shown in Figure 11.10. A history should be kept for all items on the menu—appetizers, salads, entrees, and desserts. After the forecasted day has transpired, the actual results of that

FIGURE 11.10 *Example of how a sales history tracks the percentage of the total number of guests that tend to order each item on the menu. That percentage is the item's popularity index.*

	Sales History			
	60 Day Avg.		**Wed., April 23**	
Entrees	**# Sold**	**Popularity Index**	**# Sold**	**Popularity Index**
Surf and Turf	42	20%	43	21%
Baked Stuffed Haddock	60	30%	63	31%
Chicken Marsala	71	35%	70	35%
Lamb Kabob	29	15%	25	13%
Total	202	100%	201	100%

FIGURE 11.11 *The sales forecast projects how many people are expected to order each item, based on the percentage of total guests who have ordered that item in the past.*

Sales Forecast: Wednesday, April 30			
	# of Customers Expected	Popularity Index	# of Items Forecast
Surf and Turf	209	21%	44
Baked Stuffed Haddock	209	30%	63
Chicken Marsala	209	33%	69
Lamb Kabob	209	16%	33
		Total	209

day should be posted to the sales history chart, as was done for Wednesday, April 23 in the sample history to keep the history up to-date.

A sales forecast can be calculated by multiplying the number of guests estimated for the day being planned by the popularity index obtained from the sales history. This is done for each item on the menu, as shown in Figure 11.11. In this example, 209 customers are estimated on April 30.

The popularity index should be based on a meaningful period of time—60 days is often used. A single week's figures would not be adequate, because they can be distorted by bad weather or competing events that may not recur on the day you are projecting.

Because comparing normally busy days with normally quiet days would be meaningless, a separate sales history should be kept for each day of the week—Tuesdays should be compared with Tuesdays and Saturdays with Saturdays.

The last step in the process is to update the 60-day average popularity index by dropping the oldest day and adding the latest one.

SUPERVISION IS IMPORTANT

It is easy to relax and not look for problems when things appear to be going well. That is why some restaurant owners lose sizable sums of money each year, without realizing it is happening. A lax operator may never know just how profitable the business might have been, if only better controls had been maintained. Profit leaks can occur from mistakes, waste, and dishonest practices. To plug the leaks, control procedures should be installed in all profit centers, and close supervision should be initiated to ensure that the procedures are being carried out.

Following is a list of situations that can cause a restaurant to lose profits. They are correctable but not until management realizes that they exist.

- Not obtaining competitive prices before placing orders with vendors
- Excessive buying—carrying too much stock in relation to sales volume (tying up working capital that could be better used)
- Not securing the storerooms and taking precautions to prevent theft
- Not following up on credits for merchandise that was returned because of damage or that was back-ordered
- Not taking advantage of discounts for payment on time—the result is the same as overpaying for products
- Not checking invoices and payments against receiving records to detect any shortages, back orders, or incorrect prices
- Not safeguarding the keys to the storeroom by making them available only to responsible persons whose duties require access
- Not using standard portion tools, such as ladles, scoops, and measuring cups and spoons to ensure proper portion sizes
- Letting leftover foods spoil by not covering and refrigerating them quickly
- Not keeping a daily record of food items sold to compare with the quantity of food consumed that day
- Overstaffing by scheduling extra kitchen staff and waitstaff when not needed
- Not keeping adequate sales records to track customer menu preference trends
- Making menus so complicated as to be confusing to customers and dampen sales
- Not buying products in consistent sizes and consequently applying incorrect values when taking inventory

- Failing to record additions to and subtractions from inventory accurately in the computer system, in a perpetual inventory book, or on bin cards
- Allowing excessive spoilage due to mishandling products and not having a management person verify spoilage when it occurs
- Not taking a complete physical inventory at frequent intervals to calculate the food and beverage cost percentages and also to reconcile the computer or perpetual inventory book figures with the actual stock on hand
- Failing to take corrective action quickly when the cause of a problem is discovered
- Failing to orient and train new employees properly
- Not assigning clear responsibility for inventory control to any one management person
- Not using a system of forced issues to get rid of very slow-moving items when cash flow needs improvement
- Cooks not adhering to standard recipes
- Improperly pricing menu items and thus not yielding the desired food cost percentage
- Not staffing properly and thus not capitalizing on rush-hour potential
- Allowing unauthorized removal of products from premises by employees and delivery people who enter the establishment unsupervised
- Failing to advertise specials effectively
- Failing to meet customers' wants and expectations in regard to the menu items offered
- Not establishing standard house policies and explaining them to all personnel

Observers of the retail industry indicate that pilferage is a major problem and acknowledge that employees represent a significant segment of the pilferers. Unfortunately, the restaurant industry is no exception to this indictment.

Products or services can be given away, customers can be overcharged or undercharged, or products can be rung but not recorded. The list of possibilities is lengthy. How then can management deal with the problem? The answer is to hire the best employees possible, train them well, maintain tight controls, and—above all—supervise them closely.

The object of a good security program is to keep people honest. This can be done by removing temptations, setting policies and standards for conduct, and letting people know their actions are being observed. These are important deterrents to dishonest practices, but the first line of defense is to interview applicants thoroughly, check their references carefully, and hire only the best people available. Be wary of applicants who do the following:

- Show impatience with answering questions.
- Appear untidy or seem to have a dependency that could affect their job performance.
- Behave unprofessionally or overfriendly during an interview.

Beware of the applicant who brags about all the famous places they have worked. An unusually long list of previous employers may indicate the applicant could not hold a job for very long.

ENTERTAINMENT

Restaurants sometimes put entertainment in their dining room or lounge as a business builder. Good entertainment can attract new customers and keep your existing customers from drifting to competitors, but not all entertainment is good. In fact, ineffective entertainment can drive customers away and be a financial drain on your business. When considering adding entertainment, you should ask yourself the following questions:

- What type of entertainment best fits my restaurant's format?
- Do I have excess seating capacity? Can I accommodate additional volume with my present facilities?
- Are my competitors using entertainment successfully? If so, what kind?
- Are my customers asking for a certain type of entertainment, or in the case of a new restaurant, will my target market expect it?

Three types of entertainment may be considered for a restaurant lounge: individual performers, bands or groups, and mechanical background music. Mechanical background music includes jukeboxes and tape or wireless systems. It is the least expensive type and, when supplied by a jukebox, can be an income producer. Individual performers, such as piano and guitar players, are the next least expensive. If they are good, they can add a distinctively pleasant quality to a lounge. But be aware that poor entertainment, or entertainment that does not match well with your guests' expectations, can have negative consequences. Bands can be good attractions if they are popular; however, the more popular they are, the more expensive they are. Bands are better suited to high-volume venues with large promotional budgets.

Entertainment should be evaluated regularly to determine if it is attracting business. Ask the following questions:

- Are sales increasing?
- Is it attracting the type of clientele I am seeking?
- Are profits increasing as a result of the addition of entertainment?

How to Calculate Your Break-Even Point for Entertainment

Assume that your restaurant lounge has excess capacity. That is, on certain nights of the week, you have lots of empty seats. This concerns you, because your overhead costs go on whether the house is half filled or jam-packed. Consequently, you could increase your business volume without incurring any additional overhead costs.

Let us assume that you decide to offer entertainment to attract more people on slow nights, so you hire a piano player. In addition, you run an advertisement in the local newspaper to let the community know that you have entertainment.

Your main concern at this point is that the entertainment, at the very least, pays its own way—it must break even. If it does not do that, it will not have accomplished its intended purpose of increasing business, instead actually draining your profits further.

The following example illustrates how you can calculate a break-even point for entertainment. Let's also assume that you operate with a 22 percent pouring cost (i.e., 22 cents out of each dollar of liquor sales goes to pay for the liquor required to make the drink).

If sales increase by $2,244, the lounge will have taken in just enough additional money to break even. The increase will cover the cost of the liquor in the additional drinks sold, the cost of the advertisement, and the piano player's fee. There would be neither a profit nor a loss at this point. Hopefully, as the entertainment catches on, sales will increase substantially above the break-even point and produce profits.

Step 1: Determine the total cost of the entertainment.

Cost of piano player ($200 × 4 nights)	$800
Cost of advertisement	950
Total Cost	**$1,750**

Step 2: Establish your contribution margin.

100% – Pouring Cost Percentage = Contribution Margin

100% – 22% = 78%

Step 3: Calculate your break-even point.

Total Cost ÷ Contribution Margin = Break-even Point

$1,750 ÷ .78 = $2,244 Break-even Point

EQUIPMENT MAINTENANCE

An effective maintenance program more than pays for itself. It can help avoid accidents, reduce downtime, and add dollars to your profit line.

It makes sense to keep your equipment in top shape. Reducing equipment repairs is another key to making greater profits. Aside from the fact that repair calls are expensive, it is hard to find good service technicians. Here are five steps for developing a sound equipment maintenance program:

1. *Announce it.* Explain to all employees the need for the program and the benefits it will bring. Unless everyone cooperates, the program will not work well.
2. *Set up records.* Create a file folder, either in a drawer or on your computer, for every piece of major equipment. Each folder should contain the name of the product, the manufacturer's name, the model year, the style, the warrantee form, the service agency's name and contact information, a record of service calls with costs and dates, the specification sheets, and the owner's operating manual. Much of the product information can be downloaded from manufacturers' Web sites.

3. *Follow a check list.* Formalize the program by developing a check list for inspections. With such a list, no piece of equipment is overlooked, and the right things are looked at.
4. *List the procedures.* Develop a set of maintenance procedures for each piece of equipment. They should be readily available and easy to understand. Keep a spare set in a safe place—you can be sure one will get lost.
5. *Assign responsibility.* Assign the responsibility for equipment inspection to a specific person. The frequency and extent of inspections should be clearly understood.

A good maintenance program lets employees know that the restaurant cares, and as a result, employees will strive to ensure its success. Management must, of course, set the tone by keeping the program updated and by providing the necessary tools and supplies to properly maintain the equipment.

Action Guidelines

☐ Obtain food and beverage lists from distributors and select initial inventories.

☐ Create an inventory sheet that includes all of your food and beverage stock for taking physical inventories.

☐ Keep a perpetual inventory of all items carried. Once set up, this can be done easily on a computer spreadsheet.

☐ Demonstrate your understanding of turnover rates by calculating the food turnover rate for a restaurant with the figures shown below:

Beginning inventory 11/1	$3,800
Purchases 11/1–11/30	9,200
Ending inventory 11/30	4,100

☐ Develop a sales history sheet to track the popularity of items on your menu.

☐ Forecast your production needs from week to week by using the popularity indexes developed with your sales history sheet.

12

MANAGING YOUR PERSONNEL

Wages and employee benefits together constitute the biggest expense on the profit and loss statements of many restaurants, and dealing with personnel matters is one of the more frustrating aspects of a manager's job.

Why is this so? Not just because payroll costs keep creeping upward. To a great extent, it is because the food service industry has a high labor turnover rate—employees are constantly coming and going in some jobs—and high turnover is costly.

WHAT KEEPS CUSTOMERS COMING BACK

The way a waitperson approaches a customer, presents menu information, answers questions, and makes the customer feel welcome has a great influence on how often that customer will return.

Equally important is the work of employees that the customer does not see, the workers in the back of the house. An inferior meal, soiled utensils, or an unclean restroom may irritate a customer to the point that they will not return. Usually, disgruntled customers will try another restaurant, and if they have a pleasant experience there, you may never see them again.

The true cost of a lost customer is often minimized by statements like, "You can't win them all," but a lost customer does in fact mean significant lost revenue. For example, if a restaurant loses a regular customer who brings a guest once a week and spends an average of $50 each visit, the establishment has a potential revenue loss of approximately $26,000 over a ten-year period. Unfortunately, most restaurateurs have no idea how many customers they have lost, because people rarely complain to management—they just disappear.

Essential to ensuring excellent customer service is to maintain high morale and low turnover among your employees.

EMPLOYEE RETENTION AND TURNOVER

Management must realize that the true cost of labor turnover is higher than generally thought, so it must institute initiatives that enhance labor retention. Everyone wins when a restaurant staff is stable. To achieve stability, a restaurant must train its employees well, give them the right tools to work with, pay them adequately, and strive to use them to the fullest of their abilities.

High Labor Turnover—A Clue to Greater Problems

The rate at which employees terminate employment may be a clue to problem areas that need attention. Labor turnover has a significant impact on the profitability of a restaurant, because the true cost of replacing employees is very high. Turnover costs include the following:

- The cost of exit interviewing time
- The hidden cost of lost production, due to lower morale among the remaining employees who have to pick up the slack
- The cost of advertising job openings
- The cost of time spent interviewing new candidates
- The cost of training new employees
- The cost of additional waste while the new employees learn their jobs
- Possibly an unemployment compensation tax increase

To calculate a labor turnover rate, divide the number of employees that terminated employment during a given period by the number of jobs in the restaurant and multiply the result by 100.

$$\frac{\text{\# of employees who terminated}}{\text{\# of jobs}} \times 100 = \text{labor turnover rate}$$

For example, if a restaurant had 11 of its 42 employees terminate employment last year, its labor turnover rate would be 26.2 percent.

$$\frac{11}{42} \times 100 = 26.2\%$$

Slowing Down the Revolving Door

Employees need to experience growth in their jobs by being given greater responsibility and recognition. For example, a dishwasher can be challenged to reduce the rate of dish breakage. When it is lowered, the employee should be recognized for the achievement and be told that if the reduction is maintained for, say, three or six months, it will be rewarded with a bonus. This way, the employee participates in the savings without elevating the regular payroll, and the restaurant benefits by lowering its dish breakage expense.

Employees will develop a sense of pride and stay longer if they feel they are doing a good job and are appreciated, and those feelings translate to more productivity than if the employee is demoralized. Most importantly, the restaurant's clientele will be better served.

Although waitstaff and bartenders are the only ones who have actual contact with customers, all employees of a restaurant need to know the importance of their role in the process of satisfying customers. They must be cultivated into the culture of the restaurant, and when the pride of the brand becomes the pride of its employees, the revolving door will slow down and the restaurant's profitability will rise.

Following are a few suggestions for improving pride, performance, and loyalty; your imagination can produce more. The prizes may be monetary or in benefits or even symbolic, such as the recognition of employees in front of their peers.

- Use personal incentives, such as generating publicity articles and commercials that feature a chef's skills and accomplishments.
- Create awards, such as a "Rising to the Occasion Award" for unusually fine performance in a difficult situation.
- Give employees customized restaurant T-shirts to create a community spirit.
- Recognize exemplary attendance and punctuality.
- Have a holiday party for employees and families. Let employees participate in the planning and give gifts to children.
- Send cards when you find out that an employee's family member is ill or a baby is born.

Such recognition is not a substitute for money and benefits, but if employees are also being paid fairly, it does give them great satisfaction, and they will be apt to stay in your employ longer.

HOW TO GET THE MOST OUT OF YOUR PERSONNEL

Management should develop clear and reasonable policies and explain them to all employees so that everyone knows exactly what is expected of them. Getting the most out of employees begins with hiring the best people you can afford. Also, you must do the following:

- Train them properly.
- Provide them with up-to-date equipment that is safe and increases efficiency.
- Supervise them carefully.
- Let them know that you care about how things are done.
- Solicit ideas for improvement from them and let them know that they are important to the organization.

Payroll Analysis

Restaurants are vulnerable to seasonal ups and downs—consequently, employers must react quickly to changes in sales to avert losses. Overstaffing and low productivity are major threats to profitability. It is important to measure productivity at regular intervals, because it can get out of line quickly.

Employee productivity can be rated on three measurements:

1. The number of customers served (covers) per employee
   covers per employee = covers served ÷ # of employees
2. Sales dollars generated per employee
   sales per employee = sales ÷ # of employees
3. Sales per hour worked
   sales per hour worked = sales ÷ actual hours worked

FIGURE 12.1 *Illustration of a process for analyzing weekly payroll and evaluating employee efficiency*

Payroll Analysis								
Date: Week of	Sales	Covers Served	Number of Employees	Actual Hours Worked	Payroll	Covers per Employee	Sales per Employee	Sales per Hour Worked
Jun 2	$20,500	2,344	18	730	$2,550	130	$1,139	$28.08
Jun 9	$18,640	2,110	19	750	2,458	111	981	24.85
Jun 16	$16,580	2,045	20	790	2,556	102	825	20.98
Jun 23	$15,850	2,084	21	805	2,610	99	755	19.69
Jun 30	$20,950	2,550	21	848	2,706	121	998	24.71

Orientation for New Employees

New employees should be informed immediately of what you expect of them and what they may expect of you. Orientation sessions should be well planned if you wish to convey the same information to all employees in a clear and consistent way. The content of the sessions will vary with the type and size of organization, but certain kinds of information are of interest to all employees. Following is a check list of topics that might be covered in an orientation:

- History of the establishment
- Who the owner is

- Who the management personnel are and who the employee reports to and takes orders from
- Hours, including the regular workweek and when and where the schedule is posted
- Vacation policy, including how much time is given, when, and how to request time off
- Overtime policy, including if it is allowed and who authorizes it
- Holiday work policy
- Smoking and coffee break policies
- Compensation, including the hourly rate, deductions, payday, and tip income-reporting requirements
- Fringe benefits, including insurance, sick days, etc.
- Meals, if applicable, including when and what items
- Absenteeism and tardiness policy
- How to call in, in case of emergency, including when and whom to call (with phone numbers)
- Probationary period and warning policies
- How training will occur, including when, where, by whom, and how long
- Employee evaluation and advancement policies
- Lost guest check policy
- How to handle customer complaints
- Breakage policy
- Portion control policy
- Dress code, including who will supply uniforms, if required, and how many
- Who will launder uniforms
- Deposits, if required for uniforms
- Appearance of employee, including fingernails and cleanliness
- Policy on jewelry, hair restraints, and types of shoes
- Tour of establishment, including:
  - Where things are
  - Where to park
  - Which restrooms to use and where they are
  - Where to enter and leave the establishment
  - Where employees' lockers are (if any)

- Actions that may result in termination of employment
- Personal behavior, including the consequences for profanity and vulgar actions
- Personal phone call policy
- Policy on patronizing the establishment before or after work hours
- What to do in case of accidents or fire
- Use of safety guards on equipment

Some items need only be touched upon, while others may need to be discussed in detail. In any case, you should clearly explain the policies that apply and give employees an opportunity to ask questions—this may avert problems later on.

Training Your Employees

An often-made mistake is to turn a new employee over to a present employee for training. The problem with that practice is that bad habits can be passed on by the present employee to the new person. Besides that, it is said that less than 80 percent of an employee's knowledge tends to get passed on in such training situations. Consequently, if an establishment has a high labor turnover rate, the amount of original information passed on will dwindle drastically.

This dilemma may be alleviated by giving present workers instructions on how to train others. A four-step method of training that has been used very effectively by manufacturing industries can also be used by the food service field:

1. Show the employee how to do the task. Demonstrate it.
2. Simultaneously, tell the employee what you are doing and why you are doing it.
3. Let the employee do it once or twice, under supervision. If the employee does it right, allow the employee to continue on their own.
4. Check back periodically to make sure the employee continues to do the task properly.

This technique is effective with tasks such as computer training, where numerous small but easy-to-forget steps are involved. Most restaurants try to hire employees with training and experience. But even with such a background, they need to learn your policies and procedures.

In addition to providing training, management has a responsibility to provide the necessary equipment to do a job properly. It is unacceptable for employees to be producing inferior products simply because they lack the proper tools. Another impediment to doing good work is a poorly laid-out work center. The physical arrangement of a restaurant kitchen should allow safe and efficient movement for workers. It should also be well lit and ventilated. Any of these features, if not properly planned, can adversely affect productivity and profits.

REPORTING TIP INCOME

As an employer, you have a responsibility to report tips received by employees in accordance with IRS regulations.

Employees who customarily receive tips are required to report their cash tips to their employers at least monthly, if they receive $20 or more in the month. *Cash tips* are tips received directly in cash or by check and charged tips. You have a liability to withhold and pay Social Security and Medicare tax on your employees' reported tips, to the extent that wages or other employee funds are available. If the employee does not report tips to you, you are at risk of possible assessment of the employer's share of the Social Security and Medicare taxes on the unreported tips.

If you are a large food or beverage establishment—more than ten employees work on a typical day, and food or beverages are consumed on the premises—you are required to allocate tips if the total tips reported to you are less than 8 percent of gross sales. Report the allocated amount on the employee's W-2 at the end of the year.

If the employees are reporting more than the 8 percent, there is no allocated tip amount. However, the employer must still file Form 8027, "Employer's Annual Information Return of Tip Income and Allocated Tips."

This is a partial summary of tip reporting, intended only to alert you to the existence of such requirements. For complete details on reporting tip income, refer to IRS Publication 531, "Reporting Tip Income," and consult your certified public accountant.

INITIAL INTERVIEWS

It pays for a restaurant to hire the best people it can afford. Applicants should be interviewed carefully to avoid hiring individuals who will not last long. It is not worth investing in training people who may leave soon. Such departures can have a demoralizing affect on the remaining staff and negatively affect customer service. Ask applicants about their future plans and their reasons for wanting this job. Beware, as well, of people who have unexplained gaps in the chronology of their work experience: seek explanations.

EXIT INTERVIEWS

Reasons for an employee's departure that might have been avoided will often be revealed in an exit interview. Exit interviews can clue management in to needed changes. For example, sometimes an employee leaves a job because it is boring. Knowing this, management may be able to restructure the job to make it more interesting for the next person.

On occasion, employees leave a job because they see another employee doing something that they disapprove of and do not want to become involved in. Exit interviews can sometimes reveal information that would otherwise be difficult to obtain, because employees don't like to be "tattletales."

HOW TO GAIN YOUR EMPLOYEES' COOPERATION

Cooperative and loyal employees are the most important assets a business can have. Regrettably, most restaurants do not have many such employees—often because supervisory personnel do not realize that cooperation must be earned, not dictated. Employees listen more attentively and perform better for a good leader.

The good news is that leadership qualities can be learned. A good leader treats employees fairly and leads by example. Here are five ways to win cooperation from your employees:

1. Make your employees *want* to cooperate with you. The old notion of demanding cooperation does not work. Instead, try the following:
   - Let them know what you are asking of them and why.
   - Let them know how they can personally benefit by working toward the accomplishment of your objectives. For example, their job may become safer or more efficient.
   - Appeal to their professional pride and desire to be on a winning team.
2. Have an open mind and be receptive to employees' suggestions and views. They are closest to their job and, on occasion, may reveal useful information. Listening to them shows you are concerned and sympathetic, even when you have to say no.
3. Acknowledge a job well done, particularly on an undesirable task—it is a good way of winning an employee's cooperation the next time you need to get a tough job done. If it is honest praise, it is important that you give it, because the employee knows they deserve it.
4. Avoid arguments with employees. Time has a calming effect—use it. Let the employee tell their side of the story and acknowledge that you heard it and understand what they said. Then arrange a time to discuss it. Just a few minutes is often enough time for tempers to settle. Even the thorniest problems can be dealt with more easily when the parties are in control of their emotions.
5. Do not hesitate to admit an error on your part. It will not change your status or authority. Instead, it will humanize you in the eyes of your staff.

WAYS TO IMPROVE EMPLOYEE MORALE

Low morale inevitably leads to poor work habits, excessive waste, accidents—and lost profits. An effective manager keeps close watch on the morale of the organization and takes corrective action quickly if it declines. Low morale is usually the manifestation of a problem; therefore, the underlying problem should be identified as soon as possible.

Some jobs, because of their long hours and weekend and holiday work schedules are not conducive to normal family routines or a personal life, and these jobs have a higher turnover rate. However, with a bit of creative thinking and the implementation of flextime, an employee's arrival or departure time might be adjusted to accommodate a day care schedule, for example, or a transportation problem might be solved. Lowering the turnover rate in those jobs can reduce labor costs noticeably.

Some ways to improve morale are:

- Try to find out what every employee's strength or special skill is and, when possible, provide the opportunity to make use of it.
- Be responsive to employees' concerns. You may not agree with them, but do not try to avoid them. If the complaints are valid, they won't go away. In any case, explain the reasons for your thinking.
- Provide employees with the environment to do a good job. This not only includes the proper tools but also sanitary and safe equipment, lighting, sound control, and physical comforts (such as rubber floor mats on a hard tile floor).
- Do not ignore false rumors. Debunking them quickly will set employees at ease.
- Discuss the impact of any proposed changes as soon as possible with the employees who will be affected, so that baseless rumors do not get started.
- Let your employees know how they are doing. Employees often believe they are overlooked when they do something good but are immediately reprimanded when they make a mistake. Try to eradicate that notion by giving them positive feedback when deserved and suggestions on how to correct their deficiencies when needed.
- Be firm but fair—make reasonable assignments and enforce rules in an impartial manner.
- Work through your chain of command—don't undercut your supervisors by throwing your weight around or by dealing directly with subordinate employees.
- Create a comfortable break room for employees, where they can relax and eat with some music or TV. It needn't be fancy, just clean and comfortable, to improve morale.

- Be aware of seven statements that, when uttered with sincerity in appropriate situations, can help to improve morale immensely:
  1. "Please."
  2. "Thank you."
  3. "Can I help?"
  4. "You did a fine job."
  5. "What do you folks think?"
  6. "I'm sorry. I made a mistake."
  7. "I realize it was not your fault."

KEEP THE LINES OF COMMUNICATION OPEN

Allow your employees to communicate with you. A good practice is to hold employee meetings where they have a chance to offer constructive ideas. Discuss problems such as high food cost percentages, adverse customer comments, and critical health inspector's reports. These kinds of issues can be solved better in an atmosphere of cooperation, where employees are allowed input.

Keep the meetings brief and businesslike—have a written agenda ready and be organized but not intimidating. Think of the meetings as a two-way street with information flowing from you to them and from them to you.

Employees frequently hide the real reasons for their behavior or poor performance. Fears, jealousies, antagonisms, and misunderstandings among employees are often reflected in flashes of anger or mood swings that result in poor job performance. Such behavior may also be visible—and objectionable—to customers; consequently, it cannot be allowed to continue.

When such a situation occurs, bring both parties together, confront the issue, and let them know how it is affecting their work. Seek agreement from both parties on the resolution of the problem. Here are some strategies for dealing with such situations:

- Appear impartial as you listen patiently to both sides of the story before judging.
- Be tactful as you explain the reasons for your decision.
- Try to end the discussion on a positive note, leaving no doubt that the situation must improve.

FIGURE 12.2 *Job description for a chef*

Chef

Summary

Responsible to the owner. Oversees the day-to-day operations of the back of the house. Responsible for carrying out company policies and performing the following duties: menu planning, purchasing, hiring and training new employees, supervising and motivating staff, filling in as needed for cooks, performing cost control functions, and maintaining a high level of quality and service in all aspects of the operation.

Responsibilities

1. Performs all assigned duties and responsibilities according to company policies and reports to the owner in a timely and efficient manner.

2. Develops menus.

3. Prices all menu items.

4. Establishes portion sizes.

5. Obtains competitive prices for items to be bought from purveyors.

6. Purchases products necessary to satisfy menu requirements and customers' expectations.

7. Responsible for cost control programs in the areas of payroll, food, beverages, supplies, and utilities, so that maximum quality is obtained at minimum cost.

8. Coordinates service for functions.

9. Supervises and motivates employees.

10. Inspects kitchen operations regularly for cleanliness and proper functioning of equipment.

11. Monitors all production stations during rush periods to ensure that production is flowing properly.

12. Assists, as needed, in all capacities and handles customers' complaints.

13. Schedules kitchen employees so as to ensure high-quality service, while containing payroll cost within an established percentage range.

14. Responsible for hiring and terminating employees, processing time cards, conducting evaluations, and holding kitchen staff meetings, as necessary.

15. Responsible for safety and security systems in the back of the house.

16. Responsible for compliance with sanitation codes in all areas.

17. Responsible for taking inventories and calculating food cost percentages.

How to Use Job Descriptions

Job descriptions may by used for several purposes—among them to communicate the duties of a job for which a person is being hired and to tell how management wants those duties performed. Although job descriptions may exist for all jobs, it is rare for them to be shown to hourly employees when they are hired. This is unfortunate, because every new employee can benefit from knowing what is expected.

Job descriptions can also serve as check lists when training new employees. For a sample job description with a composite list of typical duties and responsibilities, see Figure 12.2, a job description for a chef. As with all jobs, the duties of a chef will vary depending on the size and type of restaurant and the degree of autonomy the owner grants to the chef.

Action Guidelines

☐ Prepare job descriptions for the following jobs:

cook	baker
salad maker	general kitchen worker
dishwasher	

☐ Design an appropriate form to be used for weekly payroll analysis.
☐ Develop a personnel manual to be given to new employees.
☐ Outline a check list of questions to be used as an interview guide.
☐ Construct an employment application.

13

MAINTAINING FINANCIAL CONTROL

There is a big difference between appearing to do well and actually generating the kinds of returns that a restaurant may be capable of producing. Likewise, it is not unheard of for a restaurant that seemed to be doing well by all outward signs to fail. Such occurrences often result from a lack of understanding of financial controls. It is not necessary to be an accountant to operate a restaurant successfully, but owners and managers must be familiar with financial statements—in particular with the income statement and the balance sheet.

The *income statement* (also called the *profit and loss statement*) is important because it indicates whether the business made a profit or suffered a loss in a given period. The *balance sheet* tells what the business owns and what it owes to others as well as how much equity or net worth the owner has in the business.

The income statement can be likened to a movie. It has a beginning and an end (the profit or loss) and a middle that tells the reader what happened in between that lead to the ending. The balance sheet, by comparison, can be likened to a candid snapshot—it is a picture that shows how the business appears at one instant of time, usually the end of a month or a year.

When creating an estimated income statement for a new restaurant start-up, it is wise to use the services of a qualified accountant who has experience with the restaurant industry.

UNDERSTANDING THE INCOME STATEMENT

An income statement contains four types of information—*revenues, costs, expenses,* and *profit or loss.* In essence, it tells the reader how much money came in and from what sources, the cost of the raw materials that went into the products that were sold, the expenses that were incurred in the course of operating the business, and whether a profit or a loss resulted. Following is an example of the essential elements of an income statement:

Total revenues	$1,166,700
Less: Cost of sales	(370,428)
Less: Expenses	(693,817)
Net profit before tax	$102,455

While the above information tells us that the business produced a profit, it is relatively useless as a management tool to solve problems and establish goals. Only when an income statement is fleshed out, as illustrated in Figure 13.1, can it be used as an analytical tool.

COMPARISONS ARE INFORMATIVE

An income statement with percentages allows you to compare costs, expenses, and profits against sales. If sales rise, profits should also rise, but if costs or expenses are out of line, profits may not increase as expected. The income statement is a valuable analytical tool—its percentages reveal good performance as well as problem areas that need attention. Industry statistics for similar operations may be obtained from the National Restaurant Association and can be compared with your restaurant's performance.

Your current income statement can also be compared with those of previous months, or years, to assess the growth, stagnation, or decline of your business.

FIGURE 13.1 *An income statement such as the following sample can help owners analyze their establishment's financial operations.*

Income Statement for
The Harborside Restaurant and Lounge
for the period of January 1 through December 31, 20__

			Percent
Sales			
Food sales	$875,025		75.0
Beverage sales	291,675		25.0
Total sales		$1,166,700	100.0
Cost of sales			
Food cost	$306,259		35.0
Beverage cost	64,169		22.0
Total cost of sales		370,428	31.8
Gross profit from operations		$796,272	68.2
Controllable expenses			
Payroll	$332,177		28.5
Employee benefits	56,865		4.8
Direct operating expenses	54,835		4.7
Advertising	33,834		2.9
Music and entertainment	11,667		1.0
Utilities	37,334		3.2
Administrative and general expenses	46,668		4.0
Repairs and maintenance	23,334		2.0
Total controllable expenses		596,714	51.2
Profit before occupancy costs		$199,558	17.0
Occupancy costs			
Rent (triple-net lease)	$49,502		4.2
Property taxes	7,000		0.5
Other taxes	2,333		0.2
Property insurance	9,100		0.8
Total occupancy costs		67,935	5.7
Profit before interest and depreciation		$131,623	11.3
Interest		$ 5,834	0.5
Depreciation		23,334	2.0
Net profit		$102,455	8.8

Such analyses can also raise a number of questions about a business:

- Have costs gotten out of line, possibly reflecting poor purchasing practices?
- Is the nature of the business changing—is it selling more liquor than food, for instance?
- Are all profit centers contributing to profits as well as they should?
- Are any visible trends emerging?

UNDERSTANDING YOUR BALANCE SHEET

The basic purpose of a balance sheet (see Figure 13.2) is to inform the reader as to what the business owns, what it owes others, and what its worth is. The things a business owns are called its *assets*, the things it owes to others are called its *liabilities*, and the owner's equity is referred to as its *net worth*. The statement is called a balance sheet because total assets must always equal total liabilities plus net worth. If they do not, the statement is out of balance and, therefore, incorrect.

RATIOS—VALUABLE ANALYTICAL TOOLS

Numbers are more meaningful when they are related to other significant numbers, such as sales. When sales rise or fall, it is reasonable to expect certain expenses to increase or decrease accordingly. Other relationships between numbers on statements can reveal the health of a business—its strengths and weaknesses. To facilitate such comparisons, the following analytical tools have been developed:

- Food cost percentage
- Pouring cost percentage
- Labor cost percentage
- Expense percentages
- Percentage of net profit on sales
- Rate of return on investment
- Current ratio

FIGURE 13.2 *A balance sheet shows the business's financial position at a certain point in time.*

Balance Sheet
for the year ending December 31, 20—

Assets

Current assets

Cash on hand		$9,400
Cash in bank		37,000
Accounts receivable		3,800
Food inventory		9,500
Beverage inventory		6,800
Supplies inventory		2,600
Marketable securities		21,000
Prepaid expenses		12,500
Total current assets		**$102,600**

Fixed assets

Furniture, fixtures, and equipment	$150,100	
Less: Depreciation reserve	33,200	116,900
Leasehold improvements	154,000	
Less: Depreciation reserve	6,000	148,000
Total fixed assets		**$264,900**
Total Assets		**$367,500**

Liabilities and Net Worth

Current liabilities

Accounts payable	23,000
Taxes collected	8,500
Accrued expenses	13,645
Current portion of long-term loan due	3,501
Total current liabilities	**$48,646**
Long-term loan balance (12%)	121,855
Less: Current portion due	3,501
Total long-term loan	**$118,354**

Net worth

Partner A (45%)	90,225
Partner B (35%)	70,175
Partner C (20%)	40,100
Total partners' equity	**$200,500**
Total Liabilities and Net Worth	**$367,500**

- Acid test ratio
- Working capital
- Average guest check
- Seat turnover ratio

Percentages for food, beverage, labor, and expense costs may be calculated daily, weekly, monthly, or annually. However, it is not advisable to go for more than a month without calculating them, because facts are quickly forgotten and problems become harder to solve with the passage of time. The formula is the same in each instance, but only the figures for the particular period desired should be used in the calculations.

Food cost percentage. This percentage can be calculated for a single entree or for all the food consumed in a given period. It tells you what percentage of the selling price of a food product goes to pay for the ingredients from which it was made. Food cost percentages vary depending on the style of service, sales promotional objectives, and the efficiency of each restaurant, but most table service restaurants tend to operate between 30 percent and 40 percent overall, with some lower and others higher, depending on their use of convenience and pre-preped foods. Restaurants that prepare most items from scratch tend to have lower food costs but higher labor costs, whereas restaurants that use a large number of convenience (pre-preped) foods have a higher food cost percentage but a lower labor cost. Food and labor costs also vary significantly by geographic location. The formula for calculating a monthly food cost percentage is the following:

cost of food sold ÷ food sales = food cost percentage

$$\$25,521 \div \$72,918 = 35\%$$

Pouring cost percentage. The pouring cost percentage (PC) tells you what percentage of the selling price of a drink goes to pay for the liquor used to make it. Typically, pouring cost percentages range from 20 percent to 30 percent, with some lower and some higher depending on style of service, sales promotion objectives, desired profit margin, and efficiency. The PC can be calculated daily, weekly, or monthly for one drink or for all of the liquor consumed during a certain period. The percentage is calculated as follows:

cost of beverages sold ÷ beverage sales = pouring cost percentage

$$\$5,347 \div \$24,306 = 22\%$$

Labor cost percentage. This percentage indicates how efficiently you are using your workforce. It tells you what percentage of your sales dollar goes to pay for labor costs. Causes of high labor cost percentages include allowing too much overtime, overstaffing, inadequate training, and not supervising the workforce well enough. Industry statistics can be used to compare your expenses with those of other similar establishments. Percentages tend vary due to the style of service offered, seasonal swings of sales, the extent to which convenience and pre-prepped foods are used, and external influences such as a tight labor market. The formula for calculating a labor cost percentage is:

(payroll + employee benefits) ÷ total sales = labor cost percentage

$$(\$27,681 + \$4,739) \div \$97,225 = 33.3\%$$

Expense percentages. Every restaurant has a number of expense categories that can be abused if not controlled properly, such as heat, light, paper goods, linens. This percentage tells you how well those expenses are being contained within acceptable limits. Despite your efforts, external forces beyond your control, such as rising fuel and heating costs, may affect your percentage. Those situations should be identified as soon as possible so that actions can be taken in other areas to compensate for them. The following formula calculates the percentage relationship of any expense item to total sales (here, the monthly advertising expense is calculated):

advertising expense ÷ total sales = expense percentage

$$\$2,820 \div \$97,225 = 2.9\%$$

Percentage of net profit on sales. This percentage reflects a business's ability to operate profitably. A restaurant may do a superb job of increasing sales, but unless it does a good job of controlling expenses, it may not produce a proportionate increase in profits. The formula, as shown below, relates annual profits to annual sales (in the case of a corporation, net profit after taxes would be used).

net profit ÷ total sales = percentage of net profit on sales

$102,455 ÷ $1,166,700 = 8.8%

Rate of return on investment. This measures how well a business is using the funds its owners invested. It is also an essential piece of information to consider when buying or selling a business, because it indicates how fast the business will be able to pay back the funds invested. Beyond that, it is useful when comparing alternative investment opportunities (in the case of a corporation, net profit after taxes would be used).

net profit ÷ investment = rate of return on investment

$102,455 ÷ $500,000 = 20.5%

Current ratio. This ratio reflects a restaurant's ability to pay its bills as they come due and is, therefore, of great interest to suppliers and lenders. Only current assets may be used in this calculation—those are cash, receivables, marketable securities, inventories, and prepaid expenses (such as insurance premiums that are paid in advance). The ratio relates total current assets to total current liabilities—obligations that must be paid on a current basis. They include such things as accounts payable, notes payable, and accrued expenses (for example, wages payable). In the following example, the business has 2.1 times as many current assets as current liabilities. In general, a current ratio of at least 2 to 1 is considered adequate for the payment of current bills in a timely manner.

current assets ÷ current liabilities = current ratio

$102,600 ÷ $48,646 = 2.1 : 1

Acid test ratio. If a restaurant's current ratio is less than the desired 2 to 1, another test can be applied to determine a firm's ability to pay its current bills—the acid test ratio. Only cash and other "quick assets" that can be rapidly converted to cash, such as accounts receivable and marketable securities, can be used in this calculation. The sum of those three categories is divided by current liabilities, as shown below:

$$\frac{\text{cash + accounts receivable + marketable securities}}{\text{current liabilities}} = \text{acid test ratio}$$

$$\frac{\$46,400 + \$3,800 + \$21,000}{\$48,646} = \frac{\$71,200}{\$48,646} = 1.5 : 1$$

The firm analyzed above has 1.5 times as many quick assets as it has current liabilities. Because a 1:1 ratio is considered acceptable, this business is in sound financial condition and is capable of paying its current bills on time.

Working capital. Working capital is the funds needed to operate a business from week to week. Sometimes new businesses spend so much money on equipment and buildings that, if they fail to produce the cash flow they were expecting in their first year, they run out of money to pay wages and bills. Lack of adequate working capital is one of the main causes of business failures.

Working capital is the difference between a business's current assets and its current liabilities, as shown below:

$$\text{current assets} - \text{current liabilities} = \text{working capital}$$

$$\$102,600 - \$48,646 = \$53,954$$

Average guest check. This is the amount that, on average, a customer spends when patronizing your restaurant. Due to the differences between meal periods and your bar business, it is more meaningful to do a separate calculation for each meal period and for the bar. Average guest check is an important number to monitor, because a declining amount may indicate that a service or quality problem exists or perhaps that the waitstaff is not practicing suggestive selling. The average guest check may be calculated for any period, but monthly, seasonal or semi-annual periods are the best indicators of trends. It is calculated as follows:

$$\text{total sales} \div \text{\# of guests served} = \text{average guest check}$$

Lunch: $\$305,250 \div 33,000 = \$ 9.25$

Dinner: $556,010 \div 23,660 = \$23.50$

Bar only: $146,300 \div 16,700 = \$ 8.76$

Seat turnover ratio. This is an indicator of how effectively you are attracting people to your restaurant and how efficiently you are serving them when they are there. A declining ratio may indicate that your service is too slow or that you are experiencing an erosion of your customer base. The latter is a major concern and, if not corrected, will lead to business failure. The illustration below shows how a seat turnover ratio can be calculated for the preceding year. It could also be calculated for a week or a month, simply by substituting the appropriate figures.

# of customers annually ÷ # of seats ÷ 365 = seat turnover ratio
Dining room: 56,660 ÷ 100 ÷ 365 = 1.6 times a day
Bar only: 16,700 ÷ 60 ÷ 365 = 0.8 times a day

HOW MUCH CONTROL IS ENOUGH?

A certain amount of control is inherently present if the owner is actively involved in the business. But that type of control should not be relied upon, because the owner cannot physically work every hour of every day. When the owner is absent, there is a management void, and then conditions often break down.

The ideal control system incorporates management oversight with a variety of control procedures and reporting mechanisms that do not require the owner always to be present.

It should be noted, however, that the cost of any control procedure should not exceed its potential savings. Put simply, one should not spend dollars to chase after pennies.

A Simple Control System for a Small Restaurant

The following cost control system is easy to install and can work well for small restaurants that want to avoid more paperwork. It is a substantial improvement over having no controls and requires only three things:

1. A periodic inventory
2. A record of purchases
3. A record of sales

The system involves taking an inventory at the beginning of a period and again at the end of the period. The period may be whatever duration you desire, from one week to one month, but should not exceed a month. A record of sales and purchases is kept during the period, and at the end of the period, the cost of food sold is calculated as illustrated below.

Beginning inventory 8/1	$ 5,900
Plus: Purchases 8/1–8/31	16,500
Total	$22,400
Less: Ending inventory 8/31	6,400
Cost of food sold	$16,000

Assuming food sales of $45,000 for the period, use the cost of food sold to calculate the food cost percentage, as follows:

$$\frac{\text{cost of food sold}}{\text{food sales}} = \frac{\$16,000}{\$45,000} = 35.6\% \text{ food cost}$$

The food cost percentage is an indicator of a number of things: how well the purchasing function is being conducted, how much waste may be occurring in the kitchen as a result of carelessness and over-portioning, and the possibility of pilferage. When a food cost percentage remains high over time, you should analyze the menu to ascertain whether the prices being charged are adequate. If not, prices or portion sizes may need to be adjusted, or high-food-cost items may need to be replaced with lower-cost ones.

Even the minimal amount of control such as that illustrated above can bring about important results in an operation that currently has no controls. The system can be installed easily, without professional assistance—all that is needed is a supply of inventory forms.

SUPERVISION REDUCES UNDESIRABLE PRACTICES

No matter how well management tries to screen applicants and hire the best people, the possibility always exists that undesirable practices may set in. Management must monitor operations carefully to deter, or at least quickly discover, unwanted activities. Here are some things to look for when percentages get out of line:

- Unauthorized removal of property from the restaurant
- Overportioning food or beverages due to carelessness or to get bigger tips
- Giving unauthorized discounts or not charging friends
- Covering up for merchandise taken undetected by changing inventory counts
- Collusion among employees
- Accepting gifts in return for buying inferior or overpriced products
- Tampering with counters or meters on machines or bottles
- Faking petty cash payouts, breakage, or lost guest checks
- Leaving the cash drawer open and not ringing up or entering every sale

With close supervision, control procedures go a long way toward preventing unwanted practices from getting started. Observers of retail industries indicate that pilferage by employees is a major problem. Management's challenge is to eliminate any temptations by having well-understood procedures for controlling all aspects of its operations, particularly inventories and cash.

AUTOMATED SYSTEMS FOR RESTAURANTS

Many automated systems for controlling restaurant operations are available, and the technology is advancing rapidly. For example, integrated POS systems cover every aspect of a transaction and supply data for accounting controls. Liquor dispensing systems and cashiering systems can integrate with inventory systems and produce informative reports.

The degree to which a restaurant automates depends upon its size and volume, its available funds, and its management's perception of its control problems and potential. Numerous reasons for installing automatic systems are put forth by their manufacturers. Prominent among them are the following:

- Promote consistency of products.
- Control inventories.
- Prevent overportioning.
- Eliminate pricing errors.
- Ensure that house policies will be followed.
- Remove temptation.
- Reveal cash shortages.

Most systems are very good at doing what they purport to do, and users regard them highly. Most are modularized so that a business can start out with a basic installation and expand its capabilities as the business grows. As with any investment in equipment, the potential savings and benefits should be examined carefully before buying a system.

Action Guidelines

☐ Prepare an estimated income statement and calculate the following measurements of the health of the business:
- Food cost percentage
- Pouring cost percentage
- Labor cost percentage
- Percentage of net profit on sales
- Fire department
☐ Prepare an estimated balance sheet and calculate the following measurements of the financial strength of the business:
- Working capital
- Current ratio
- Acid test ratio

14

MARKETING

As the restaurant industry's annual sales pass the half-trillion dollar mark, nothing is more evident than the importance of its marketing strategies. While on the surface, one may say our products are food and beverages, in reality they are much more—convenience, relaxation, entertainment, and nourishment—and we must market each one of these products creatively to reach the population that values them.

Restaurants typically have several types of customers—luncheon guests, dinner guests, bar guests, entertainment seekers, and function planners—and each type has its own wants and needs. Our challenge is to to identify them and use the best means to reach them with the message that *we can satisfy their desires.*

In the restaurant business, marketing may be defined as "the process of getting the right products and services to the right customers, at the right time and place, and at the right price." The key word in each instance is *right.*

IS A MARKETING PLAN NECESSARY?

Without a marketing plan a restaurant is like a ship without a rudder—it will drift aimlessly. A marketing plan helps it stay on the right course to achieve its goals. When clearly communicated to employees, a marketing plan also creates a team spirit that brings out the best performance from everyone, focusing their efforts on achieving the restaurant's goals.

A Seven-Step Process for Developing a Marketing Plan

1. Establish your overall objective. For example, "To increase sales by 40 percent next year."
2. Identify your strengths and weaknesses. Examples might be:

Strengths	Weakness
Excellent food and drinks	Lack of seating capacity
Excellent service	

3. List the alternative strategies available to you. For example, your options might include:
   • Add on to the existing building.
   • Convert a function room to general dining.
   • Increase seat turnover.
4. Select the best strategy. In this example, let's assume that "increase seat turnover" is believed to be the best option.
5. Develop a detailed plan of action, such as:
   • Review menu offerings that require lengthy preparation times. Try to pre-prep more items to speed up the production process. Where necessary, replace difficult-to-prepare items with popular but easier-to-prepare ones.
   • Offer early-bird specials to attract people before the usual rush hours, thereby gaining additional turnover.
   • Speed up service by retraining waitstaff to use digital handheld devices for order taking and electronically transmitting orders to the kitchen and bar through the integrated POS system.
   • Add a lighter, late-evening menu to be offered after the dinner rush. Advertise it to appeal to theater and sports event attendees.
   • Have theme nights planned for normally slow nights.
6. Implement the plans, as follows:
   • Establish a timetable for execution of the plans.
   • Advertise externally and promote internally.

- Start doing it.
- Keep careful records of results.
- Observe the good and bad points of what you are doing.
- Refine and adjust specific actions as you go along.
- Reinforce good features.
- Correct flaws.

7. Evaluate the results of your efforts. Decide whether to continue, modify, or terminate the plan.

Successful marketing programs are based on in-depth knowledge of your prospective customers' wants and needs. The programs may include a broad range of tools, called "the marketing mix." Among the tools are market research, product and concept development, packaging, pricing, advertising, sales promotion, and personal selling strategies. Which to use is determined partly by the current stage of the restaurant's life cycle.

Every Business Has a Life Cycle

Typical of all businesses, restaurants pass through a life cycle consisting of the following five stages. It is essential at each stage to know where you are, because your marketing activities should be based on what that stage requires.

Life Cycle Stage	Characteristics of That Stage
1. Introduction	Your restaurant has just started. It is trying to survive and become established. Your systems are still being perfected.
2. Conservative growth	A period of slow and steady sales growth ensues as more people learn about your restaurant. New ideas are tried to attract more people.
3. Rapid growth	Your reputation spreads. The word is out that you have a unique restaurant and serve good food and drinks. Your popularity grows rapidly, as do your sales. Competitors notice your success.
4. Leveled maturity	Competition intensifies as others copy your ideas and new competitors emerge. Growth ceases, and you try to hold on to your share of the market.
5. Rejuvenation or decline	Competitors and new entrants not only take your ideas but improve on them. You must reinvent your business by introducing new ideas that differentiate and position you ahead of the pack, or your restaurant's business will decline.

At first, a restaurant focuses its advertising on letting the public know that it exists, what it offers, and where it is. Then its advertising changes to promotions that bring in first-time patrons and increase the frequency of patronage by existing customers. After that, it attempts to hold its market share by capitalizing on the reputation it built in the previous stages. It reminds people about its quality and the reasons it became popular. Finally, if it succeeds in rejuvenating itself, its advertising emphasizes what is new or improved, and the whole process starts over.

MARKET RESEARCH PAYS OFF

The more you know about the people in your marketing area, the better you can serve them. You will be aware of their customs and special holidays; when, where, and how they spend their money; how you should price your menu; and what level of service will be expected.

Three types of information about prospective customers can help a restaurant plan a marketing strategy. They are:

1. Demographic information
2. Geographic information
3. Psychographic information

Demographics are facts about people such as their age, income, education, occupation, race, religion, and nationality.

Geographic information tells you where people live and work. It also tells you something about their dining and drinking patterns. For example, harried commuters are more apt to rush to their cars after work than in-town dwellers, who might stop by for cocktails or dinner.

Psychographic information can tell you such things as whether people are brand conscious, influenced by peer groups, socially oriented, or feel a need to keep up with others. Some persons are attracted to prestigious establishments where people of influence or celebrities are known to frequent. Psychographics deals with lifestyles and motivational influences on people's spending behavior.

Market research firms sell market information to businesses, and their names are available at the reference department of your local library and in business and telephone directories. However, if you cannot afford to purchase information, you can gather a great deal of it on your own through observation and discreet questioning. Public information agencies—such as chambers of commerce, state and city agencies, as well as newspapers and radio stations—can provide much information.

In addition to researching your prospective customers, check out your competition. It is a good way to glean new ideas. The success of a competitor may, in some cases, indicate how well you will do.

Investigate the economic trend of your community. Do not focus too much on what it was like in the past but consider where is it headed—conditions may change in the future. Your market research will influence decisions that may make or break you. Following is a list of questions that your research should address:

- Who are your competitors? What are they offering? Menu? Style of service? Entertainment? Atmosphere and decor?
- Are they successful? What seems to make them successful?
- What kinds of customers do they attract?
- What special things are they doing to attract their clientele?
- What are their merchandising and pricing policies?
- What are their apparent strengths?
- Do they have any weaknesses on which you can capitalize?

You cannot be sure that your concept is truly distinctive until you research your competitors. Your research will also help you identify the merchandising styles to which particular segments of the market respond, and it may guide you to marketing strategies that will reach your desired clientele effectively. Beyond that, it will give you some idea of the degree of difficulty you can expect to encounter in your effort to penetrate the market.

Personal Research Is Valuable

The most direct way to gather information about your competitors is to patronize their restaurants. Don't be bashful about your research efforts; you can be sure that they will be researching your business as soon as you open. Observe everything about them that may be of help to you. Chat with waitstaff. Question suppliers and delivery people. Talk to other business owners and anyone else who might give you valuable information. Find out who your competitors will be and which ones are most successful. Dine there and check out their operations. Everything you learn will help you develop a competitive strategy. Here are some things to look at when researching another establishment:

- Kind of restaurant: its concept, style of service, and type of clientele
- Approximate seating capacity
- Waiting time to be seated and to be served
- Efficiency and friendliness of the host and waitperson
- Number of menu offerings, both food and beverages
- Variety of offerings
- Quality of food and drinks
- Cost relative to quality
- Arrangement of dining room and appearance of table settings
- Atmosphere and decor of rooms
- Apparent cleanliness of the facility
- Availability of waitperson when needed
- Smoke-free section—how smoke-free is it?
- Background music
- General ambiance of establishment
- Type of sales promotional techniques, including displays, price inducements, and personal selling
- Bill—is it timely? Correct?
- Payment collected quickly
- Being thanked for your patronage

KNOW YOUR TARGET MARKET

Not everyone likes the same thing—people over 50 do not generally have the same taste for music or ambiance or even foods as people in their early 20s. Unfortunately, because restaurateurs want everyone to feel welcome in their establishment, many make the mistake of thinking their target market is "everyone." In fact, their target market is the segment of the population that strongly wants or needs what they offer and is most apt to patronize their establishment.

FIGURE 14.1 *Market Segmented Pie Chart*

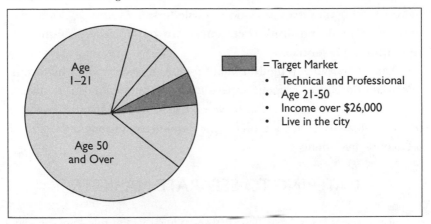

= Target Market
- Technical and Professional
- Age 21-50
- Income over $26,000
- Live in the city

Most restaurants have a stronger following within certain demographic groups than they do within others. The best way to identify your target market is to segment the market according to demographic, geographic, and psychographic variables. Figure 14.1 depicts how a particular market may be segmented to measure a targeted population.

RECOGNIZE YOUR CUSTOMERS' WANTS AND NEEDS

Observe what your customers ask for when they come to your establishment and determine what you can offer to satisfy their wants or needs.

Recognize the differences in behaviors and consumption patterns of the various generational waves of our population. For example, the Y generation, which includes young adults born between 1981 and 1995 and numbers more than 57 million, has distinct characteristics. Gen Yers tend to be financially responsible, because many were raised by a single parent, often a working mother, and helped with grocery shopping and other necessary purchases. They search for ways to save money, time, and effort and assume product claims are hype that should be distrusted. They expect promises to be kept and have little brand loyalty, but they do reward outstanding service. This population segment appears to respond most to believable marketing that makes use of humor, irony, and truth.

Information on consumer trends and preferences can be obtained by researching industry association newsletters and journals. Popularity indexes of food and drink preferences are periodically published in restaurant trade journals.

Another resource is the National Restaurant Association, which compiles data on customer spending patterns and other industry statistics. Their annual publication, *The Restaurant Industry Operations Report*, can provide valuable information on the performance of various kinds of food service establishments.

CATERING TO SEPARATE MARKETS

Some restaurants have two distinct types of clientele—in the daytime, they may cater to workers, shoppers, and tourists, while at night they may cater to a social, fun-seeking clientele. With careful planning, you may be able to serve more than one type of customer, provided they are acceptable to each other and your desired image is not compromised. The following example illustrates how customer wants and needs may be analyzed and satisfied.

Type of Guest	Want or Need	Response
Workers, lunchtime	Nourishment	Offer good, healthy food
Workers, after work	Relaxation	Offer comfortable seating, soft music
Dinner guests	Excitement	Offer interesting food and drinks
Entertainment seekers	Stimulation	Offer high-energy music and dancing
Social guests	Meet people	Offer an informal lounge atmosphere with close, comfortable seating and stand-up bars

STRATEGIES FOR MEETING THE COMPETITION

There are three types of competitive strategies you may consider when starting out—market penetration, differentiation, and concentration.

Using the *market penetration strategy*, you penetrate the market with lower prices than your competitors. This is an often-used strategy, but it is feasible only when accompanied by tight cost controls in all expense areas, allowing you to make a profit even though you charge lower prices.

The *differentiation strategy*, which refers to setting your business apart from your competitors, stresses such things as uniqueness or higher quality in your advertising. Uniqueness can take many forms. A restaurant's unusual atmosphere and decor, music, specialized style of service, or menu offerings can differentiate it from its competitors.

You can also make your restaurant appear to be different simply by the way you position your competitors in your advertising. An example of this would be the following statement in an advertisement: "Have It Both Ways—Now You Can Enjoy Healthy Dining in a Totally Smoke-Free Environment." If your competitors are not totally smoke-free or offer only deep-fried foods, your restaurant would appear quite different to your target market.

Concentration involves focusing on a particular customer group, geographic location, or style of service. While the cost-based and differentiation strategies are aimed at the entire potential market, the concentration strategy aims at a particular need of a specific segment of your target market.

THE SECRET TO GROWTH—GETTING NEW CUSTOMERS

Some customers may come to your restaurant because it is the newest place in town. Others come because you are close by or because they have heard good things about it. Many more intend to come someday but will never get around to doing so, unless you do something special to draw them in.

Researchers have found that consumers go through a decision-making process before making purchases. Restaurant patrons, knowingly or unknowingly, pass through the same five stages. The process may be described as follows:

1. *Awareness.* A person first realizes that your restaurant exists.
2. *Interest.* They hear something good about your place from a friend or see an enticing advertisement.
3. *Evaluation.* They mull over what they have seen or heard and either decide to try it sometime or forget it.
4. *Trial.* The customer visits your restaurant to see if they like it.

5. *Adoption or rejection.* This result depends on whether the customer is pleased or not by their first experience at your establishment.

It is important to understand a consumer's decision-making process, because it reflects how hard it is to get new customers and it points out the importance of taking good care of your present customers.

New customers are your key to growth. To get them, you must make people aware of your existence through creative advertising and sales promotion programs aimed at first-time customers. You can also gain new customers by doing an exceptional job with your present customers— satisfying them so well that they tell their friends about your restaurant. Without question, the most effective form of advertising is word-of-mouth.

HOW TO MAKE THE MOST OF YOUR GRAND OPENING

People are attracted to grand openings because they represent something new and exciting—perhaps a better deal. A grand opening is a very important time for a restaurant to do things right. This is when it can really impress new customers and gain valuable word-of-mouth advertising. Unfortunately, many establishments waste the opportunity to cash in on their grand opening and, in some cases, do such a poor job that it takes months to recover from an initial flurry of bad word-of-mouth advertising. Here are some ways to make a grand opening successful:

- Carefully preplan a schedule of preliminary activities to ensure that you will be ready on the big day. Do not have your grand opening until you are ready to do everything right.
- Thoroughly train your staff prior to the grand opening.
- Make sure all equipment is assembled properly, cleaned, and tested. This should be done enough in advance to allow technicians time to come back and make corrections if necessary.
- Be certain all of your licenses and permits will be issued before the grand opening date is announced. More than one opening has had to be postponed because of a last-minute snag. Work closely with the licensing authorities.

- Communicate regularly with your suppliers to make certain their deliveries will arrive in advance to avoid distractions, back orders, or returned merchandise during the grand opening.
- Schedule a dry-run party before going public with your grand opening. A dry run is a private function to which you invite your relatives and close friends, business associates, and anyone who can ever do you any good such as media people; suppliers; politicians; liquor, fire, and health authorities; lenders; investors; and contractors.

You can expect a high rate of attendance, because the event is free. This is a chance to strut your stuff in a friendly atmosphere, when no one will complain if something goes wrong (because the price is right). Nonetheless, every detail, including mistakes and problems, should be handled as though the attendees were paying guests. The reason for having a dry-run party is to iron out any wrinkles in your operation.

Get the Word Out

The best-planned grand opening will be of little value if people do not know about it. So you must advertise and publicize it well in advance for people to talk it up with their friends. A frequently used technique for announcing grand openings with a big splash is to have all of your contractors and suppliers sponsor a full-page newspaper advertisement that congratulates you on your opening and wishes you well. The contractors have made money on you, and your suppliers will make a lot in the future if you are successful, so it is in their best interest to do this. Besides, it puts their name in the public's eye, because most ads of this type have the sponsors' business cards arranged as a border around the perimeter of the ad. Everybody wins.

Other ways to announce a grand opening are:

- Visit nearby businesses to introduce yourself to their owners. In addition, make yourself known to their employees, because retail store clerks are frequently asked for recommendations on a place to eat by their customers.
- Offer an introductory discount to employees of neighboring businesses.

- Mail a copy of your menu and information about your hours and facilities to all businesses within your dominant marketing area. Be sure to emphasize your name and address prominently so that if the recipient does not read the entire mailing, they will at least know who and where you are.
- Supply all visitor information centers in your community with literature about your restaurant to be displayed in their racks. Give a gift certificate for a free lunch to the person at the visitor information center who dispenses information.
- Put an eye-catching "Coming Soon" sign in your front window announcing the date of the grand opening. This should be done well in advance to attract the attention of the most people possible.
- Have a press kit prepared to give to all media representatives before the grand opening. It should include an article that describes the restaurant and extols its features and benefits as well as photos.

FREE PUBLICITY CAN BE YOURS FOR THE ASKING

Newspaper editors, who have the responsibility of filling many pages with print, welcome newsworthy publicity articles from businesses. On slow news days, press releases are heavily used.

Publicity articles can be about a wide variety of topics such as grand openings, new products, significant contributions to charities, awards bestowed by professional associations, a change of name, or a promotion of a key person. They must be of genuine interest to the public and cannot be blatantly self-serving, contain unsubstantiated claims, or be critical of competitors or products. In short, they cannot be advertisements. But if they are truly newsworthy, well written, and submitted on time, they stand an excellent chance of being published.

Free publicity is more valuable than paid advertising, because readers tend to believe news articles much more than advertisements. Most people do not realize that publicity articles are usually written by the business that they are about or by its publicist. They are thought to have been written by an unbiased person and, therefore, must be true.

Photographs make publicity articles much more interesting and increase their chances of being placed in a good location in a newspaper. They increase the readership rate dramatically, and editors like to run them. To be used, however, they must be of good reproduction quality or, if in digital image form, be at least 300 dots per inch (dpi). It is worth trading a meal and a couple of drinks to have a professional photographer take a picture for you.

Following are some tips for writing successful publicity articles:

- Submit time-sensitive articles adequately in advance of the paper's deadline. Find out your local newspaper's deadlines for copy.
- Send articles to the appropriate editor. For example, an article announcing a promotion in your organization should be sent to the business editor, while an article announcing the sponsorship of a softball team by your restaurant should be sent to the sports editor.
- Articles should be typed, double-spaced on plain white paper or e-mailed. Call first to find out the newspaper's preference. If you have a really important, time-sensitive story that cannot wait, e-mail it to the editor.
- Summarize the "Who, Why, What, When, and Where" of the story in the first paragraph. Then proceed to give details in subsequent paragraphs. This is done so that if a person reads only the first paragraph, they at least know your name and the important facts.
- In the case of a longer feature article, let the editor know if the article was written exclusively for that newspaper.
- If an article is not time-sensitive, indicate it is being "submitted for publication on a space-available basis." This notation gives it a greater chance of being published when space becomes available.
- Run a paid advertisement, preferably with a photograph, on the same page where the publicity article appears. You can make claims and self-serving statements in your ad, and the credibility given to the publicity article will tend to transfer to what is said in the paid ad, thereby giving it greater acceptance.

It pays to relate well to your community—become involved with civic groups and projects. If public speaking is something you enjoy, that is a good way to gain favorable exposure. Many groups are constantly looking for interesting speakers and would love to have a presentation on cooking, wines, or beers or a tour of your restaurant. Public speaking is a good way to make acquaintances, elevate the image of your establishment, and get additional publicity, because speaking events are often announced by the sponsoring group in a press release.

GIVE CUSTOMERS REASONS TO COME BACK

Special attention gives customers a feeling of being appreciated and makes them want to come back soon. There are many ways to give special attention to customers. A friendly greeting when they arrive and a thank-you when they leave makes their visit much more personal. This is especially effective when done by the manager—everyone likes to know the manager.

Table tents and lobby posters that announce future events, such as New Year's Eve and Mothers' Day or dinner/theater combination packages, can be effective tools to bring people back.

Theme nights are very successful in some restaurants, particularly where customers are given the opportunity to participate in events. Listed below is a collection of ideas for theme nights. Some are straightforward, such as holiday observances, while others require a creative flair and the right setting. But all of them will stimulate your creativity and lead you to other ideas. Consider all of the possibilities associated with themes—contests, prizes, special music, costumes, and decorations.

Special Events and Theme Suggestions

Salute to the Armed Forces	Hockey Games
Calypso Beach Party	Basketball Games
Old Time Hollywood Night	Sidewalk Sales
Après Ski	Carnival Day
New Year's Day	St. Patrick's Day
Super Bowl Day	April Fool's Day
Homecoming Weekend	Easter
Olympics	Mother's Day
Labor Day	Father's Day
Back to College Days	Graduation Day
Columbus Day	Independence Day
Veterans Day	Cajun Festival

Football Day	Washington's Birthday
Thanksgiving Day	Lincoln's Birthday
Christmas Day	Fashion Show
Mardi Gras	Art Exhibit
Patriot's Day	Opera Night
May Day	Country Fair
Dollar Days	Halloween Party
Theater Night	Marathon Mania
Baseball Party	Chinese New Year
Kentucky Derby	Hawaiian Cruise
Gay Nineties	Sing Along
Roaring Twenties	Election Day Party
Wine Tastings	Sadie Hawkins' Day
Cabaret Night	Mystery Dinner
Masked Ball	Chicago 1920s
Cartoon Night	Soap Opera Night

ACQUIRING YOUR DESIRED IMAGE

How do you want to be perceived? The answer to this question will direct your advertising, merchandising, sales promotion, and publicity activities. Once you decide how you want the public to view your restaurant, you must scrutinize every activity you conduct to be certain that it clearly signals that image.

The hard- or soft-sell message of your ads, your choice of radio stations, the tone of your advertisements—all transmit an image of your business. If they are not well thought out to convey the precise image you want, you may be wasting your money. Advertising budgets for restaurants typically range from 2 percent to 3 percent of sales, although some do very little or no advertising and others as much as 5 percent.

It is important for everyone in your organization to have a clear understanding of your desired image and to work to achieve it—particularly service employees, who are at the point of contact with your customers.

SHOULD YOU ADVERTISE?

Advertising has become a fact of life in the business world. People expect it, look for it, and in spite of its many abuses, still place a great deal of trust in it. There are many reasons to advertise restaurants. The most common reasons are listed below:

- To introduce a new restaurant
- To attract new customers
- To test new ideas
- To let the public know what you are doing
- To announce special holiday and theme events
- To publicize a new or changed menu
- To position your establishment a certain way
- To reposition your competition
- To resell lost customers
- To introduce new management
- To report your achievements to the public
- To create and maintain a certain image
- To increase sales
- To keep your name in the public's eye, particularly if your competitors advertise
- To stimulate conversation and word-of-mouth advertising

Effective Use of Advertising Media

Every year, a great deal of money is wasted on advertising by restaurants desperately seeking to reach new customers. Many ads are poorly written or placed in inferior locations in newspapers, and radio commercials are often aired on the wrong stations. An ad must be run in the newspaper or on the radio or television station that is read or listened to by the target market. It also has to be run at the right times and in the right position. For example, the inside, lower corner of a newspaper page is a poor location for a small ad, because many people read newspapers while sitting with their legs crossed and drape the paper across their lap. Consequently they rarely see the ads in the lower, inside corners of their paper.

Frequency is also important in advertising. The chances of a reader noticing an ad that is run one time is pure luck. If an ad is run regularly, however, the chances of its being seen are much greater. In general, it is better to run a smaller ad more often than to run a larger ad just once. This is especially true with radio advertising, where the listener has no opportunity to clip out and save a commercial as they can with a newspaper ad. Figure 14.2 lists some of the advantages and disadvantages of different media.

ESTABLISHING REALISTIC SALES GOALS

Enthusiastic entrepreneurs can easily overestimate sales. This error is very risky in the restaurant business, because all other budgeted cost and expense projections are based on sales. Exaggerated sales can delude a planner into budgeting too much money for expenses and lead to a loss on operations.

There are many approaches to setting sales goals, but the best approach is to use a combination of several methods and temper it with your own gut feeling. Industry sources, such as the National Restaurant Association's *Annual Restaurant Operations Report*, can give you typical sales ranges for various types of establishments. The figures are expressed in total dollar amounts as well as sales per seat. Trade journals also conduct surveys and publish useful information. These are all good numbers to use as cross-references, but you should calculate your own figures based on your seating capacity, expected seat turnovers meal by meal and day by day, and average guest check.

Following is an illustration of one method for estimating sales.

Tips for Achieving Sales Goals

- Be prepared for the rush seasons and their busy periods. Have your staff fully trained and your equipment in peak condition. That is the secret to maximizing sales. Take advantage of the opportunities when they are there—be ready to handle a crowd.
- Believe in yourself and set high standards. Serve good food and beverages, and keep your establishment clean and attractive. Offer a good value for the prices you charge, and you will soon get valuable word-of-mouth advertising from your customers.

FIGURE 14.2 *Media analysis*

Media Analysis	
Radio	**Advantages**
	• It's easy to target market through choice of station.
	• Has a captive audience during drive times.
	• 99 percent of homes are said to have radios.
	• Over 95 percent of all cars are said to have radios.
	Disadvantages
	• Audio only—listener can't save or cut out.
	• Lacks visual appeal.
Newspapers	**Advantages**
	• Timely, they contain news of the day.
	• Ads are easy to change on short notice.
	• They are published frequently.
	• Can tie in advertisements with local events.
	• Ads are less expensive than in magazines and broadcast media.
	Disadvantages
	• They have a short life—usually discarded daily.
	• Ads may get buried among many others.
	• Some people read certain sections only.
	• They're not as well read on certain days.
	• They're not well suited for high-quality photos.
Television	**Advantages**
	• Has both audio and visual appeal.
	• It's easy to target market through choice of program.
	• Can be heard from another room without viewing.
	• TV is viewed in most households.
	Disadvantages
	• It's relatively more expensive.
	• A longer time is required to produce commercials.
	• Remotes allow muting of commercials.
	• VCRs allow fast-forwarding through commercials.
	• Better-quality commercials that use professional actors must be produced by a specialized production company.
	• Can't be saved as with print media (unless taped).

(continued on next page)

FIGURE 14.2 *(Continued)*

Magazines	**Advantages** • Can be highly targeted to demographic groups, geographic areas, particular lifestyles, and special interests. • Have a long life and may be saved. • May have multiple readers as they are shared and re-read. • May lend prestige to the advertiser. • Better-quality paper allows high-quality photos. **Disadvantages** • Advertiser may pay for wasted circulation outside of the restaurant's marketing area. • Require long lead times, up to several months. • May be expensive.
Billboards	**Advantages** • They are useful for giving directions. • They are good for reminder messages. **Disadvantages** • Viewers are limited mainly to motorists. • They are not allowed in many locations. • Can only accommodate short messages.
Car Cards	**Advantages** • Can be located very precisely. • Are most effective in mass transportation vehicles. **Disadvantages** • Are useful only for short messages or reminder ads. • Viewers are largely limited to riders.
Internet	**Advantages** • This fastest-growing medium has huge potential. • Can be targeted regionally. • Works best when supported by links, blogs, and print media. **Disadvantages** • Pop-ups are often considered spam. • Web site must be promoted aggressively. • Are available only to computer users.

(continued on next page)

FIGURE 14.2 *(Continued)*

Direct Mail	**Advantages**
	• Computerized mailing lists are available.
	• Can be personalized.
	• It's highly selective; good targeting is possible.
	• Ads can be saved or passed on to others.
	• Ads can include coupons.
	Disadvantages
	• Has a low percentage of return, usually under 5 percent.
	• Direct mail is very expensive.
	• Ads are often thrown out as "junk mail."

- Keep a positive attitude. All months are not created equal, and there will be slow times. You can offset slow periods to some degree by being creative and coming up with sales promotional ideas that "keep smoke in the chimneys," but your main focus should be on maximizing your sales when people feel like coming out and are ready to spend their money.
- Let your customers know you care about them. Establish a rapport with them. That way, if they have a complaint, you will be able to handle it without their becoming resentful toward you.
- Get feedback from your customers. Listen to their compliments and their complaints—they are telling you what they like and don't like.
- Never embarrass customers for mispronouncing something or a faux pas of etiquette. Be sympathetic and helpful—do not ever diminish them in any way.

Ways to Increase Food and Beverage Sales

The three basic purposes of a menu are:

1. To let customers know what you offer
2. To let them know how much things cost
3. To promote the sale of certain highly profitable items

The following is a method for developing a sales objective.

Step 1: Estimate the *number of customers* you expect to patronize your establishment during each meal period, for each day of the week.

	Mon.	Tue.	Wed.	Thur.	Fri.	Sat.	Sun.	Total
Lunch	75	75	80	90	100	90	85	595
Dinner	35	45	60	65	85	90	80	460
Bar only	20	25	40	50	65	70	30	300

Total customers per week 1,355

Step 2: Calculate the *average menu price* for each category of items on your menu. A weighted average that takes into account the popularity and sales of each item, in comparison to the others, is best. But until you are in business for a while and have a sales history, this simple average method will suffice.

Sandwiches or salads	$ 7.50
Entrees include demi-salad	16.95
Desserts	3.80
Drinks	4.50

Step 3: Determine the amount of an *average guest check* by estimating what a typical guest is apt to order. If you expect that only one out of every two guests will order a drink or a salad, you may indicate the item as 0.5 salad or 0.5 drinks and value it at half price. This will keep your estimate on the conservative side.

Lunch	Sandwich or salad plus 0.5 drinks	$ 9.75
Dinner	Entree includes demi-salad, 0.5 dessert, plus 2 drinks	27.85
Bar only	Average 2 drinks	9.00

Step 4: Multiply your average guest check by the number of customers expected per week to determine your estimated weekly sales.

595 lunch customers   × $ 9.75 = $ 5,801
460 dinner customers   ×   27.85 =   12,811
300 bar only customers ×   9.00 =   2,700

Total Weekly Sales $ 21,312

Step 5: Finally, multiply your estimated weekly sales by 52 to arrive at your estimated annual sales.

52 weeks × $21,312 = $1,108,224

The benefit of this process is that it tailors your sales objective to your specific business and local conditions. The resultant annual sales figure may then be compared to industry averages.

Sales may be enhanced by bringing certain items to the attention of customers. For example, boxing an item makes it stand out on a menu (see Figure 14.3). The location of items on a menu also can affect their sales. Knowing this, you can place certain high-profit items in strategic places where they are apt to be selected more often. Studies have shown that people's eyes tend to follow certain patterns when reading menus (see Figure 14.4).

Suggestive Selling Works

Waitstaff should be taught the art of suggestive selling. When done in an informational manner, it can be very helpful to customers. Some other helpful hints for increasing sales are:

- Reduce confusion in customers' minds by using menu descriptions that clearly describe food items and wines.
- Make it easy for people to order. Assign numbers to wines, and where it fits into the style of service, do the same for entrees. This gives customers the opportunity to order by number if they cannot pronounce the name of an item.
- Use large type sizes. It makes names seem less intimidating to inexperienced diners and assists people with visual impairments.
- Print menus on white or light-colored stock for easy reading. The covers of a wine menu should coordinate with the colors of the decor and the mood of the atmosphere.
- Use menus that are appropriate to your table sizes. Oversized and odd-shaped menus can be cumbersome on a crowded tabletop and annoy guests.
- Proofread menus and wine lists carefully before approving them for printing, especially when they include foreign names and terms.

Some restaurants use contests and incentive plans to stimulate waitstaff to promote certain items to guests. Table tents and menu clip-ons can also be used to highlight specialties. A successful tactic for increasing wine sales in small, upscale restaurants is to place an unopened bottle of wine on each table and include wine glasses in the table setting. If the guests do not wish to order wine, the glasses are removed. Displaying a wine rack in the restaurant lobby has also proven successful in increasing wine sales.

FIGURE 14.3 *Boxing an item on a menu emphasizes it.*

DOWNEAST
LOBSTER BAKE

Whole Maine Lobster,
Heap of Steamed Clams,
Local Com on the Cob,
Sausage, Boiled Egg,
Onion, Baked Beans &
Seedless Watermelon

Only $28.00

FIGURE 14.4 *A typical reading pattern for a three-fold menu*

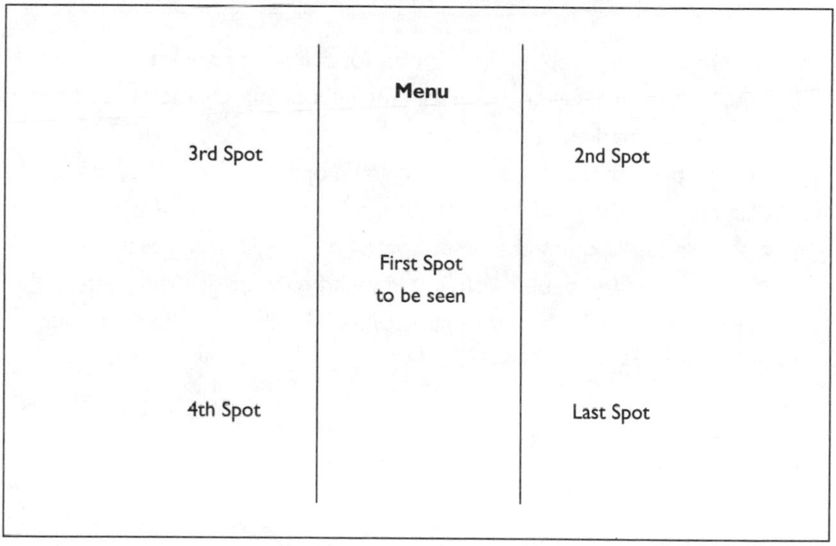

Menu

3rd Spot   2nd Spot

First Spot
to be seen

4th Spot   Last Spot

USE THE POWER OF THE INTERNET, AND DON'T FORGET THE PHONE

Web sites are wonderful tools to present information about your function rooms and banquet packages. They can give directions and show off the facilities with stunning photos to stimulate interest. E-mail is also a popular way to let customers know of special promotions. Interest in your restaurant can be raised as well with a planned telephone call to function planners and area businesses. Such calls are most productive when they contain the basic elements of any sales call, namely:

- A introduction that tells the listener who you are and the purpose of your call
- An attention-getting statement that gives the listener a reason for continuing to listen
- A discussion of the features and benefits that you are offering
- An opportunity for the listener to ask questions or voice any objections
- An appeal for action of some sort or a personal meeting

Action Guidelines

- ☐ Develop a seven-step marketing plan for a new restaurant.
- ☐ Describe in a detailed paragraph the identifying characteristics of your target market.
- ☐ Write a press release announcing the grand opening of your restaurant.
- ☐ Plan an advertising campaign, based on 2 to 3 percent of your estimated sales, allocating the funds among the media you select.
- ☐ Make a list of the people you would invite to your dry-run party.
- ☐ Prepare a timetable for the marketing tasks that will lead to your grand opening.

Chapter

15

SANITATION, SAFETY, AND RESPONSIBILITY

Can you recall a time when you patronized a restaurant with high expectations, only to find that your table had not been thoroughly cleaned after the previous party left, your water glass was slightly chipped, or the restroom was in need of attention? These are but a few of the details that can tarnish a dining experience and cause guests to wonder what else, that they can't see, may be wrong. People go out to eat expecting that they will dine in a safe environment and will not have to worry about becoming sick from the food they eat.

As a manager, you have responsibilities beyond the bottom line of your income statement. You hold a public trust to serve wholesome food in a safe establishment and to dispense alcoholic beverages in a prudent manner. To uphold that public trust, a manager must be informed on and closely monitor three areas of concern:

1. Food sanitation
2. Safety
3. Responsible service of alcoholic beverages

WHAT IS FOOD SANITATION?

In common parlance, the term *food sanitation* refers to all activities and conditions that ensure the delivery of safe and wholesome food to consumers. It includes employee hygiene, work habits, food preparation and processing, holding equipment, and the physical facilities of a restaurant—and the food supply itself.

Purchasing Food

An effective sanitation program starts with good purchasing practices. Restaurants must buy commercially produced products from reliable vendors who, in turn, acquire their food supplies from food-packing and processing plants that are inspected and adhere to specified health standards.

When you start out in the restaurant business, you must select the purveyors from which you will buy. It is advisable to interview several of them in each food category to find out their policies and how they handle their products and rotate stock. Visit their establishments to see how clean and orderly they are. Ask questions about their policies on rotating stock and taking back items that are overripe or showing defects. Prices are important but should not be your only consideration when choosing suppliers.

Receiving Shipments

The receiving function in your restaurant is also an important part of a good sanitation program. Every shipment of food should be checked for broken packages, dented or swollen cans, proper color and stage of maturity, as well as signs of rodent or insect damage.

Check the temperatures of products. Frozen and refrigerated products should be delivered in vehicles that hold them at the proper temperature. Temperature is especially critical for fish and poultry products, which are highly perishable.

Storing Food

Once inspected and signed for, food should be put into the proper storage location immediately. Frozen products should be put away first, followed by refrigerated products and, finally, dry storage products. It is advisable to check your freezer and walk-in refrigerator thermometers regularly to make sure they are holding foods at the proper temperatures. If they are inaccurate, they should be calibrated by a refrigeration technician.

To prevent contamination while in refrigeration, raw products should be stored on lower shelves, below cooked products, and items that may drip should be wrapped tightly and placed on lower shelves as well. All foods in storage should be raised off the floor. Dry storage rooms should be dry, dark, and preferably cool. The following are recommended temperatures for refrigerated storage of certain food groups.

Product	Temperature	Humidity
Meat and poultry	32 to 36°F	75 to 85%
Fish	30 to 34°F	75 to 85%
Dairy products	38 to 40°F	75 to 85%
Most fruits and vegetables	40 to 45°F	85 to 95%

Food Handling

The food-handling phase requires constant training and supervision by management. Employees must be taught the basics of food spoilage and contamination. Several excellent courses on food sanitation are available in a variety of media formats from the National Restaurant Association.

The food service industry relies heavily on entry-level employees, many from cultures that do not have the same standards as ours in matters of personal hygiene and food handling. They must be trained and supervised closely until they demonstrate that they understand the public health implications of food sanitation and can dependably apply the techniques they have learned.

Local health inspectors can be very helpful when developing training programs. See Appendix B in the back of this book for state health department addresses.

Serving Food

The holding and serving stage is critical, because cooked food should not be held on the serving line for long periods of time. It is recommended that food be cooked in smaller batches and that the serving line be resupplied periodically. This not only cuts down on the amount of time the food is held on the serving line, it also tends to reduce the amount of leftovers at the end of each shift. Someone should check the serving line with an instant-read thermometer every meal period to make sure that hot foods are being kept hot, over 140°F, and cold foods are being kept cold, 40°F or lower.

Cleaning and Sanitizing

The proper cleaning and sanitizing of equipment is another vital component of an effective sanitation program. Training must be ongoing for dishwashers because of the high turnover rate in that job. Detergent salespeople are excellent resources for dishwashing machine training. They want you to continue using their products, so most of the companies will supply you with audiovisual aids and do demonstrations for you on request. The dishwashing function should receive constant supervision to control dish breakage and chipping as well.

For proper dishwashing, soiled ware should be prescraped and loaded neatly into dish racks to ensure that everything will be washed thoroughly. Dishes and utensils should be washed with water of 140°F to 160°F and sanitized with water of 180°F. Clean dishes should be stored quickly at their point of next use to reduce the chances of contamination by unwashed hands.

Beware of the Disposable Glove Fallacy

Many employees do not understand that disposable gloves simply serve as a barrier between their hands and the food products and equipment that they touch. But unless employees exercise extreme care about what they do or touch while wearing disposable gloves, the gloves themselves can transmit dangerous germs and toxic substances. For example, if an employee empties a smelly garbage can while wearing latex gloves, then goes back to work handling food, the latex gloves will serve no purpose and will, in fact, be as dangerous as contaminated hands.

Employees must be taught to discard their soiled latex gloves immediately after use on an unsanitary task and to wash their hands frequently and thoroughly. It is important that management keep an ample supply of disposable gloves on hand at all times, provide clean and well-stocked restrooms, and install sufficient hand-washing sinks.

DEALING WITH PESTS

Pest control can be a difficult problem in many inner-city locations, because pests are a community problem. You may operate a very clean establishment, but insects and rodents may be all around you in the neighborhood. They can enter your premises through open doors or cracks in walls or floors, or they may come in on the food products and supplies that you buy. The most effective way to deal with pests is to contract a professional exterminator to deal with the problem on a regular basis through an ongoing preventative program. Professionals know what to look for and where to look for it. They also know the proper way to use the chemical agents and devices needed to eradicate the problem, and they are insured. You should also seal off any points of entry that may be located.

PLANNING FOR GOOD SANITATION

Much can be done when you are building or renovating a restaurant to facilitate a sound sanitation program, such as choosing easily cleanable floor and wall materials, equipment, and work surfaces. Food service equipment should bear the NSF label on it—the label signifies that the equipment design was inspected and found to meet the standards of the National Sanitation Foundation.

Another aspect of planning for good sanitation is providing the necessary cleaning tools and supplies and assigning responsibility for cleaning certain work areas and equipment to particular individuals.

New products that help keep food and equipment sanitary, such as fruit and vegetable wash additives that reduce pathogen levels and disposable pan liners that minimize manual pot and pan washing, become available every year.

WHAT IS HACCP TRAINING, AND HOW CAN IT HELP RESTAURANTS?

Essentially, Hazard Analysis and Critical Control Point (HACCP) is a preventive program developed by the Food and Drug Administration for the food production and food service industries. It breaks down every food-related process, from the raw state to consumption by a consumer, and identifies the critical points at which hazards are likely to occur. The HACCP program contains recommended measures for each critical point, such as storing, handling, cooking, and cooling, and stipulates minimum cooking times and temperatures and the procedures required for controlling or eliminating potential hazards.

The HACCP program in its entirety goes beyond the issues that concern restaurants, but the National Restaurant Association offers its ServSafe training program, which was developed in accord with the HACCP principles and is specifically designed for restaurant and institutional food service operations.

One of the worst public relations problems for a food service establishment to endure is a food-borne illness outbreak. The risk of such incidents can be greatly reduced by giving employees sanitation training by using such tools as the ServSafe program.

EMPLOYEE SAFETY

The true costs of accidents in the workplace often go unnoticed. Aside from the pain inflicted on an injured person, there is the loss of the employee's skills, a possible increase in the restaurant's workers' compensation rate, and a lowering of morale if accidents occur frequently.

Most accidents can be attributed to unsafe acts, unsafe equipment, or unsafe working conditions. In a restaurant kitchen, the most common accidents are cuts, burns, and falls. All of these can be prevented with proper training, proper equipment, and proper supervision, but management must first be aware of the potential hazards. The causes of the problems must be identified, and solutions to each must be developed. This can be done by conducting a hazard analysis of the facility—and inspecting it from one end to the other.

Management must provide safe equipment with protective guards and other safety features; then the employees must be taught how to use the equipment properly and perform their duties safely. It is useful to post safety procedures near any piece of potentially hazardous equipment to remind employees of the possible dangers if misused.

CUSTOMER SAFETY

Patrons do not return to establishments that are unsafe. When evaluating your customer safety program, it's important to walk through the entire dining process that a customer experiences starting in your driveway. Following is a partial list of potential hazards you should evaluate:

- Is your driveway well marked?
- Is your parking lot well lit?
- Are parking spaces large enough and clearly painted?
- Has snow been removed, and have ice patches been sanded?
- Are there any loose steps or otherwise unsafe stairs?
- Are any carpets torn or loose?
- Are any tables or chairs weak or damaged?
- Have cracked dishes or glassware been removed from service?
- Are emergency exits clearly marked with lighted signs?
- Are your servers' practices such that they protect guests from accidental spills?
- Do you have safety procedures in place to handle emergencies?

FIRE SAFETY

The most common type of restaurant fires are grease fires in exhaust hoods. Ordinances in most communities require that fire suppressant equipment be installed in restaurant kitchens, but such equipment does not prevent fires. Regular cleaning of equipment and ductwork, where grease can build up and become heated to ignitable temperatures, is the only way to prevent this type of fire.

The next most common fires are electrical. Electrical fires can be avoided best by training employees how to handle electrical equipment properly. Teaching them such things as not to pull cords from wall receptacles by yanking on the cord (but rather by grasping the plug) and to turn off equipment when it will not be used for a while. Employees also should be taught how to use the various types of fire extinguishers and to report any defective electrical equipment immediately.

ALCOHOL RESPONSIBILITY

Not all restaurants need to serve alcoholic beverages—it depends on the market niche you wish to occupy. Although it is estimated that 70 percent of the adult population drinks alcoholic beverages to some degree, one can safely assume that very few people want a drink with breakfast. Therefore, alcohol service should be considered in the context of the wants and needs of your desired clientele.

Where alcohol service is feasible, it can be a significant profit center, provided the bar operations are controlled well and service is rendered responsibly. Dram shop laws and negligence statutes place a formidable responsibility on proprietors of alcoholic beverage establishments.

Know the Signs of Intoxication

All servers of alcohol should be trained to look for signs that indicate the state of a customer's sobriety. The challenge to a server is not to "shut off" a person after they have consumed too much, but rather to help them drink in such a way that they have an enjoyable time without becoming intoxicated. The following four stages can be considered signs on the road to becoming intoxicated. By recognizing each sign, the server can intervene to slow down the customer's rate of consumption as necessary.

1. Lessening of inhibitions
2. Exercising poor judgment
3. Displaying an impairment of reaction time
4. Exhibiting a loss of coordination

People tend to relax when they have a drink—their *inhibitions lessen.* As a result, they may act differently; some turn quiet while others become talkative, but all are relaxing in their own way. People can drink for quite a while without becoming intoxicated if they drink at a slow enough pace and do not consume more alcohol than their liver can metabolize per hour (one ounce or less, depending on body size).

The next noticeable affect of intoxication is *exercising poor judgment.* This occurs when a person drinks too fast. Their blood alcohol content rises, and they begin to do things that they probably would not do if not under the influence of alcohol. They might irritate other customers with loud outbursts of laughter or off-color remarks, becoming argumentative, or chug-a-lugging or ordering doubles in rapid succession.

Further drinking leads to a *loss of reactions.* This stage of intoxication is reflected by such behaviors as slurring speech, fumbling with money or cigarettes, and being unable to concentrate. At that point the drinker's brain and motor skills are not synchronized.

The last stage, *loss of coordination,* is exhibited by stumbling and weaving, spilling drinks and dropping money, falling asleep, and a general inability to function normally.

In the last two stages, drinkers can do serious harm to themselves and to others, so it is very important to prevent drinkers from entering those stages. This can be done by intervening with strategies that will slow a drinker's consumption. Servers should be aware of the conditions that influence the speed with which drinkers become intoxicated and take precautions.

Following are some of those conditions:

- Drinking too fast
- Repeatedly ordering strong drinks
- Taking medications while drinking
- Drinking on an empty stomach
- Drinking when depressed, stressed, or exhausted

In general, females have more fatty cells than males and tend to be smaller in body size. For those reasons, they tend to absorb alcohol into their bloodstream faster than males. In the same manner, a small male will be affected faster by alcohol consumption than will a large male.

When servers are aware of a drinker's need to be slowed down, they can intervene by serving snacks that do not create thirst and by not asking for reorders right away. When such measures are done tactfully, the customer may not even realize what is happening.

Responsible Business Practices

A great deal has been done by state agencies, the Training for Intervention Procedures by Servers of Alcohol (TIPS) program, the National Restaurant Association, and the major brewers and distillers of alcoholic beverages to educate the restaurant industry on the need for responsible business practices.

Licensees and servers of alcoholic beverages cannot eliminate their liability involving alcohol, but they can certainly reduce their risk by establishing and adhering to responsible business practices, including:

- Conducting periodic, in-house training sessions on alcohol responsibility
- Letting their customers know their policies by putting up posters and spelling out their policies on table tents, menus, and wine lists
- Checking the ID of anyone who does not appear to be at least 30 years old. This allows a comfortable margin of safety, as opposed to trying to determine if a person is 21.
- Making sure that all servers are acquainted with the restaurant's policies and practice them
- Keeping a list of all the things the bar does to abide by the law, such as conducting training sessions and checking IDs
- Keeping an incident log at the bar into which bartenders and servers enter a record of any situations where they had to shut off someone or refuse to serve a person
- Not soliciting refills until the customer asks for one
- Setting a limit on the number of stronger drinks that may be served to a person or developing recipes for weaker versions of those drinks
- Sending your servers to training programs such as the TIPS program

- Not having happy hours or similar programs that encourage people to consume excessive amounts of alcohol in short periods of time
- Making nonalcoholic drinks available
- Staffing adequately for peak periods so that servers can check IDs without being rushed and can monitor their customers properly
- Controlling the level of the lighting and music so that it does not encourage rapid drinking
- Offering free snacks to slow down consumption rates
- Offering free coffee to departing customers
- Calling taxicabs or arranging for safe transportation

These kinds of activities establish you as a prudent, law-abiding businessperson who runs an ethical establishment with well-trained employees and high standards. Those attributes can contribute positively to a legal defense, should one ever become necessary.

LIQUOR LAWS

If you sell alcohol, you should abide by both the spirit and the letter of the liquor laws. The alcoholic beverage control agency of each state publishes its regulations, which are based on the statutes of that state. A copy of the regulations may be obtained by writing to or calling the alcohol control agency in your jurisdiction (see Appendix D for contact information). The laws and regulations vary from state to state, but two things are common throughout the 50 states and the District of Columbia:

1. You cannot legally serve a minor. For the purposes of drinking, a minor is defined as any person under 21 years of age.
2. You cannot legally serve a person who is visibly intoxicated.

Checking IDs

It is imperative for a server of alcohol to check the ID of any person of questionable age. A helpful manual, the "I.D. Checking Guide," can be purchased from the Drivers License Guide Company (*www. driverslicenseguide.com*). This publication describes in detail the specific features of the driver's licenses of every state.

Following are some useful tips for checking the IDs of persons of doubtful age:

- Hold the license in your hand. Do not check it in a wallet. It is easier to see and feel indications of tampering when you hold a license.
- Compare the picture on the license with the face of the person. Pay particular attention to the mouth and chin. Holding the license in a line of vision directly under the person's chin makes comparisons easier.
- Check the date of birth on the license and ask the person what it is.
- Feel the surface of the license for rough spots and look for discolorations, separations, white-outs, or erasures.
- Check the thickness of the license to determine if the picture has been superimposed.
- Refer to the "I.D. Checking Guide" for out-of-state licenses.

Determining Who Is Visibly Intoxicated

Intoxication is determined by levels of blood alcohol content, and law enforcement officers have precise equipment for measuring such levels. Severs, however, don't have such equipment. Beyond that, except for blood alcohol levels, few laws stipulate a standard for determining "visible intoxication."

It is therefore important for servers to be trained to recognize the signs of intoxication discussed above and to use intervention techniques to slow down drinking before a person becomes legally intoxicated. Most importantly, a server should be familiar with the liquor laws as they pertain to servers and always act as would a prudent person who is guided by the intention to obey the law.

Action Guidelines

☐ Order a food sanitation code book from the public health agency of your state.

☐ If you plan to serve alcoholic beverages, order a liquor law book from the alcoholic beverage control agency of your state.

☐ Obtain a list of food sanitation and safety practices from your local health inspector.

☐ Develop a list of responsible business practices and prepare a policy manual for your bar and servers.

☐ Create an outline for a training session on sanitation and safety for kitchen employees and another one on responsible beverage service for your bar employees and dining room servers.

Chapter

16

WHAT IF YOU SUCCEED?
WHAT NEXT?

Some restaurants become an immediate success. Those rare occurrences are usually the result of being in the right place at the right time with a unique concept that is well received by the target market. Most new restaurant ventures are not so lucky as to have all of those crucial factors intersect at the same time. For them, success comes slowly as the result of much hard work, experimentation, and concerted management.

If your restaurant survives the first five years, it quite likely will continue to flourish, provided you remain enthusiastic about it and adhere to the sound business principles that enabled you to succeed in the first place. However, when a new business stabilizes and gives indications that it can continue to flourish, some people begin to tire of it. They discover that their main satisfaction came from building the business, not from operating it on a day-to-day basis. The question for them becomes: What next?

Whether or not a restaurateur continues to be enthralled with the business, a number of questions inevitably surface. Should you sell the business and enjoy the fruits of your labor? Or should you stay as you are and continue to enjoy the business? Should you expand? If you are highly successful, you might ponder the question: Should I franchise? Many chains started from humble beginnings and grew to national

225

proportions. Drive down the main business strip in most communities and count the success stories.

To decide on the right choice for you, you will have to go back to square one: redefine your goals and evaluate the options. You will need to consider the sacrifices required by each option and its implications for your lifestyle.

SHOULD YOU STAY THE SAME?

Changes are constantly occurring in the restaurant field. New foods come into vogue, technology changes, consumer tastes change, economic conditions vacillate, and new trends emerge. A restaurant must respond to change to survive over the long run. Few businesses can remain the same.

The trick is to incorporate changes without sacrificing the concepts that initially made the restaurant successful. Managing change is said to be the biggest challenge most businesses will face this millennium.

SHOULD YOU EXPAND?

All restaurants should at least consider expansion when they initially start up. It is unfortunate when a business has to move because it outgrows its present location. One never knows if the dynamics that worked so well in the original setting will happen again in another location. Customers sometimes resent change and will try a competitor before following a business, and if the competitor treats them well, they probably will not return.

The question of expansion has two facets:

1. Should you?
2. Can you?

It may appear from your growth pattern that you should expand, but do you have the physical space to enlarge your operations? If you add on to your building, can you add on to your parking lot? How would the additional space integrate with your existing production system and flow of traffic? Can new equipment be placed where it is most needed?

Sometimes, when a restaurant cannot expand at its present location, it will open a second one at another site. If it has good name recognition, the second location may achieve quick customer acceptance. If it does not have name recognition, a long, hard struggle may be required to make the second location succeed. The question that must then be asked is: Are the additional profits worth the additional burden of managing two locations?

SHOULD YOU FRANCHISE?

Many people think about franchising their business, but very few consider it seriously. It requires a great deal of legal and financial expertise as well as a substantial amount of capital. One must be realistic in assessing whether the business is franchisable. Does it have universal appeal? Is it distinctive enough to fill an existing market niche?

Selling franchises is very different from selling food—is that what you want to do? Are you willing and able to take on the monumental volume of legal and marketing activities involved in franchising? Legal, accounting, and marketing professionals should be consulted before this avenue is given any serious consideration.

Some restaurant companies prefer to open up additional company-owned locations as an alternative to franchising and all of its complexities.

SHOULD YOU SELL YOUR RESTAURANT?

If you are one of those people who enjoy the challenge of creating a successful restaurant but care very little about running it once the fun is over, you should consider selling it. There are individuals whose principal activity is starting, growing, and selling restaurants for substantial gains on their investment.

If your restaurant is successful, you will be in the enviable position of being able to ask a higher price without the financial pressure of needing to sell quickly.

You must ask yourself if you are happy with your lifestyle. Are you getting the satisfaction you anticipated from being in the restaurant business? If the answer to that question is no, you should probably sell the business and enjoy the profit. On the other hand, if the answer is yes and you remain in the business and continue to do a good job, you should make a very good living and be happy in your work.

Action Guidelines

☐ List your various options.
☐ Reassess your goals and objectives.
☐ Tabulate, in balance sheet form, the pros and cons of each option.
☐ Select the one choice that most closely matches your goals and objectives.

A

SAMPLE BUSINESS PLAN FOR A RESTAURANT

It is essential for any business seeking to attract investors or to obtain funds from lending institutions to have a business plan. Prospective investors and lenders will expect it to be complete, accurate, and defendable. A good business plan reflects conservative goals and expectations for the start-up period that are, above all, believable. Beyond its objective of obtaining capital, the business plan, if properly completed, ensures that you have considered, to the best of your ability, all of the contingencies that can make or break a start-up business.

Following is an illustration of how a business plan for a medium-priced, full-service restaurant in an urban/vacation city might appear.

BUSINESS PLAN

THE CHECKERED FLAG STEAK HOUSE
1340 Competition Drive
Raceway City, FL 30001

January 10, 20—

Robert Wiggins, Sarah Wiggins, Richard Wiggins
240 Palmetto Drive
Yourtown, FL 30002

Telephone: (396) 000-0000

Copy No. 1

CONTENTS

STATEMENT OF PURPOSE

Robert Wiggins, Sarah Wiggins, and Richard Wiggins—45 percent, 40 percent, and 15 percent partners respectively—seek a loan of $250,000, which together with their $250,000 personal investment will be used to obtain a lease at 1340 Competition Drive, Raceway City, Florida; acquire necessary licenses; make improvements to the leased premises; purchase furniture, fixtures, equipment, and inventories; provide working capital for two months; and cover such other preopening expenses that are necessary to open The Checkered Flag Steak House (also referred to herein as "the Checkered Flag" and "the restaurant"). It is expected that the business will produce a profit in the first year, and increased profits are expected in subsequent years, assuring a timely payback of the loan.

PART ONE: THE BUSINESS

Background

The principals recognized a need for a full-service restaurant near the site of the new SpectraDome Civic Center, scheduled to open in six months. The restaurant will be strategically located between several hotels, the SpectraDome Civic Center, and the National Speedway. It is estimated that because the SpectraDome Civic Center will house Raceway City's professional basketball team, conventions, and concerts, a stream of several million cars will pass by the restaurant each year. The restaurant will have highly visible signage and ample parking.

Research disclosed only three restaurants and two bars within a half mile of the Checkered Flag. Two of them are fast-food establishments; another is a Chinese restaurant. A survey of 1,500 people revealed that a steak-and-ribs house would be most welcome at the new site.

The Checkered Flag will occupy 2,400 square feet of space at 1340 Competition Drive and will accommodate 152 guests. It will have a capacity of 90 seats in its dining room, 30 seats in its lounge, and outside patio seating for an additional 32 guests. Its hours of service will be 11 AM to midnight every day; however, dining room seating will cease at 10:30 PM.

Entertainment on nonracing or sporting event nights will consist of two large television sets located at the bar and electronic background music in the dining room. A jazz pianist will play and sing intermittently from 7 PM to 11 PM on Thursdays, Fridays, and Saturdays.

Mission Statement

The Checkered Flag seeks to serve creatively prepared, high-quality food and beverages in a trendy, upscale atmosphere, while observing high standards of service.

The Concept

The Checkered Flag will be a medium-priced restaurant, featuring prompt service in a relaxing atmosphere. Its decor will have an auto racing theme. A refurbished, bright yellow, highly polished 1930s race car will be parked as an attention getter in the front patio. Scale models of race cars will be mounted on the interior walls. The barn-board paneled walls and rough-sawn, cedar-shingle roof facades will contrast with the luxurious carpeting and comfortable chairs so as to reflect the diversity of NASCAR racing and sporting fans. Life-size pictures of famous racing champions and racing paraphernalia, such as chrome-plated car parts, and artistically crafted neon tube signage will be displayed on the walls. An antique gas pump with gasoline priced at 23 cents a gallon will stand next to the lobby entrance. Lighting will be provided by Tiffany-style light fixtures for intimacy and be supplemented by natural lighting from large, smoked-glass windows. The menu covers will feature a racing graphic on the front panel.

Location

The restaurant will be located at 1340 Competition Drive in the east side of Raceway City, an area that is being revitalized by the development of the SpectraDome Civic Center. The restaurant will be housed on the street level of a renovated office building, with access from the street and from the lobby. Agreement on a favorable seven-year lease with an option to renew has been obtained. Occupancy costs will be $21 per square foot on a triple-net lease.

The population of Raceway City is approximately 68,000, of which 65 percent are age 21 or over. It is projected that the Checkered Flag will attract about 5 percent of the age 21-or-over segment and that local customers will patronize the restaurant 2.5 times a month on average.

Beyond the local clientele, it is estimated that annually, racing fans, basketball fans, and beach goers and concert goers will more than double that volume. The strategic location of the restaurant ensures that several million people will see the restaurant annually.

Access to the Checkered Flag is available by car, taxicab, and bus and by walking from nearby hotels. The restaurant will have 40 parking spaces reserved for its clientele in the building's parking facility. Beyond that, nearby parking lots and garages and the SpectraDome Civic Center's parking garage can accommodate several thousand cars.

Industry Trends

Studies by three state and local governmental agencies indicate that the recent economic growth of Raceway City is expected to continue as a result of the city's refocusing its outreach to out-of-state tourists and racing fans. The favorable weather and lovely beaches will continue to make it an attractive destination for family vacationers and winter residents. This growth will substantially benefit retail and hospitality businesses, and the city's favorable labor pool makes it an ideal location for new businesses.

Other Resources

Agreements for lines of credit have been established with the following firms:

Midstate Meatpackers, Inc.	2/10, n/30
Reliable Food Products, Co.	2/10, n/30
Superior Wares and Equipment, Inc.	2/10, n/30

Professional services will be provided by the following firms:

Taylor & Hynes, Associates	Certified Public Accountants
Carver, Kline & Golden	Attorneys at Law
The Ad-Vantage Agency	Advertising
Hospitality Services, Inc.	Foodservice Consultants

Management

The restaurant will be managed by Robert Wiggins (45 percent partner), who will also function as head chef. Sarah Wiggins (Robert's wife and 40 percent partner) will be the office manager and part-time dining room hostess. Richard Wiggins (their son and 15 percent partner) will be sous-chef.

Robert Wiggins has eight years of experience as a head chef and sous-chef for a prestigious Raceway City restaurant and six years of experience as the manager of an upscale restaurant. Richard Wiggins has an associate degree in culinary arts, two years of experience as a first cook, and four years as a sous-chef for a major hotel. Sarah Wiggins has seven years of restaurant serving experience in Miami and five years of dining room manager experience at an upscale restaurant in Fort Lauderdale, Florida. She is a graduate of Seagate Business School.

Objectives and Financial Expectations

The immediate goal of management is to generate a cash flow sufficient to meet all obligations of the business and generate a net profit before taxes of 10 percent of total sales. It is expected that this will be accomplished through creative merchandising and advertising, employee training, and the use of cost controls.

The long-term goal of management is to become one of Raceway City's culinary landmarks, yielding an annual return on investment in excess of 20 percent to its owners.

Product and Service

The Checkered Flag will be unique to the Raceway City area. Its style of service and method of food presentation will be that of a high-quality beef house, and its distinctive racing decor will give guests an interesting dining experience. Our motto will be: "Upscale, on a budget."

The clear message that The Checkered Flag Steak House will strive to communicate is, "This is a remarkable restaurant that serves excellent food and is convenient to the SpectraDome Civic Center, the beaches, and the National Speedway." Its menu will feature a variety of steaks, beef ribs, beef kabobs, chicken, and fish for dinner, as well as a luncheon menu consisting of soups, sandwiches, gourmet burgers, salad plates, and upscale appetizers. No other restaurant in the nearby area offers a similar menu in an entertaining atmosphere.

Pricing and Profitability

The Checkered Flag Steak House's dining room will operate with food cost percentage of 33 percent, and its lounge will operate with a bar cost percentage of 23 percent.

The expected breakdown of total revenues will be 73 percent from food sales and 27 percent from beverage sales. The combined total cost of sales will be 30 percent, producing a gross profit of 70 percent on total sales.

Prices will be competitive with comparable restaurants; however, the strategy of The Checkered Flag Steak House will be to give a perception of higher value than what its competitors offer through its food and drink presentation methods, pleasing service, and closeness to popular attractions.

Assuming a return on investment of at least 20 percent per year, the loan and the partners' investment will be recovered in five years or less.

Product Life Cycle

Due to the strategic location of the restaurant and the long-term loyalties of the sports fans that will go to the SpectraDome Civic Center, The Checkered Flag Steak House will have an indeterminate life cycle, as long as its high standards of food and service are maintained.

At the end of the restaurant's fifth year, however, management will conduct a self-study to ascertain whether the concept and the menu need to be rejuvenated.

It is anticipated that due to normal wear and tear, the facility will need a complete refurbishing and replacement of some equipment in seven years.

Market Analysis

The growth that will result from the opening of the SpectraDome Civic Center has been well determined by public and private researchers, and the restaurant will be in a strategic location to benefit from that growth.

A significant percentage of the retail and office employees of nearby businesses, sports fans, and tourists that will visit the area every day are expected to visit the restaurant when it opens. Our foremost goal is to give them a satisfying experience so that they will come back often.

Research indicates that after the SpectraDome Civic Center is opened, tour buses will bring thousands of sightseers into the area annually to see the unique architecture of the facility and to visit the sports paraphernalia shops.

Surveys of sports fans and employees of neighboring businesses revealed a desire for a nice place to eat near the SpectraDome Civic Center. The Checkered Flag Steak House will fill this need and, at the present time, has no competition offering the same kind of food, concept, and atmosphere within its marketing area.

Competition

There are three restaurants and two bars within a two-block radius of The Checkered Flag Steak House, but none of them is as close to the new SpectraDome Civic Center or offers the same dining experience. Two of the restaurants are fast-food, hamburger-based establishments that cater mainly to youths and lower-paid retail and service workers. The other is a Chinese restaurant. The two bars are sports bars that serve only pizzas and submarine sandwiches.

Studies of the competitors showed that none of them present substantial competition because of their different concepts and menu offerings.

Customers

The Checkered Flag Steak House will have three types of customers:

1. People going to events at the SpectraDome Civic Center or the National Speedway
2. Professional, administrative, and retail employees from nearby businesses
3. Vacationers, shoppers, and tourists

Because the SpectraDome Civic Center will be home for the city's basketball team and will accommodate conventions and concerts, it will generate a steady, year-round stream of potential customers.

The sports fans will typically be males and females over 18, from all walks of life, arriving as couples or in groups, or as families with an average of two children over seven years old.

The employees of nearby businesses will tend to walk to the restaurant, while shoppers will drive in from suburban communities and park in our lot or the nearby garages.

Marketing Strategy

The Checkered Flag Steak House will be positioned as a trendy place to have dinner on your way to or from an event at the SpectraDome Civic Center, a place where you can bring your business and social friends for an exceptionally good lunch or a steak dinner and good drinks at attractive prices, and a place where families will feel comfortable with their children.

Sunday through Wednesday, the restaurant will feature soft, electronic background music that appeals to people who want to dine in a relaxing atmosphere, as well as to tourists and sports fans who will appreciate the racing decor. On Thursday through Saturday nights, a jazz pianist will play from 8 PM to 11 PM.

Public relations contacts will be made with taxicab companies, tour group leaders, and other agencies that make recommendations to tourists.

All advertisements and commercials will position The Checkered Flag Steak House as "*the* restaurant that must be tried when you visit Raceway City." The Ad-Vantage Agency will handle all media placements and public relations releases. They have over 18 years of experience with top hospitality accounts in the Raceway City area.

Support will be given to a few highly visible charitable organizations and community causes, and the partners of the business will be active members of the chamber of commerce, Rotary, and Kiwanis clubs.

Personnel

The restaurant will rely heavily on part-time employees, because there is an ample supply of culinary and other students as well a large immigrant population seeking such employment. The projected staff includes 11 full-time employees and 19 part-time employees, who will work an average of 755 hours per week and generate a weekly payroll of $6,848 on average.

The estimated annual payroll of $356,070 is 30 percent of total sales. Table 1 shows the projected employee work schedule for The Checkered Flag Steak House. Arrangements have been made for additional, part-time, and temporary staffing on nights when special events are scheduled at the SpectraDome Civic Center and for race weeks at the National Speedway.

Risk

Risk management will be practiced from the opening day. All food service handlers will be given an in-house food sanitation and safety course, and all servers will be required to attend an accredited responsible alcohol service course. Both training courses will entitle the restaurant to substantial discounts on insurance premiums. The restaurant will carry the following insurances in its risk management portfolio:

- Named peril insurance (hurricane)
- Liquor liability and third-party liability insurance
- Workers' compensation insurance
- General liability insurance
- Business interruption insurance
- Product liability insurance
- Fire insurance
- Key-person life insurance on partners
- Personal injury liability insurance

In addition to insuring against specific risks, ongoing training programs will be conducted to ensure a high degree of professionalism among employees in their respective jobs.

PROJECTED EMPLOYEE WORK SCHEDULE

	Mon.	Tue.	Wed.	Thru.	Fri.	Sat.	Sun.	Total Hrs.	Hrs. Wage	Wkly Pay
KITCHEN										
Head Chef & Mgr (Partner)	4/11	9/5	9/5	9/5	9/5	9/5	9/5		Salary	866.00
Sous Chef (Partner)			4/11	4/11	4/11	4/11	4/10		Salary	726.00
Rounds Person	9/5	5/10		5/10	11/7	11/7	5/11	40	10.00	400.00
Boiler Person	5/9		5/9	5/9	5/9	5/9	5/9	24	9.75	234.00
Salad & Dess't Maker	11/5	11/5	11/5	11/5		11/5	11/5	36	9.00	324.00
Cooks Helper	10/2	10/2	10/2	10/2	10/2		10/2	24	8.50	204.00
GenKitchen/Dshwshr	5/10	5/10	5/10		5/10	5/10	11/7	33	8.50	280.50
Dishwasher	5/10	5/10	5/10	5/10	5/11	5/11	5/10	37	8.00	296.00
Dishwasher	11/5	11/5	11/5	11/5	11/5	11/6	5/9	40	8.00	320.00
DINING ROOM										
AM Head Waitperson	10/4		10/4	10/4	10/4	10/4	10/4	36	4.25	153.00
Waiterperson P/T	10/2	10/2	10/2	10/2	10/2	10/2		20	3.15	63.00
Waiterperson P/T	10/2	10/2			10/2	10/2	10/2	20	3.15	63.00
Waiterperson P/T	10/2	10/2	10/2	10/2	10/2	10/2	10/2	24	3.15	75.60
Waiterperson P/T	4/10	10/2	10/2			10/2	10/2	22	3.15	69.30
Waiterperson P/T	10/2			10/2		10/2	10/2	16	3.15	50.40
PM Head Waitperson		4/10	4/10	4/10	4/10	4/10	4/10	36	4.00	144.00

PROJECTED EMPLOYEE WORK SCHEDULE

	Mon.	Tue.	Wed.	Thru.	Fri.	Sat.	Sun.	Total Hrs.	Hrs. Wage	Wkly Pay
Waitperson P/T			5/9	5/10	5/10	5/9	5/9	18	3.15	56.70
Waitperson P/T	5/8		5/9	5/9		5/10	5/9	20	3.15	63.70
Waitperson P/T	5/8	5/9			5/9	5/10	5/9	20	3.15	63.00
Waitperson P/T	5/9	5/9	5/9	5/9	5/9	5/9	5/9	24	3.15	75.60
Waitperson P/T		5/9	5/9		5/9	5/9		16	3.15	50.40
BAR & LOUNGE										
AM Head Bartender	10/4	10/4	10/5	10/5	10/5	10/5		40	9.00	360.00
PM Head Bartender			5/1	5/1	5/1	5/1	5/1	40	8.00	320.00
Bartender P/T		4/8	10/2	10/2	11/2	5/12		22	7.00	154.00
Bartender P/T	4/1		5/8	5/8	5/9	10/2	10/6	31	7.00	217.00
OTHER										
Office Mgr. (Partner)	9/5	9/5	9/5	9/5	9/5	9/5	11/2		Salary	765.00
AM Host(ess)	11/2	11/2	11/2	11/2	11/2	11/2	11/2	21	8.00	168.00
PM Host(ess)	5/8	5/8	5/8	5/8	5/8	5/8	5/8	21	8.00	168.00
Maint. & Cleaning	9/12	9/12	9/12	9/12	9/12	9/12	9/12	21	8.00	168.00

Total Weekly Payroll : $6,847.50
times 52 Weeks   X52

Estimated Annual Payroll $356,070

Loan Request and Intended Use of Funds

Amount requested	$250,000
Term of loan	Fifteen years;, with first payment due three months after transaction date of loan.
Interest rate	12% fixed rate, with no prepayment penalty.
Debt-to-equity ratio	1 to 1 ($250,000 to $250,000)
Collateral	Deed of trust on the wholly owned home of Robert and Sarah Wiggins, with a current market value appraised at $475,000.
Other protections	Borrowers will carry insurance against business interruption and loss due to hazards, naming the lender as a beneficiary in the event of interruption of business.
Intended use of funds	The partners will use the borrowed funds, in conjunction with their own investment, to acquire necessary licenses; secure a lease; make improvements to the leased premises; and purchase the furniture, fixtures, equipment, and inventories necessary to open The Checkered Flag Steak House and to conduct a grand opening.

Summary of Part One

Robert Wiggins, along with his wife Sarah Wiggins and their son Richard Wiggins—45 percent, 40 percent, and 15 percent partners respectively—seek a secured loan of $250,000, which in conjunction with their combined personal investment of $250,000 will be used to open an upscale steak house, to be known as The Checkered Flag Steak House, at 1340 Competition Drive, Raceway City, Florida.

Extensive market analysis indicates a need for such a restaurant and a sufficient target population to sustain it. The new SpectraDome Civic Center, which will be located a block away, is expected to bring an estimated 2 million people into the area every year.

The restaurant will have a capacity of 90 seats in its dining room, 30 seats in its bar, and 32 seats in its outside patio. It will offer high-quality food and beverage service in a casual and comfortable atmosphere. Its racing decor will feature poster-size photos of race cars and drivers, and its menu will be that of an upscale beef house. There is no direct competition in the restaurant's dominant marketing area.

It is expected that through effective sales promotion, thorough training, and the use of cost controls, the restaurant will be profitable from the first year and will be able to pay back the loan and the partners' investment in five years.

PART TWO: FINANCIAL PROJECTIONS

Start-Up Requirements

Cash (working capital)	$92,500
Leasehold improvements	130,000
Licenses	36,000
Beginning inventories	38,000
(Food, beverages, and supplies)	
Furniture, fixtures, and equipment	133,500
Opening expenses	70,000
(Liquor liability insurance, other insurances, licenses, permits, clean-up, advertising and promotion, deposits, employee training, preopening parties, and grand opening)	
Total Start-Up Investment Required	**$500,000**

Estimated Annual Sales

Number of Customers Expected Each Day of the Week

	Mon.	Tue.	Wed.	Thur.	Fri.	Sat.	Sun.	Total
Lunch	70	75	80	90	100	90	80	585
Dinner	35	45	60	65	85	90	75	455
Bar only	20	25	40	40	50	55	25	255
					Total Customers per Week			**1,295**

Average Menu Prices

Sandwiches and salad plates	$6.95
Entrees	16.95
Desserts	4.00
Drinks	4.50

Estimated Average Guest Check per Person

Lunch	Sandwich or salad plate, plus drink	$11.45
Dinner	Entree, salad, 0.5 dessert, plus drink	30.40
Bar only	Average 2 drinks	9.00

Estimated Weekly Sales

585 lunch guests	×	$11.45	=	6,698
455 dinner guests	×	30.40	=	13,832
255 bar only guests	×	9.00	=	2,295
Total Weekly Sales				**$22,825**

Estimated Total Annual Sales

52 weeks × $22,825 weekly sales = **$1,186,900 annual sales**

* Note: The 0.5 for items such as desserts allows for the expectation that approximately one out of every two customers will order one.

List of Furniture, Fixtures, and Equipment

Qty.	Item	Cost
1	Freezer, reach-in, stainless, with racks	$ 3,725
1	Dishwasher, automatic	12,300
1	Walk-in refrigerator	7,100
2	Fryers, twin basket	7,450
1	Griddle, 3'	3,500
1	Toaster, automatic, conveyor type	1,725
2	Stainless steel prep tables	800
1	Food mixer, 20 quart	3,175
2	Restaurant ranges	4,850
1	Convection oven	5,450
1	Garbage disposer	300
2	Refrigerators, 40 cu. ft., stainless	4,475
1	Fire protection hood and exhaust system	10,000
1	Broiler	2,800
1	Coffee urn	2,100
1	Ice maker, air cooled, 600-pound capacity	3,000
1	Remote, 6-keg capacity, beer refrigerator	2,500
2	Cocktail stations, 30"	1,800
2	Three compartment bar sinks, with speed racks and double drain boards	1,500
1	Direct draw, 3-keg beer box, with taps	2,100
2	Post mix soda dispensing systems, with carbonator and 50' lines	2,000
1	Three door bar refrigerator	2,400
1	Glass froster, 3', 120-mug capacity	1,200
1	Beer bottle cooler, 4'	900
20"	Front bar with top and foot rail	4,020
14"	Back bar with cabinets and shelves	2,038
15	Bar stools, upholstered	3,901
8	Booths, 4'	4,013
12	Tables, with bases, seat 4	2,388
10	Tables, with bases, seat 2	1,750

(continued on next page)

100	Chairs	12,500
2	Television sets, large screen	5,500
	Glassware	1,100
	Small wares and supplies	1,800
1	Safe, fireproof	2,500
1	POS system, cash register	3,250
1	Desk, mahogany and swivel chair	625
1	Desk, steel and secretary's chair	450
1	Planter, divider, 3' high	515
Total Cost of Furniture, Fixtures, and Equipment		**$133,500**

Leasehold Improvements

Heating, ventilation, and air-conditioning	$41,000
Electrical	22,000
Plumbing	21,000
Carpeting, floor tile, and other related equipment	46,000
Total Leasehold Improvements	**$130,000**

Sources and Uses of Funds

Uses of Funds	Source of Funds		
Start-Up Expenses	**Partners' Equity**	**Loan**	**Total**
Furniture, fixtures, and equipment	$66,750	$66,750	$133,500
Leasehold improvements	29,000	101,000	130,000
License	36,000	0	36,000
Food, beverage, and supplies inventories	19,000	19,000	38,000
Opening expenses (liquor liability insurance, other insurances, licenses, permits, advertising, lease deposit, clean up, employee training, preopening parties and grand opening)	35,000	35,000	70,000
Working Capital	46,250	46,250	92,500
Total Funds	**$232,000**	**$268,000**	**$500,000**

Income Statement for
The Checkered Flag Steak House
for the period of January 1 through December 31, 20___

			Percent
Sales			
Food sales	$866,437		73.0
Beverage sales	320,463		27.0
Total sales		$1,186,900	100.0
Cost of sales			
Food cost	$285,924		24.1
Beverage cost	73,706		6.2
Total cost of sales		359,630	30.3
Gross profit from operations		$827,270	69.7
Controllable expenses			
Payroll	$356,070		30.0
Employee benefits	48,663		4.1
Direct operating expenses	54,597		4.6
Advertising and promotion	21,364		1.8
Music and entertainment	11,667		1.0
Utilities	36,794		3.1
Admin. and general expenses	29,673		2.5
Repairs and maintenance	17,804		1.5
Total controllable expenses		576,632	48.6
Profit before occupancy costs		$250,638	21.1
Occupancy costs			
Rent (triple-net lease)	$50,400		4.2
Property taxes	7,000		0.6
Other taxes	2,333		0.2
Property insurance	9,100		0.8
Total occupancy costs		68,833	5.8
Profit before interest and depreciation		$181,805	15.3
Interest		$ 5,834	0.5
Depreciation		23,334	2.0
Net profit		**$152,637**	**12.8**

Twelve-Month Projected Income Statement

Projected Income Statement
The Checkered Flag Restaurant
for the period Jan. 1 thru Dec. 31, 20_

	Jan	Feb	Mar	Apr	May	Jun	Jul	Aug	Sep	Oct	Nov	Dec	Total
Sales													
Food	67,203	68,203	69,203	70,203	71,203	72,203	72,203	73,203	74,203	75,203	76,203	77,204	866,437
Beverage	26,705	26,705	26,705	26,705	26,706	26,705	26,705	26,705	26,705	26,705	26,705	26,705	320,463
Total Sales	93,908	94,908	95,908	96,908	97,909	98,908	98,908	99,908	100,908	101,908	102,908	103,911	1,186,900
Cost of Sales													
Food	22,177	22,507	22,837	23,167	23,497	23,827	23,827	24,157	24,487	24,817	25,147	25,477	285,924
Bev	6,142	6,142	6,142	6,142	6,142	6,142	6,142	6,142	6,142	6,142	6,142	6,142	73,706
Total Cost of Sales	28,319	28,649	28,979	29,309	29,639	29,969	29,969	30,299	30,629	30,959	31,289	31,619	359,630
Gross Profit from Operations	65,589	66,259	66,929	67,599	68,270	68,939	68,939	69,609	70,279	70,949	71,619	72,292	827,270
Controllable Expenses													
Payroll and Emplee Benefits	32,023	32,364	32,705	33,046	33,387	33,728	33,728	34,069	34,410	34,751	35,092	35,434	404,733
Direct Operating	4,320	4,366	4,412	4,458	4,504	4,550	4,550	4,596	4,642	4,688	4,734	4,780	54,597
Advertising and Promotion	1,690	1,708	1,726	1,744	1,762	1,780	1,780	1,798	1,816	1,834	1,852	1,870	21,364
Music and Entertainment	939	949	959	969	979	989	989	999	1,009	1,019	1,029	1,039	11,667
Utilities	2,911	2,942	2,973	3,004	3,035	3,066	3,066	3,097	3,128	3,159	3,190	3,221	36,794
Administrative and Gen.	2,348	2,373	2,398	2,423	2,448	2,473	2,473	2,498	2,523	2,548	2,573	2,598	29,673
Repairs and Maintenance	1,409	1,424	1,439	1,454	1,469	1,484	1,484	1,499	1,514	1,529	1,544	1,559	17,804
Total Controllable Expenses	45,639	46,125	46,611	47,097	47,584	48,069	48,069	48,555	49,041	49,527	50,013	50,501	576,632
Profit Before Occupancy Costs	19,950	20,134	20,318	20,502	20,686	20,870	20,870	21,054	21,238	21,422	21,606	21,791	250,638
Occupancy Costs													
Rent	4,200	4,200	4,200	4,200	4,200	4,200	4,200	4,200	4,200	4,200	4,200	4,200	50,400
Property Taxes	583	583	583	583	583	583	583	583	583	583	583	583	7,000
Other Taxes	194	194	194	194	194	194	194	194	194	194	194	194	2,333
Property Insurance	758	758	758	758	758	758	758	758	758	758	758	758	9,100
Total Occupancy Expenses	5,735	5,735	5,735	5,735	5,735	5,735	5,735	5,735	5,735	5,735	5,735	5,735	68,833
Profit Before Int. and Depr.	14,215	14,399	14,583	14,767	14,951	15,135	15,135	15,319	15,503	15,687	15,871	16,056	181,805
Interest	486	486	486	486	486	486	486	486	486	486	486	486	5,834
Depreciation	1,945	1,945	1,945	1,945	1,945	1,945	1,945	1,945	1,945	1,945	1,945	1,945	23,334
Net Profit	11,784	11,968	12,152	12,336	12,520	12,704	12,704	12,888	13,072	13,256	13,440	13,625	152,637

Cash Flow Statement—By Month
The Checkered Flag Restaurant
for the period of January 1 through December 31, 20___

Sources of Cash	Preopening	Jan.	Feb.	Mar.	Apr.	May	June	July	Aug.	Sept.	Oct.	Nov.	Dec.	Year Total
Partners' Equity	$250,000													$250,000
Loan	250,000													250,000
Net Profit	0	$11,784	$11,968	$12,152	$12,336	$12,520	$12,704	$12,704	$12,888	$13,072	$13,256	$13,440	$13,625	152,637
Depreciation		1,945	1,945	1,945	1,945	1,945	1,945	1,945	1,945	1,945	1,945	1,945	1,945	23,340
Total	500,000	13,729	13,913	14,097	14,281	14,465	14,649	14,649	14,833	15,017	15,201	15,385	15,570	675,977
Disbursements														
Liquor License	36,000													35,000
Leasehold	130,000													130,000
Improvements														
Furn./Fix./Equip.	133,500													133,500
Beg. Inventories	38,000													38,000
Opening Costs	70,000													70,000
Monthly Loan Payments	0	0	2,500	2,500	2,500	2,500	2,500	2,500	2,500	2,500	2,500	2,500	2,500	27,500
Total	407,500	0	2,500	2,500	2,500	2,500	2,500	2,500	2,500	2,500	2,500	2,500	2,500	434,000
Mo. Cash Flow	92,500	13,729	11,413	11,597	11,761	11,965	12,149	12,149	12,333	12,517	12,701	12,885	13,070	240,769
Cum. Cash Flow	92,500	106,229	117,642	129,239	141,000	152,965	165,114	177,263	189,596	202,113	214,814	227,699	240,769	240,769

Daily Break-Even Analysis

Monthly Fixed Costs	
Rent	$ 4,200
Salaries	10,214
Utilities	3,325
Insurance	2,758
Taxes	3,047
Depreciation	1,945
Total Monthly Fixed Costs	$25,489
Daily Fixed Costs (Total monthly fixed costs ÷ 30 days)	$850
Daily Variable Costs	
Cost of food (1 day's supply)	$ 794
Cost of liquor (1 day's supply)	205
Cost of additional staff essential to sales	649
Total Daily Variable Costs	$1,648
Daily Sales Volume Required to Break Even	$2,498

Cash-Flow Statement for 12 Months

Conclusion and Summary

This request is for a secured loan in the amount of $250,000, which together with an investment of $250,000 by Robert Wiggins, Sarah Wiggins, and Richard Wiggins—45 percent, 40 percent, and 15 percent partners respectively—will be used to start The Checkered Flag Steak House. Specifically, the funds will be used to acquire necessary licenses; obtain a lease for premises at 1340 Competition Drive, Raceway City, Florida; make improvements to leased premises; purchase furniture, fixtures, equipment, and inventories; hire and train staff; and for pre-opening expenses and working capital.

All financial projections have been made conservatively, with a 10 percent safety factor used to overstate costs and understate revenues. It is expected that The Checkered Flag Steak House will operate profitably in its first year of operation and be able to meet all of its obligations in a timely manner.

The opening of the nearby SpectraDome Civic Center will attract several million sports fans and tourists to the dominant marketing area of The Checkered Flag Steak House each year. In addition, a program of aggressive marketing and strict cost controls should enable the restaurant's profits to grow for the foreseeable future.

Based on the foregoing documentation and the research upon which it is based, the proposed restaurant should be viable and generate a very satisfactory return for its owners.

PART THREE: SUPPORTING DOCUMENTS

Resumes of Partners

Robert Wiggins
240 Palmetto Drive
Yourtown, FL 30002
(396) 000-0000

Education:
Tri-town Regional High School, Centerville, Connecticut
Institute of Culinary Arts, diploma 1985

Employment:
The Gulf Stream Restaurant, Raceway City, Florida, 1991–1999
    Positions: head chef and sous-chef
Atlantic Seafood House, Fort Lauderdale, Florida, 1999–2006
    Position: general manager

Personal Credit References:
Onshore Savings Bank, Raceway City, Florida
    House mortgage, paid up in 2001
Second Federal Bank, Raceway City, Florida
    Automobile loan, 24 months, paid up in 2004

References:

Thomas Holder, President	Bart Fender, Sales Manager
Onshore Savings Bank	Precise Insurance Company
1503 Flint Street	520 Metal Road
Raceway City, Florida 30001	Raceway City, Florida 30001

Sarah Wiggins
240 Palmetto Drive
Yourtown, Florida 30002
(396) 000-0000

Education:
Strafford Business School, Atlanta, Georgia
Accounting and clerical diploma, 1985

Employment:
The Top of the Tower Restaurant, Miami Beach, Florida, 1993–2000
    Positions: server, host
Atlantic Seafood House, Fort Lauderdale, Florida, 2000–2006
    Position: dining room manager

Personal Credit References:
Sun City Savings Bank, Sun City, Florida
    Automobile loan, paid up in 2005
Seaside Finance Company, Raceway City, Massachusetts
    Personal loan, 12 months, paid up in 2002

References:

Alice Maxfield, Executive Director
Bayside Charities, Inc.
390 Pondview Street
Morcland, Georgia

Charles Bookman, Manager
Flashwell Business Services
17 Jackson Street
Elmore, Georgia

Richard Wiggins
1123 Central Street
Yourtown, Florida 30002
(396) 000–0000

Education:
Harbor Community College, Raceway City, Florida, AAS degree 1997
Institute of Culinary Arts, diploma 1999

Employment:
Uptown Hotel, Embassy Room, Raceway City, Florida, 2000–2006
    Positions: first cook, sous-chef

Personal Credit References:
Bayside Savings Bank
    Automobile loan, paid up in 2003
Uptown National Bank, Raceway City, Florida

References:

Ann Carswell, Executive Director
Bayside Chamber of Commerce
690 Water Street
Raceway City, Florida

Calvin Binder, Advertising
Manager
Finer & Hapwell Advertising
Agency
417 Maryland Street
Raceway City, Florida

Personal Balance Sheets of Partners

Robert Wiggins
(as of November 1, 20—)

Assets

Cash in bank—savings	$ 8,000
Checking	3,000
Marketable securities	75,000
Life insurance	35,000
Home equity (50% equity in jointly owned home valued @ $376,000)	188,000
Automobile	22,500
Other personal assets	21,000
Total assets	**$352,500**

Liabilities

Accounts payable	$ 3,400
Home improvement loan	39,000
Total liabilities	**$ 42,400**

Net worth	**$310,100**
Total liabilities and net worth	**$352,500**

Sarah Wiggins
(as of November 1, 20—)

Assets

Cash in bank—savings	$ 28,200
Checking	7,000
Marketable securities	90,000
Automobile	17,000
Home equity (50% of equity in jointly owned home)	188,000
Other personal assets	18,000
Total assets	**$348,200**

Liabilities

Accounts payable	$3,500
Total liabilities	**$3,500**
Net worth	**$344,700**
Total liabilities and net worth	**$348,200**

Richard Wiggins
(as of November 1, 20—)

Assets

Cash in bank—savings	$12,200
Checking	2,000
Marketable securities	40,000
Automobile	12,000
Other personal assets	8,000
Total assets	**$74,200**

Liabilities

Accounts payable	$ 3,500
Automobile installment loan balance	1,200
Total liabilities	**$ 4,700**
Net worth	**$69,500**
Total liabilities and net worth	**$74,200**

Floor Plan of The Checkered Flag Steak House

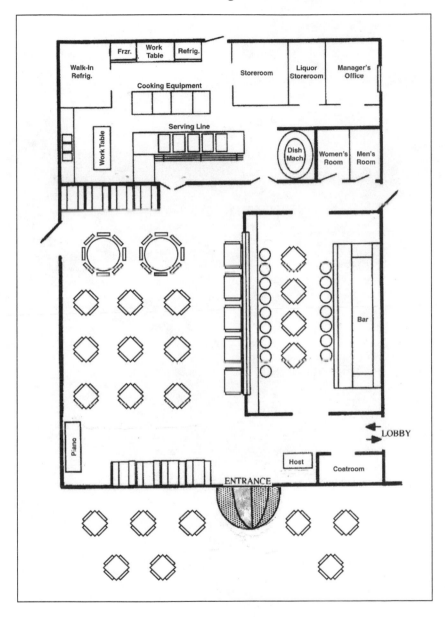

B

STATE HEALTH DEPARTMENTS

Following is a list of state agencies that issue permits and regulate and enforce the public health laws of the state.

Alabama
Department of Public Health
201 Monroe Street
Montgomery, AL 36104
(334) 206-5200

Alaska
Division of Public Health
Department of Health and
    Social Services
PO Box 110601
Juneau, AK 99811
(907) 465-3030

Arizona
Department of Health Services
150 N 18th Avenue
Phoenix, AZ 85007
(602) 542-1001

Arkansas
Department of Health
4815 W. Markham Street
Little Rock, AR 72205
(501) 682-2111

California
Health and Human Services
    Agency
1600 9th Street, Room 460
Sacramento, CA 95814
(916) 654-3345

Colorado
Department of Public Health and
    Environment
4300 Cherry Creek Drive S.
Denver, CO 80246
(303) 692-2100

Connecticut
Department of Public Health
410 Capitol Avenue
Hartford, CT 06106
(860) 509-7101

Delaware
Department of Health and Social
  Services
Herman Holloway Sr. Campus
1901 N Du Pont Highway,
  Main Building
Newcastle, DE 19720
(302) 255-9040

Florida
Department of Health
2585 Merchants Row Boulevard,
  Suite 140
Tallahassee, FL 32399
(850) 245-4321

Georgia
Division of Public Health
2 Peachtree Street NW
Atlanta, GA 30303
(404) 657-2700

Hawaii
Department of Health
PO Box 3378
Honolulu, HI 96801
(808) 586-4410

Idaho
Department of Health and Welfare
450 W. State Street
Peter T. Cenarrusa Building
Boise, ID 83720
(208) 334-5500

Illinois
Department of Public Health
535 W. Jefferson Street, 5th Floor
Springfield, IL 62761
(217) 782-4977

Indiana
State Department of Health
2 N. Meridian Street
Indianapolis, IN 46204
(317) 233-7400

Iowa
Department of Public Health
Lucas Building
321 E. 12th Street
Des Moines, IA 50319
(515) 281-8474

Kansas
Department of Health and
  Environment
1000 SW Jackson, Suite 540
Topeka, KS 66612
(785) 296-0461

Kentucky
Cabinet for Health and
  Family Services
275 E. Main Street
Frankfort, KY 40601
(502) 564-7042

Louisiana
Department of Health and
  Hospitals
PO Box 629
Baton Rouge, LA 70821
(225) 342-9500

Maine
Department of Human Services
State House Station #11
Augusta, ME 04333
(207) 287-2736

Maryland
Department of Health and
  Mental Hygiene
201 W. Preston Street, 5th Floor
Baltimore, MD 21201
(410) 767-6505

Massachusetts
Department of Public Health
250 Washington Street
Boston, MA 02108
(617) 624-5200

Michigan
Department of Community Health
Lewis Cass Building, 6th Floor
320 S. Walnut
Lansing, MI 48913
(517) 373-0408

Minnesota
Department of Health
85 E. 7th Place, Suite 400
Saint Paul, MN 55101
(651) 215-5806

Mississippi
State Department of Health
PO Box 1700
Jackson, MS 39215
(601) 576-7400

Missouri
Department of Health
PO Box 570
Jefferson City, MO 65102
(573) 751-6001

Montana
Department of Health and
  Human Services
111 N. Sanders, Room 301/308
Helena, MT 59601
(406) 444-5622

Nebraska
Department of Health
PO Box 95007
Lincoln, NE 68509
(402) 471-3121

Nevada
Health Division
Department of Human Services
505 E. King Street, Room 600
Carson City, NV 89706
(702) 687-4740

New Hampshire
Department of Health and
  Human Services
129 Pleasant Street
Concord, NH 03301
(603) 271-4331

New Jersey
Department of Health
PO Box 360
Trenton, NJ 08625
(609) 292-7837

New Mexico
Department of Health
1190 Saint Francis Drive
Santa Fe, NM 87504
(505) 827-2613

New York
Department of Health
Corning Tower Building
Empire State Plaza
Albany, NY 12237
(518) 474-2011

North Carolina
Department of Health and
    Human Services
2001 Mail Service Center
Raleigh, NC 27699
(919) 733-4534

North Dakota
Department of Health
600 E. Boulevard Avenue,
    2nd Floor
Bismarck, ND 58505
(701) 328-2372

Ohio
Department of Health
246 N. High Street
Columbus, OH 43216
(614) 466-2253

Oklahoma
State Department of Health
1000 NE 10th Street
Oklahoma City, OK 73117
(405) 271-2771

Oregon
Health Services
500 Summer Street NE,
    Suite E-41
Salem, OR 97301
(503) 947-1175

Pennsylvania
Department of Health
PO Box 90
Health and Welfare Building
Harrisburg, PA 17108
(717) 787-6436

Rhode Island
Department of Health
3 Capitol Hill
Providence, RI 02908
(401) 222-2231

South Carolina
Department of Health and
    Human Services
PO Box 8206
Columbia, SC 29202
(803) 898-2504

South Dakota
Department of Health
600 E. Capitol Avenue
Pierre, SD 57501
(605) 773-3361

Tennessee
Department of Health
Cordell Hull Building, 3rd Floor
425 5th Avenue N
Nashville, TN 37247
(615) 741-3111

Texas
Department of Health
1100 W. 49th Street
Austin, TX 78756
(512) 458-7375

Utah
Department of Health
288 N. 1460 W.
Salt Lake City, UT 84114
(801) 538-6111

Vermont
Department of Health
108 Cherry Street
Burlington, VT 05402
(802) 863-7280

Virginia
Department of Health
109 Governor Street
Richmond, VA 23219
(804) 786-3561

Washington
Department of Health
PO Box 47890
Olympia, WA 98504
(360) 586-5846

West Virginia
Department of Health and
   Human Resources
State Capitol Complex Building 3,
   Room 206
1900 Kanawha Boulevard E.
Charleston, WV 25305
(304) 558-0684

Wisconsin
Department of Health and
   Family Services
PO Box 7850
Madison, WI 53702
(608) 266-0667

Wyoming
Department of Health
Hathaway Building, 1st Floor
2300 Capitol Avenue
Cheyenne, WY 82002
(307) 777-7656

District of Columbia
Department of Health
825 N. Capitol Street NE
Washington, DC 20002
(202) 442-5199

Source: *Directory of Administrative Officials*, 2004, published by the Council of State Governments

C

STATE LABOR DEPARTMENTS

Following is a list of state agencies that are responsible for administering and enforcing the state's labor laws:

Alabama
Department of Labor
PO Box 303500
Montgomery, AL 36130
(334) 202-3460

Alaska
Department of Labor
PO Box 21149
Juneau, AK 99801-1149
(907) 465-2700

Arizona
Industrial Commission
PO Box 19070
Phoenix, AZ 85005-9070
(602) 542-4515

Arkansas
Department of Labor
10421 W. Markham, Suite 100
Little Rock, AZ 72205
(501) 682-4541

California
State Labor Commissioner
455 Golden Gate Avenue,
  9th Floor
San Francisco, CA 94102
(415) 703-4810

Colorado
Department of Labor and
  Employment
1515 Arapahoe Street
Denver, CO 80202-2117
(303) 318-8468

Connecticut
Department of Labor
200 Folly Brook Boulevard
Wethersfield, CT 06109
(860) 263-6505

Delaware
Department of Labor
4425 N. Market Street, 4th Floor
Wilmington, DE 19802
(302) 761-6621

Florida
Department of Labor
Caldwell Building, Suite 100
107 E. Madison Street
Tallahassee, FL 32399
(850) 245-7105

Georgia
Department of Labor
148 International Boulevard NE
Atlanta, GA 30303
(404) 656-3011

Hawaii
Department of Labor and
   Industrial Relations
830 Punchbowl Street, Room 321
Honolulu, HI 96813
(808) 586-8844

Idaho
Labor and Industrial Services
317 W. Main Street
Boise, ID 83735-0001
(208) 332-3579

Illinois
Department of Labor
160 N. LaSalle Street, Suite C1300
Chicago, IL 60601
(312) 793-1808

Indiana
Department of Labor
IGC-South, Room W195
402 W. Washington
Indianapolis, IN 46204-2739
(317) 232-2738

Iowa
Division of Labor Services
Department of Employment
   Services
1000 E. Grand
Des Moines, IA 50319
(515) 281-3447

Kansas
Department of Human Resources
401 SW Topeka Boulevard
Topeka, KS 66603-3182
(785) 296-7474

Kentucky
Kentucky Department of Labor
1047 U.S. 127 S., Suite 4
Frankfort, KY 40601-4381
(502) 564-3070

Louisiana
Department of Labor
PO Box 94094
Baton Rouge, LA 70804-9094
(225) 342-3011

Maine
Department of Labor
State House Station #45
Augusta, ME 04333-0045
(207) 264-6400

Maryland
Division of Labor and Industry
Department of Licensing and
 Regulation
500 N. Calvert Street, Suite 401
Baltimore, MD 21202
(410) 230-6020, ext. 1393

Massachusetts
Department of Labor
1 Ashburton Place, Room 2112
Boston, MA 02108
(617) 727-6573

Michigan
Department of Labor
PO Box 30004
Lansing, MI 48909
(517) 373-3034

Minnesota
Department of Labor and
 Industry
443 Lafayette Road
Saint Paul, MN 55155
(651) 284-5010

Mississippi
Department of Employment
 Security
PO Box 1699
Jackson, MS 39215-1699
(601) 321-6100

Missouri
Department of Labor and
 Industrial Relations
PO Box 599
Jefferson City, MO 65102-0599
(573) 751-2461

Montana
Department of Labor and
 Industry
PO Box 1728
Helena, MT 59624-1728
(406) 444-9091

Nebraska
Department of Labor
PO Box 94600
Lincoln, NE 68509
(402) 471-9000

Nevada
Labor Commission
555 E. Washington Avenue,
 Suite 1400
Las Vegas, NV 89101
(702) 486-2650

New Hampshire
Department of Labor
95 Pleasant Street
Concord, NH 03301
(603) 271-3171

New Jersey
Department of Labor
PO Box 110
Trenton, NJ 08625-0110
(609) 292-2323

New Mexico
Department of Labor
PO Box 1928
Albuquerque, NM 87103-1928
(505) 841-8409

New York
Department of Labor
State Office Building #12,
    Room 500
Albany, NY 12240-0003
(518) 457-2741

North Carolina
Department of Labor
4 W. Edenton Street
Raleigh, NC 27601-1092
(919) 733-0359

North Dakota
Department of Labor
State Capitol, 6th Floor
600 E. Boulevard Avenue,
    Department 406
Bismarck, ND 58505-0340
(701) 328-2660

Ohio
Department of Labor Relations
50 W. Broad Street, 28th Floor
Columbus, OH 43215
(614) 644-2239

Oklahoma
Department of Labor
4001 N. Lincoln Boulevard
Oklahoma City, OK 73105-5212
(405) 528-1500, ext. 200

Oregon
Bureau of Labor and Industries
800 NE Oregon Street, #32
Portland, OR 97232
(503) 731-4070

Pennsylvania
Department of Labor and
    Industry
Labor and Industry Building,
    Room 1700
7th and Forster Streets
Harrisburg, PA 17120
(717) 787-5279

Rhode Island
Department of Labor
1511 Pontiac Avenue
Cranston, RI 02920
(401) 462-8870

South Carolina
Department of Labor
PO Box 11329
Columbia, SC 29211-1329
(803) 896-4300

South Dakota
Department of Labor
700 Governors Drive
Pierre, SD 57501-2291
(605) 773-3101

Tennessee
Department of Labor
710 James Robertson Parkway
Nashville, TN 37243-0655
(615) 741-6642

Texas
Department of Labor Laws
Workforce Employment
  Commission
101 E. 15th Street, Room 674
Austin, TX 78778
(512) 463-0735

Utah
State Labor Commission
PO Box 146610
Salt Lake City, UT 84114-6610
(801) 530-6880

Vermont
Department of Labor and Industry
National Life Building
PO Drawer 20
Montpelier, VT 05620-3400
(802) 828-2288

Virginia
Department of Labor and Industry
13 S. 13th Street
Richmond, VA 23219
(804) 786-2377

Washington
Department of Labor and
  Industries
PO Box 44001
Olympia, WA 98504-4000
(360) 902-4203

West Virginia
Division of Labor
State Capitol Complex, Building 6,
  Room B749
Charleston, WV 25305
(304) 558-7890

Wisconsin
Department of Labor and Human
  Relations
PO Box 7946
Madison, WI 53707-7946
(608) 267-9692

Wyoming
Department of Employment
1510 E. Pershing Boulevard
Cheyenne, WY 82002
(307) 777-7672

District of Columbia
Department of Employment
  Services
54 New York Avenue NE,
  Suite 3007
Washington, DC 20002
(202) 671-1900

Source: U.S. Department of Labor, 2005, *www.dol.gov.esa*

D

STATE ALCOHOLIC BEVERAGE CONTROL BOARDS

Following is a list of the state agencies that administer and enforce the laws and regulations regarding licensing, production, distribution, and service of alcoholic beverages.

Alabama
Alcoholic Beverage Control Board
(334) 271-3840
www.abcboard.Alabama.gov

Alaska
Alcoholic Beverage Control Board
(907) 269-0350
www.DPS.state.ak.us/abc

Arizona
Department of Liquor License
    and Control
(602) 542-5141
www.azliquor.gov

Arkansas
Alcoholic Beverage Control
    Division
(501) 682-1105

California
Department of Alcoholic
    Beverage Control
(916) 419-2513
www.abc.ca.gov

Colorado
Liquor Enforcement Division
(303) 205-2300
*www.revenue.state.co.us/
    liquor_dir/toc.htm*

Connecticut
Department of Consumer
   Protection
(860) 713-6200
www.ct.gov/dcp

Delaware
Office of the Alcoholic Beverage
   Control Commissioner
(302) 577-5222
*http://dabcte.state.de.us/dabcpublic/
   index.jsp*

Florida
Division of Alcoholic Beverages
   and Tobacco in Tallahassee
(850) 488-3228
www.state.fl.us/dbpr/abt/index/shtml

Georgia
Alcohol and Tobacco Law
   Enforcement Division
(404) 417-4900
*www.etax.dor.ga.gov/alcohol/
   index.shtml*

Hawaii
Department of Taxation
Oahu (808) 527-6280
County of Hawaii (808) 961-8218
Kauai (808) 241-6580
Maui (808) 243-7753
*www.co.honolulu.hi.us/liq/
   lcrules.htm*

Idaho
Alcoholic Beverage Control
   Division
(208) 947-9400
www.liquor.Idaho.gov/td>

Illinois
Illinois Liquor Control Commission
(312) 814-2206
www.state.il.us/lcc

Indiana
Alcohol and Tobacco Commission
(317) 232-2430
www.in.gov/atc/

Iowa
Iowa Alcoholic Beverage Division
   (515) 281-7407
www.iowaabd.com

Kansas
Alcohol Beverage Control
   Division
(785) 296-7015
www.ksrevenue.org/abc.htm

Kentucky
Office of Alcoholic Beverage
   Control
(502) 564-4850
www.abc.ky.gov/

Louisiana
Office of Alcohol and Tobacco
   Control
(225) 925-4054
*www.atc.rev.state.la.us/atcweb/
   home.htm*

Maine
Bureau of Liquor Enforcement
   and Licensing
(207) 287-3721
www.maineliquor.com

Maryland
Alcohol and Tobacco Tax Bureau
Annapolis (410) 260-7314
Montgomery County
   (240) 777-1900
Baltimore (410) 396-4380
compnet.comp.state.md.us/
   red/attb

Massachusetts
Alcoholic Beverages Control
   Commission
(617) 727-3040
www.mass.gov/abcc/

Michigan
Liquor Control Commission
(517) 322-1345
www.cis.state.mi.us/lcc/home.htm

Minnesota
Department of Public Safety
   Liquor Control Division
(651) 296-6159
www.dps.state.mn.us

Mississippi
Alcohol Beverage Control
(601) 856-1301
mhicks@mstc.state.ms.us

Missouri
Division of Alcohol Control
(573) 751-2333
www.atc.dps.mo.gov

Montana
Customer Service Center, Liquor
   Licensing
(406) 444-6900

Nebraska
Liquor Control Commission
(402) 471-2571
www.lcc.ne.gov

Nevada
Department of Taxation
Las Vegas (702) 486-2300
Reno (775) 688-1295
Carson City (775) 687-4892
Elko (775) 738-8461
www.tax.state.nv.us

New Hampshire
State Liquor Commission
(603) 271-3134
www.state.nh.us/liquor

New Jersey
The Division of Alcoholic
   Beverage Control
(609) 984-2830
www.state.nj.us/lps/abc

New Mexico
Alcohol and Gaming Division
Regulation and Licensing
   Department
(505) 476-4875
www.rld.state.nm.us.AGD

New York
State Liquor Authority
(518) 474-0810
www.abc.state.ny.us

North Carolina
Alcoholic Beverage Control
   Commission
(919) 779-0700
www.nc.abc.com

North Dakota
Office of State Tax Commissioner
Alcohol Tax Section
(701) 328-2702
www.nd.gov/tax

Ohio
Department of Commerce,
  Division of Liquor Control
(614) 644-2360
www.liquorcontrol.ohio.gov

Oklahoma
Alcoholic Beverage Laws
  Enforcement Commission
(405) 521-3484
www.able.ok.us

Oregon
Liquor Control Commission
(503) 872-5000
www.olcc.state.or.us

Pennsylvania
Liquor Control Board
(717) 787-5986
www.lcb.state.pa.us

Rhode Island
Division of Commercial Licensing
Liquor Control Administration
(401) 222-4016
www.dbr.state.ri.us/liquor_comp.html

South Carolina
Department of Revenue, Alcohol
  Licensing
(803) 898-5864
www.sctax.org

South Dakota
Department of Revenue and
  Regulations, Special Tax
  Division
(605) 773-3311
www.state.sd.us/drr2/revenue.html

Tennessee
Alcoholic Beverage Commission
(615) 741-1602
www.state.tn.us/abc/

Texas
Alcoholic Beverage Commission
(512) 206-3333
www.tabc.state.tx.us

Utah
Department of Alcoholic
  Beverage Control
(801) 977-6800
www.alcbev.state.ut.us

Vermont
Department of Liquor Control
(802) 828-4929
www.state.vt.us/dlc

Virginia
Department of Alcoholic
  Beverage Control
(804) 213-4400
www.abc.Virginia.gov

Washington
Washington State Liquor Control
  Board
(360) 664-1600
www.liq.wa.gov

District of Columbia
Alcoholic Beverage Control Board
(202) 442-4423
www.abra.dc.gov

West Virginia
Alcohol Beverage Control
   Commission
(304) 558-2481
www.wvabca.com

Wisconsin
Alcohol-Tobacco Enforcement
   Unit
(608) 261-2772
www.dor.state.wi.us

Wyoming
Liquor Commission
(307) 777-6255
www.revenue.state.wy.us

Source: National Conference of State Liquor Administrators website

E

DIRECTORY OF STATE RESTAURANT ASSOCIATIONS

Alabama
Alabama Restaurant Association
61B Market Place
Montgomery, AL 36124-1413
(334) 244-1320

Alaska
Alaska Cabaret, Hotel, Restaurant,
   and Retailers Assoc.
1111 E. 80th Avenue, Suite 3
Anchorage, AK 99518
(907) 274-8133

Arizona
Arizona Restaurant and
   Hospitality Association
   Foundation
2400 N. Central Avenue, Suite 109
Phoenix, AZ 85004
(602) 307-9134

Arkansas
Arkansas Hospitality Association
PO Box 3866
Little Rock, AR 72203
(501) 376-2323

California
California Restaurant Association
   Education Foundation
1011 10th Street
Sacramento, CA 95814
(916) 431-2747

Colorado
Colorado Restaurant Association
   Education Fund
430 E. 7th Avenue
Denver, CO 80203
(303) 830-2972

Connecticut
Connecticut Restaurant
   Association
100 Roscommon Park, Suite 320
Middletown, CT 06457
(860) 635-5600

Delaware
Delaware Restaurant Association
PO Box 8004
Newark, DE 19714
(302) 227-7300

Florida
Florida Restaurant Association
230 S. Adams Street
Tallahassee, FL 32301
(850) 224-2250

Georgia
Georgia Restaurant Association
480 E. Paces Ferry Road, Suite 7
Atlanta, GA 30305
(404) 467-9000

Hawaii
Hawaii Restaurant Association
1451 S. King Street, Suite 503
Honolulu, HI 96814
(808) 536-9105

Idaho
Idaho Lodging and Restaurant
   Association
134 S. 5th Street
Boise, ID 83702
(208) 342-0777

Illinois
Illinois Restaurant Association
200 N. LaSalle Street, Suite 880
Chicago, IL 60601
(312) 787-4000

Indiana
Restaurant and Hospitality
  Association of Indiana
200 South Meridian, Suite 350
Indianapolis, IN 46225-1076
(317) 673-4211

Iowa
Iowa Hospitality Association
  Education Foundation
8525 Douglas Avenue, Suite 47
Des Moines, IA 50322
(515) 276-1454

Kansas
Kansas Restaurant and Hospitality
  Association Education
  Foundation
359 S. Hydraulic
Wichita, KS 67211
(316) 267-8383

Kentucky
Kentucky Restaurant Association
133 Evergreen Road, #201
Louisville, KY 40243
(502) 896-0464

Louisiana
Louisiana Restaurant Association
  Education Foundation
2700 N. Arnoult Road
Metairie, LA 70002
(504) 454-2277

Maine
Maine Restaurant Association
PO Box 5060
Augusta, ME 04332-5060
(207) 623-2178

Maryland
Maryland Restaurant Association
6301 Hillside Court
Columbia, MD 21046
(410) 290-6800

Massachusetts
Massachusetts Restaurant
  Association Hospitality Institute
Southborough Technology Park
333 Turnpike Rd, Suite 102
Southborough, MA 01772-1775
(508) 303-9905

Michigan
Michigan Restaurant Association
225 W. Washtenaw Street
Lansing, MI 48933
(517) 482-5244

Minnesota
Minnesota Restaurant Association
305 E. Rosclawn Avenue
Saint Paul, MN 55117
(651) 778-2400

Mississippi
Mississippi Restaurant Association
130 Riverview Drive, Suite A
Flowood, MS 39232
(601) 420-4210

Missouri
Missouri Restaurant Association
1810 Craig Road, Suite 225
Saint Louis, MO 63146
(314) 576-2777

Montana
Montana Restaurant Association
1537 Avenue D, Suite 320
Billings, MT 59102
(406) 256-1005

Nebraska
Nebraska Restaurant
    Association
PO Box 83086
Lincoln, NE 68501-3086
(402) 488-3999

Nevada
Nevada Restaurant Association
1500 E. Tropicana Avenue,
    Suite 114-A
Las Vegas, NV 89119

New Hampshire
New Hampshire Lodging and
    Restaurant Association
14 Dixon Avenue, Suite 208
Concord, NH 03301
(603) 228-9585

New Jersey
New Jersey Restaurant
    Association
126 W. State Street
Trenton, NJ 08608
(609) 599-3316

New Mexico
New Mexico Restaurant
    Association
9201 Montgomery Boulevard NE,
    Suite 602
Albuquerque, NM 87111
(505) 343-9848

New York
New York State Restaurant
    Association
409 New Karner Road
Albany, NY 12205
(518) 452-4222

North Carolina
North Carolina Restaurant
    Association
204 West Millbrook Road
Raleigh, NC 27609-4304
(919) 844-0098

North Dakota
North Dakota Hospitality
    Association
PO Box 428
Bismark, ND 58502
(701) 223-2284

Ohio
Ohio Restaurant Association
1525 Bethel Road, Suite 301
Columbus, OH 43220
(614) 442-3535

Oklahoma
Oklahoma Restaurant
    Association
3800 North Portland
Oklahoma City, OK 73112-2948
(405) 942-8181

Oregon
Oregon Restaurant Association
  Education Foundation
8565 SW Salish Lane, Suite 120
Wilsonville, OR 97070
(503) 682-4422

Pennsylvania
Pennsylvania Restaurant
  Association
100 State Street
Harrisburg, PA 17101-1024
(717) 232-4433

Rhode Island
Rhode Island Hospitality and
  Tourism Association
832 Dyer Avenue
Cranston, RI 02920
(401) 223-1120

South Carolina
Hospitality Association of South
  Carolina
1338 Main Street, Suite 505
Columbia, SC 29201
(803) 765-9000

South Dakota
South Dakota Retailers
  Association—Restaurant
  Division
3612 Landmark Drive, Suite B
Columbia, SD 29204
(605) 224-5050

Tennessee
Tennessee Restaurant Association
720 Cool Springs Boulevard,
  Suite 150
Franklin, TN 37067
(615) 771-7056

Texas
Texas Restaurant Association
1400 Lavaca
Austin, TX 78701
(512) 457-4100

Utah
Utah Restaurant Association
420 E. South Temple, #355
Salt Lake City, UT 84111
(801) 322-0123

Vermont
Vermont Lodging and Restaurant
  Association
13 Kilburn Street
Burlington, VT 05401
(802) 660-9001

Virginia
Virginia Hospitality and Travel
  Association
2101 Libbie Avenue
Richmond, VA 23230-2621
(804) 288-3065

Washington
Washington Restaurant Association
  Education Foundation
510 Plum Street SE, Suite 200
Olympia, WA 98501-1587
(360) 956-7279

District of Columbia
Restaurant Association of Metro
  Washington, Inc.
1200 17th Street NW, Suite 110
Washington, DC 20036
(202) 331-5990

West Virginia
West Virginia Hospitality and
  Travel Association
PO Box 2391
Charleston, WV 25311
(304) 342-6511

Wisconsin
Wisconsin Restaurant Association
  Education Foundation
2801 Fish Hatchery Road
Madison, WI 53713
(608) 270-9950

Wyoming
Wyoming Restaurant
  Association
211 West 19th, Suite 201
Cheyenne, WY 82001
(307) 634-8816

Source: National Restaurant Association, Educational Foundation, 2006